# Indigenous Imaginaries

*Also by E. V. Ramakrishnan*

**Locating Indian Literature: Texts, Traditions, Translations**

# Indigenous Imaginaries

## Literature, Region, Modernity

E. V. Ramakrishnan

Orient BlackSwan

INDIGENOUS IMAGINARIES

**ORIENT BLACKSWAN PRIVATE LIMITED**

*Registered Office*
3-6-752 Himayatnagar, Hyderabad 500 029, Telangana, India
*Email*: centraloffice@orientblackswan.com

*Other Offices*
Bengaluru, Bhopal, Chennai, Guwahati, Hyderabad, Jaipur, Kolkata, Lucknow, Mumbai, New Delhi, Noida, Patna, Vijayawada



First published 2017

ISBN 978 93 86689 45 0

*Typeset in* Adobe Garamond Pro 10.5/13 *by*
Akhil Offset Printers
Hyderabad 500 020

026017
13092017

*Printed at*
Glorious Printers, Delhi

*Published by*
Orient Blackswan Private Limited
3-6-752 Himayatnagar, Hyderabad 500 029
*Email*: info@orientblackswan.com

# Contents

# Preface

In December 2015 I was invited to deliver the Birinchi Kumar Barua Memorial Lecture in Gauhati. I chose to speak on 'Literature, Region, Modernity: A Perspective on Indian Literature in the Context of Assamese Literature', where I attempted to make sense of Assamese literature in its modern phase, drawing parallels from my understanding of the historical trajectories of Malayalam literature. My objective was to bring out the reciprocity between two literary traditions without erasing their differences. Birinchi Kumar Barua (1908–64) was a cosmopolitan critical insider who chose to express himself in several genres such as the novel, short story, essay and drama, besides achieving remarkable success in a variety of fields ranging from folklore and linguistics research to academic administration and institution building. His ability to cross boundaries was evident in whatever he did. My initiation into Assamese literature, through Barua's life and works, deepened my awareness of the multiple worlds we inhabit in the Indian subcontinent and once again, brought home to me the constraints one faces in cultivating a level of intimacy with another linguistic/literary tradition with any degree of inwardness. The Northeast region contains multiple worlds, made up of a plurality of languages and cultures – and postcolonial or postmodernist theories of literature are of no help in making sense of the vitality or complexity of these cultures.

I begin on this personal note, recounting my encounter with Assamese, to emphasise that the issue of modernity in India has to be mapped back to its regional historical variations with its own sub-regional clusters of knowledge traditions, for a fuller understanding of the dynamics of literary traditions in India. In theorising about India, we have lost sight of the significance of *kshetra* with its implicit semiotics of place, territory, body, sanctity, work, fertility and origin. Sreekanteswaram G. Padmanabha Pillai's Malayalam lexicon, *Sabdataravali*, defines *kshetra* in these terms: fertile land, an abode of God or a place of worship, the physical body, a place of work, or place of origin (1986, 700). *Kshetra* is not the same as 'region'. 'Region' is derived from Latin and Old French, suggesting 'territory', 'district', or 'province'. According to the *Concise Oxford English Dictionary*, the word comes to Middle English from Old French and originally from Latin (Soanes and Stevenson 2009, 1211). The Latin word '*regionen*' meant 'a district' or 'territory', while '*regere*' in Old French meant 'to direct', or 'to rule'. *Kshetra*, thus, exceeds 'region' in its suggestion of the sacred and its resonance of the physical. This has nothing to do with religion or spirituality. *Kshetra* implies a semiotic field of linguistic and cultural interrelationships woven through language, collective memory, oral narratives and performance traditions, and multiple forms of expression. My attempt here is to problematise our received notions of the 'region' as a fragment, and to make it a productive category that can contest the essentialist claims of both the 'national' and the 'local'. Region as *kshetra* is a crossroad where several narratives meet and diverge.

To illustrate this further, let us see how *kshetra* informs a modern Indian novel like *Dhorai charit manas* (1949–51) by Satinath Bhaduri, written in Bengali but set in the Hindi-speaking area of Purnea in Bihar. There are many varieties of Hindi and tribal languages spoken here, apart from Bengali and English. And all these languages, with their multiple dialects and registers, find their way into the texture of the narrative. The inter-textual relation with the great Hindi poem, *Ramcharit manas,* suggested in the title, projects a horizon of orality through which the written narrative is stitched into a complex whole cutting across horizontal and vertical divisions of language, religion, caste and class. As Ipshita Chanda, who translated this novel into English, asks, 'A landscape, a way of life, a world woven into a fabric of many colours, in a range of spoken-language registers: what is it that makes Bangla claim Satinath as its own, when his text is modelled on the version of the epic that is not local to Bengal but to the Hindi-speaking people?' (2013, xv). The *kshetra* revealed in this novel has the oral epic embedded in its collective memory and hence, it transcends the linguistic boundaries of the people living within its ambit, to constitute them into a larger community, even as they remain divided along the axis of power, material wealth and beliefs.

Another example for the cultural economy of *kshetra* would be the fictional works of VKN (Vadakkke Koottala Narayanankutty Nair) in Malayalam. For a fuller understanding of his complex deployment of carnivalised speech (words such as 'humour', 'satire', 'farce' and 'irony' fail to convey the explosive and subversive energy of his stunning verbal inventiveness), one needs to plumb the depths of the performative traditions of Kerala such as *koothu* (which literally means 'dance' but is a solo performance by an accomplished scholar-actor who uses both Sanskrit and Malayalam to narrate myths from classics interspersed with devastating sarcasm, mostly aimed at the ruling elite) and *thullal* (which uses dance and carnivalised narrative verse). Both these performances use the masked face of a *vidushaka*-like figure along with elaborate stylised narration replete with innuendoes and word-play. VKN's narratives stage his critique of contemporary society through verbal gestures that recover the acoustics of speech resonating with inter-textual echoes from the collective memory of shared texts which include Sanskrit classics, mainstream Malayalam literature, folk narratives, colonial history and popular culture. Here, *kshetra* invokes a subliminal cultural cosmos of lived traditions, shared memories and collective attitudes and assumptions that inform the social imaginary of the people. Inwardness to these traditions enables an informed reader to enter the inter-textual space of cultural memory in the personal act of reading VKN. In both these authors, the settings of their novels are far away from where their languages are spoken; and hence, it is the addressivity of the language that embodies *kshetra*.

One argument that runs through the chapters of this volume is that we need to recover a deeper level of embedded cultural cosmologies in the literary texts of Indian languages: we need to 'regionalise' Indian literature. (Needless to say, here I use the word 'region' in the sense of *kshetra*, as explained above.) I first presented this argument in a seminar at Baroda, in 2011, where Gayatri Chakravorty Spivak was the main speaker. The argument was later taken up by Spivak and elaborated in her inimitable style in an interview with David Damrosch:

> In a paper presented in Baroda, in February, Professor Ramakrishnan suggested that we regionalise the multilingual Indian literatures, that we not try endlessly to find one example and translate it into English and put it side by side with something else. He asked us rather to "regionalise" these – his word – multilingual Indian literatures by way of context and language in order paradoxically restore their Indianness that is best a theoretical geopolitical fiction like "Europe", pleading perhaps for comparative literature, all world literature, to include something

> "Indian" as a historical sign system to be traced post-theoretically rather than sketched in here through Global English alone. (2011, 477)

Spivak further illustrated the implications of 'regionalising' literature, when she spoke of the Tagore she had internalised intimately as a girl growing up in Bengal, as different from the declamatory figure he is made out to be in world literature. As she says, 'You really have to think about singularity in a collectivity and put geo-politics over against this' (478). The region as *kshetra* realises the singular which enables us to recover the universal: 'It simply implies that what is singular in any text is universalizable' (478). When you read as an insider, reading becomes a communal act of recovery and bonding with 'a historical sign system'. Just as there are 'thick descriptions', there are also dense ways of reading.

Though I do not use this as a prescriptive approach for my critical practice, some of the implications of the above approach are worked out in most of the chapters of this volume. The five chapters in the first section, titled 'Configuring Contested Epistemologies: The Literary across Cultures', take up questions of theoretical nature regarding modernity, nation, multilingualism, secularism, globalisation and dissent, in the context of Indian literatures. The second section, 'Reading as Recovery: Textual Worlding of the Singular', presents close readings of seminal texts that enact the transformation of indigenous imaginaries in the wake of the epistemic violence brought about by colonialism. The texts, drawn from different Indian languages, focus on issues of gender and desire, marginality and modernity, memory and history as well as ethnicity and violence, in contemporary Indian society and even beyond. The authors discussed here include Rabindranath Tagore, Vaikom Muhammad Basheer, Mahasweta Devi, Amitav Ghosh, Anand, Jean Arasanayagam and Agha Shahid Ali. The choice of authors here will also make it clear that the present volume is not making a nativist argument. Inwardness to a culture has to be painstakingly cultivated to make the act of reading a process of recovery. The third section, titled 'Colonialism to Comparatism: Translating/Historicising the Other', deals with questions of literary history and translation with an accent on changing concepts of the literary from the late nineteenth to the middle of the twentieth century.

Translation as a cultural practice figures prominently in all three sections, either directly or obliquely. The opening chapter,

'"Disciplining" India: Literature, Region, Modernity', argues that the conjunction of print and public sphere defines the moment of modernity in India which manifests itself in the impulse to modernise and standardise Indian languages across various regions in India, in ways that are not identical. Translation becomes a trope for the impulse to negotiate the alien in moments of cultural challenge from within and without. The second essay, 'Beyond the Orientalist and Postcolonial Constructs: Telos of Translation Studies from the Perspective of Comparative Literature', shows how the foundational moment of Indian languages is marked by monumental works of translations from Sanskrit, which, in effect, ended the hegemony of Sanskrit and transformed Indian languages into literary languages with their own textual traditions. Once again, in the nineteenth century, the cultural ferment of the colonial phase involved negotiations with the imperial authority of English through translations. Unlike Sanskrit, which in its long history hardly found it necessary to translate, Indian languages have been held in a state of continuous flux through translations that look beyond the narrow boundaries of language and community. As Indian languages responded to the compulsions of cultural variations embodied in the habitat of *kshetra*, they were required to confront the Other, in its various manifestations. This openness to external influences is what has enabled them to reinvent themselves in accordance with the times. The tradition of dissent in Indian literatures has contributed to the progressive democratisation of Indian society and polity. The thematic of dissent in poetic traditions from Bhakti to Dalit literature opens up the possibility of alternative paradigms of interpretation, when Euro-centric categories misrepresent and erase the singularity of lived experiences from our contexts. The readings presented in the essay 'Dialogics of Dissent in Indian Literature', from multiple Indian traditions, both oral and written, show how they resist assimilation into hegemonic discourses by embodying new moral imaginaries. This site of resistance becomes a cultural resource for survival in times of globalisation when the work of art becomes an exhibit in the market place. The essay 'Globalisation, Resistance and Social Imagination' argues that the productive power of social imagination can effectively challenge the homogenising impact of globalisation.

The questions that animate the second section are concerned with the self-divisions and dichotomies of modernity in its various phases. It shows how multi-vocal texts enact culture-specific singularities. Tagore sensed a predatory impulse in the hegemonic form of modernity he confronted in the garb of nationalism. While his fictional works dramatised its violence in discursive form, his poetry embodied a communitarian voice of intimacy and harmony, clearing an ethical space that can re-imagine the self–world relations from an inclusive space of humanity. Tagore's explication of man–woman relations is particularly relevant in grasping the dynamics of the relation between masculinity and nationalist discourse at the turn of the twentieth century. Vaikom Muhammad Basheer was caught in a moral impasse, which also became a crisis of narrativisation, as he found the ideal of the secular modern inseparable from its normative, homogenising violence. He fashioned a complex ironic mode rooted in regional experience that critiques and contests received notions of nationalist discourse. In the fictional works of Mahasweta Devi, Amitav Ghosh and Anand, memory is a contested site wrought with opposing currents of culture and power. Retrieving the layered past of a community, which is threatened by the mindless violence of the nation state, can be an act of collective resistance and survival, as shown by the close readings of some of the seminal works in this section. The significance of Bhalachandra Nemade's *Kosla* is that it finds a lexicon of lived experience to articulate the volcanic rage of the post–1960 generation against the double-speak of a self-seeking society which had no moral courage to face its failures. Nemade subjects the complex relation between the individual and his/her society to close scrutiny through the lens of an ethical perspective derived from a native tradition that goes back to the medieval *Mahanubhav* traditions. The institution of the storyteller was a defining feature of South American and Asian societies in pre-modern times. The novels of Gabriel García Márquez reinvented this figure of the storyteller in the twentieth century, enabling Latin American readers to overcome the cognitive blockage imposed by colonial violations. Close readings of a few fictional works from Malayalam suggest how the reception of Márquez's indigenous imaginaries was mediated by the crisis of authenticity that confronted these Malayalam authors. In the poetry of the Sri Lankan poet Jean Arasanayagam and the Kashmiri poet Agha Shahid Ali, one sees parallels occasioned by the conflict between ethnicity, as shared memories, and the discourse of the nation, as imagined by a ruling elite alienated from the people.

The first two sections demand new approaches to literary history. The final section, while addressing issues in translation and literary history, argues that comparatism has to be seen as an ideological response to the compulsions of colonial knowledge production. A new category of the literary that emerged in the nineteenth century enjoined upon the reader to move away from the prevailing protocols of reading. A novel cannot be read as an epic, nor can an oil painting be seen in terms of the conventions of two-dimensional figures. The reflective or argumentative essay, the proscenium play, the travelogue, the short story and the autobiography demanded new hermeneutics of textual explication. This involved a cognitive shift towards a dialogic or translational approach to the literary. Translation becomes a mode of self-fashioning as it mediates between multiple conventions of the literary, providing a critique of the hegemonic elements in the native as well as the colonial cosmologies. The role of translation in shaping the literary public sphere in Kerala and the modernist poetic discourse in Indian languages is discussed in this section. Indian languages such as Malayalam have increasingly witnessed the shift from 'macro literary histories' to 'micro literary historiographies', as a response to strident feminist and Dalit critiques of mainstream literary histories that were both exclusivist and elitist.

The present volume continues to engage with the concerns and preoccupations I had pursued in *Locating Indian Literature: Texts, Traditions, Translations.* The inter-relations between multilingualism, region and modernity are emphasised here in greater detail. This is in keeping with my search for alternative paradigms of reading as a cultural act of recovering ideological links between poetics and politics. As a bilingual writer with a 'double consciousness', I wear a bi-focal lens that constantly moves between the horizons of languages, close readings complementing distant readings, and peripheries coming into view, altering the longitudes of the discipline.

I dedicate this book to all my students who inspired me to stay focussed on these problems, in the classroom and outside, through their persistent questioning and their sceptical silence.

## References

Chanda, Ipshita. 2013. Preface. In *Dhorai charit manas,* i–xxiv. New Delhi: Sahitya Akademi.

Spivak, Gayatri Chakravarty, and David Damrosch. 2011. A discussion. *Comparative Literature Studies* 48. 4: 455–85.

Pillai, Sreekanteswaram G. Padmanabha. 1986. *Sabdataravali.* Kottayam: Sahitya Pravartaka Sahakarana Samgham.

Soanes, Catherine, and Angus Stevenson, ed. 2009. *Concise Oxford English dictionary*. New Delhi: Oxford UP.

# Acknowledgements

Most of the chapters in this volume were originally written for national and international seminars and conferences held in India and abroad. Critical pursuits and sustained engagements with questions that animate contemporary society and culture require a commitment that goes beyond mere professional requirement. In that sense, sharing these views with a large number of scholars has helped me refine my ideas and engage with the best minds in the field. The Sahitya Akademi (New Delhi), Comparative Literature Association of India (CLAI), International Comparative Literature Association (ICLA) and the Forum for Contemporary Theory, Baroda, are some of the important institutions, apart from many universities in India and abroad, which had given me opportunities to present my ideas and thoughts before they could take concrete shape in the form of the chapters presented here.

The chapter 'Narrating a Community: The Secular Modern and the Discourse of Marginality in the Fictional Works of Vaikom Muhammad Basheer' was presented as a paper at the national conference on 'Discourse, Democracy and Difference', jointly organised by Sahitya Akademi, New Delhi, and M. S. University, Baroda, in August 2003. It appeared in an earlier version in the volume *Discourse, Democracy and Difference: Perspectives on Community, Politics and Culture*, edited by M. T. Ansari and Deepta Achar and published by Sahitya Akademi, New Delhi, in 2010. 'Poet as Witness: Ethnicity and Discourse of the Nation in the Poetry of Jean Arasanayagam and Agha Shahid Ali' was first presented in a national seminar convened by Jasbir Jain at the University of Rajasthan in September 2007, on 'Crossing Borders: Post–1980 Subcontinental Writing in English'. Subsequently, it was published in *Crossing Borders: Post–1980 Subcontinental Writing in English*, edited by Jasbir Jain. 'Globalisation, Resistance and Social Imagination' grew out of a plenary lecture delivered at the international CLAI conference held at the Mahatma Gandhi University, Kottayam, in 2008. It was also published in the journal *Haritham* (No. 20, 2009) brought out by the School of Letters, M. G. University. An earlier version of the chapter titled 'Beyond Canons and Classrooms: Towards a Dialogic Model of Literary Historiography' appeared in the *Jadavpur Journal of Comparative Literature* (No. 47, 2009–10). The chapter on Tagore, titled 'Interrogating Modernity: The Social Imaginary in Tagore's Prose Works', was presented at an international conference on Tagore's works organised by the Indian Council for Cultural Relations in New Delhi in 2012.

The chapter 'Habitations of Resistance: The Role of Translation in the Creation of a Literary Public Sphere in Kerala' was presented at the Fourth Asian Translation Traditions Conference held at the Chinese University of Hong Kong, in December 2010. 'Redefining the Secular and the Modern: The Politics of Identity and the Minority Discourse in Contemporary India' was presented at an international conference organised jointly by CLAI and the Central University of Rajasthan, 'Minority Discourses across Cultures', in February 2012. The paper was included in *Discoursing Minority: In-Text and Co-Text*, edited by Anisur Rahman, Supriya Agarwal and Bhumika Sharma, published in 2014. An earlier version of 'Beyond the Orientalist and Postcolonialist Constructs: The Telos of Translation Studies from the Perspective of Comparative Literature' was presented at the national seminar jointly organised by Sahitya Akademi, New Delhi, and the Centre for Comparative Literature Studies, University of Hyderabad, on 'Multilingualism and the Literary Culture of India'. The paper appeared in *Language Policy and Education in India: Documents, Contexts and Debates*, edited by M. Sridhar and Sunita Mishra, published by Routledge London, in 2017.

'Shifting Centres and Emerging Margins: Translation and the Shaping of Modernist Poetic Discourse in Indian Poetry' was originally presented as a paper at the XX World Congress of ICLA, organised at the University of Paris-Sorbonne, in July 2013, on 'Comparative Literature as a Critical Approach'. The chapter titled '"Disciplining" India: Literature, Region, Modernity' grew out of an earlier essay, 'Is There an Indian way of Thinking about Comparative Literature?', written for the Global South Project initiated by Ngugi Wa Thiongo and Satya P. Mohanty. This essay is available on the Global South Project website: www.globalsouthproject.cornell.edu. 'Narratives of Memory: Representations of the Other in Postcolonial Indian Fiction' was delivered as a lecture at the Wilson Centre for Humanities and Arts, University of Georgia, where I was a Visiting Professor during October–November 2014. 'Hegemony, Ideology, and the Idea of the Literary' was presented at the World Sinology Conference at Renmin University, in September 2014. 'The Dialogics of Dissent in Indian Literature: From Bhakti Tradition to Dalit Literature' grew out of the key-note speech given at the UGC national seminar on 'Writing, Censorship and Democracy' organised by the English department of Calicut University in December 2015. 'Shifting Paradigms of Literary Historiography: Malayalam Literary History in the New Millennium' was presented as a paper at the national seminar on 'Indian Literary Historiography' organised jointly by Sahitya Akademi, New Delhi, and S. V. University, Tirupati, in September 2015. It has appeared in *Malayalam Research Journal* (Vol. 9, No. 1, Jan–April 2016), published by the Benjamin Bailey Research Foundation, Kottayam. 'Modernity, Memory and Magic Realism: Gabriel García Márquez and Malayalam Fiction' is based on the paper I presented at the national seminar on Márquez organised by The English and Foreign Languages University, Hyderabad, in March 2015.

I am grateful to Orient BlackSwan for undertaking the publication of this book. Sreenath's editorial contribution needs a special mention for his patience, eye for detail, diligence and commitment.

Needless to say, all scholarship is a product of collaborative work shaped by the climate of ideas that communities live in. In that sense, the books I cite in these chapters and the many more I must have read during the last few decades, the colleagues, friends, students and strangers who responded to my viewpoints in seminars, classrooms and outside, the issues and questions that I faced in the daily business of living as an ordinary citizen, have all contributed to my arguments presented here. I refrain from naming anyone, since any such list cannot do justice to the debts I have incurred in producing this work.

# Section I

# Configuring Contested Epistemologies: The Literary across Cultures

## Chapter One

# 'Disciplining' India: Literature, Region, Modernity

This chapter attempts to map the nature of changes in the cultural domain of India, in the wake of the introduction of English education, the advent of print medium, the spread of periodicals and the emergence of a public sphere. The rise of colonial institutions organised India into a discursive field and an object of study. The conjunction of print and public sphere defined the moment of modernity in India, which manifested itself in the impulse to modernise and standardise Indian languages across regions, with varying results. This can be demonstrated with reference to some of the major Indian languages such as Malayalam, Hindi and Marathi. In these languages, the emergent socio-political identities were negotiated primarily through prose genres. But this modernity was riddled with contradictions, and these inherent contradictions are best revealed in the literary works of the period, particularly in the novel, and *not* in the new disciplines that internalised colonial ideology. Comparative literature studies in India will have to recognise that categories such as 'text', 'reader' and 'tradition', constituted in the moment of modernity, are fluid and permeable, as they have to mediate the compulsions of a multilingual society. To devise an alternative narrative of modernity from indigenous intellectual and cultural resources, comparative literature as a discipline will have to discover the dynamics of dialogism that inform regional literatures.

## I

An earlier version of this chapter was titled, 'Is There an Indian Way of Thinking about Comparative Literature?' That title was a take-off from a similar question A. K. Ramanujan had asked about the Indian way of thinking. He also added that depending on where the stress was placed, it contained many questions, 'all of which are real questions' (1999, 34). This chapter will raise a few questions regarding the field of comparative literature in India, and its trajectory and thrust areas.

As an interdisciplinary field, comparative literature has to cultivate a high degree of self-reflexivity to reflect on our society and culture. Such informed discussions will invariably lead us to debates around a cluster of ideas and issues – such as the oral and the written, literacy and the literary, tradition as past and presence, the colony and the empire, print and the coming of the book, the empire and the nation, the elite and the popular, homogeneity and plurality, literary history and history of literature, speech genres and literary genres, and so on. The fact that most of these issues emerged in the nineteenth century forces us to revisit the shifts that took place in the nineteenth century with greater care. This introductory chapter will map the larger terrain of these shifts, with reference to the emergence of the public sphere in general, and the introduction of print and its cultural impact in particular. This will lead us to an understanding of some of the assumptions, attitudes and concerns that informed the foundational moments of modern Indian literature, and by extension, comparative Indian literature.

The disciplines we now include under the humanities and social sciences – from history to psychology, and from economics to literature studies – entered India in the nineteenth century. Once literature became a subject of study in the classroom, new forms of reading and interpreting literature came into being. By the end of the eighteenth century, India had emerged as an object of study in Europe. This was completely different from the kind of exchanges that had taken place between India and the West in the preceding centuries. The nineteenth century coincides with the rise of colonial institutions across India that reorganised the country into a discursive field, with its own taxonomy across several fields, from land and revenue to languages and education. As Bhalchandra Nemade comments, 'learning, throughout the nineteenth century, became synonymous with the ability to read and write the English language, a social substitute for the ancient system of learning the Sanskrit language' (1990, 3). However, what is often lost sight of is the fact that the discovery of 'Classical India' itself was part of this reconstitution of India into a discursive terrain. Tradition, as interpreted and made available to a new generation of Indians, was located in the present and *not* in the remote past of antiquity. As Foucault comments on the profound changes that overtook Europe from its transition from the Classical to the modern periods, 'the mode of being of things, and of the order that divided them up before presenting them to the understanding, was profoundly altered' (1994, xxii). In India, something fundamental to 'the mode of being of things, and of the order that divided them up before presenting them to the understanding' changed in the nineteenth century.

The introduction of English into India set in motion a series of profound changes in the very manner in which we think of language, literature and culture. The arrival of English and the advent of print shared the same *episteme*, and they reinforced control over the minds of the people of India by setting normative practices of reading and writing that had far-reaching consequences for the entire country. Nothing in the preceding centuries had prepared Indians for the massive reorganisation of culture, language and knowledge that took place subsequently in the nineteenth century. To seek continuities between an earlier era and this new period would involve bypassing disciplinary boundaries. The past can only be reconstructed from the various fragments of the present, and as can be expected in such contexts, there are multiple pasts vying with one another for legitimacy. The legitimating function of power structures in constituting the past needs to be examined in Indian contexts with greater sensitivity to their ideological implications. Much ground has been covered by eminent scholars such as Vasudha Dalmia, Veena Naregal, Gauri Viswanathan, Sudhir Chandra, Sudipta Kaviraj, Ranajit Guha, Partha Chatterjee and C. A. Bayly, with reference to the role of colonial administration in the production of India as an object of knowledge. Their insights will help us in the following discussion of the rise of print and its impact on the fashioning of a new subjectivity in the nineteenth century. That they have chosen to work with literary texts is significant; and its relevance in reinventing disciplines in contemporary contexts will be discussed later in this chapter.

## 2

Once Sanskrit and Persian were displaced from their position of distinction and dominance, English came to occupy that space; and with that, modern Indian languages came under the compulsion to approximate to the norms set by English in education and production of knowledge. The standardisation of Indian languages – enabled through the publication of books on grammar, dictionaries and textbooks, and the creation of a new script for printing – took place across Indian languages. What Nemade says in the context of Marathi is largely true of other Indian languages too: 'the transition from oral to the written and from the manuscript to the print culture was the first requisite of the new prose style, which was laboriously accomplished by the first generation of the prose writers in the period between 1818 and 1847' (1990, 5). The emergence of print media and the fashioning of a new 'standard' prose take place simultaneously in most of the Indian languages. The example of Malayalam would serve as an entry point to probe this process of modernisation further.

The first book to be printed in an Indian language was a Tamil book that was printed in Lisbon in 1544. It was, however, printed in Roman script. The first Malayalam book to come out was the New Testament (with 504 pages), printed in 1811 at Courier Press in Bombay (Govi 1998, 1–20). Printing was introduced to Kerala by 1824 when the CMS (Church Mission Society) Press in Kottayam brought out a book in Malayalam titled *Cheru paithangalku upkarartham Englishil ninnu paribhashapeduthiya kathakal* (Stories translated from English for the benefit of children). By the time the New Testament was printed in Malayalam in 1829, the modern Malayalam script fashioned by Benjamin Bailey (1791–1871), a missionary from the British Church of England who spent most of his working life in Kottayam, had become the standard script for printing in Malayalam. Bailey published a Malayalam–English dictionary in 1846 and an English–Malayalam dictionary in 1849, besides launching a periodical, *Jnana Nikshepam,* in 1846. From 1847, Hermann Gundert (1814–93), another missionary whose contributions to the development of modern Malayalam is equally seminal, had started two periodicals, *Rajyasamacharam* and *Paschimodayam,* from Tellicherry (Thalassery) in North Kerala. All this contributed to the rise of Malayalam prose, which attained a new vocabulary and syntactical form. Translations of Christian tracts were now overtaken by translations of literary classics of various kinds that the English-educated Malayalam readers found acceptable (Ramakrishnan 2012, 24–48). Debates on social reforms and the early assertion of nationalist sentiments could now be articulated in a language that addressed the common people.

The new Malayalam prose moved away from the highly Sanskritised model that had limited appeal even among the educated in the early part of the nineteenth century. The opaque nature of this Sanskritised Malayalam prose had rendered an early translation of a Dutch novel, *Akbar* – by an eminent Malayalam scholar, Kerala Varma Valiyakoyithampuran (1845–1914) – almost unreadable. However, when Valiyakoyithampuran presided over the textbook committee of the Travancore state, he played a crucial role in creating a Malayalam prose that was not cluttered with Sanskrit or dialect words. He considered the English prose of Joseph Addison, Richard Steele and Jonathan Swift as his model (Gangadharan 1984, 32). He also kept mythology and religion out of these textbooks and cultivated an inclusive, secular perspective – a defining attribute of the emerging modernity (71). By the time two newspapers, *Keralamitram* and *Kerala Patrika*, began to appear from 1881 and 1884 respectively, the former from Kochi and the latter from Calicut (Kozhikode), a common Malayalam accessible to the masses and a well-defined public sphere were firmly in place. G. Arunima has argued that through the 1890s, Malayalam periodicals, such as *Vidyavinodini* and *Bhashaposhini*, carried several articles on the changing nature of Malayalam and the need to modernise it (2006, 70–71). A common Malayali identity evolved linguistically as various communities adopted Malayalam as the medium of expression. As Arunima observes, 'Moreover, in Kerala, unlike in Punjab or in the Urdu- and Hindi-speaking regions of the United Provinces, community difference on the basis of religious origin was not mapped onto a modern linguistic identity' (73). The first Malayalam novel to become a bestseller, *Indulekha*, appeared in 1889; and issues of modernity were now in the public domain to be debated and contested. In the next two decades, about twenty novels were published in Malayalam, which included a satire on *Indulekha* as well. The emergence of the literary public sphere was the result of the modernisation and standardisation of language (Malayalam), its ability to represent all communities irrespective of their religious affiliations, and the evolution of a regional ethnic identity centred around language, which did not homogenise the inherent plurality of dialects, sub-regions or communities.

This brief discussion on print in Malayalam leads us to larger questions of modernity across the country. With the mobilisation of the people, the colonial administration introduced measures to contain freedom of the press. In 1867, the government set up a registration process that aimed at regulating newspapers. In 1878, another law was introduced specifically for controlling newspapers in Indian languages. Subsequently, in 1908 and 1910, draconian legislations were introduced to restrain press freedom. The coercive apparatus of the colonial state was intimidating and its imperial hegemony was a reality which modern Indian languages had to grasp in their formative phase.

The domain of Indian languages had an independent existence and it responded to social and political issues, which amounted to 'speaking truth' to power. We witness a schism between English and Indian languages during this phase. This was rooted in their relations of complicity or confrontation with the colonial administration. Arvind Rajagopal has explained this process:

> If, for English speakers, native society was backward and unredeemable, and required to be written over with their civilizing mission, nationalists presented national culture as the true bedrock of Indian society. By extension, the Indian language press, became not simply a medium for elite and middle class politicians and writers to exchange ideas but the representative of the real India, against which the truth claims of the English language press were suspect. (2009, 7)

Modernity has to be located in the Indian context in such contestations. The nature of these contestations will have to be probed in detail to understand the direction taken by the public sphere. The roles of English and modern Indian languages need to be understood against their ideological contexts. It is apparent that Indian languages do not subscribe to a definition of modernity embodied in the power structures of English. 'Regions' negotiated the hegemonic structures of colonial power from their respective positions. Rajagopal talks of a 'split public' in India where there was a growing schism between 'an officially maintained secular public sphere and a more heterogeneous popular culture' which took many forms in the culture of the twentieth century (2009, 208). Indian languages had to balance two influential elements of the public sphere – the English-knowing bilingual elite as well as the popular domain made up of the common people whose sense of reality was informed by their material conditions of exploitation and deprivation.

Indian languages have always had to confront and contain disparate realms of reality which are often contradictory in nature. Sudhir Chandra has brought out the deep sense of ambivalence that characterised the Indian response to colonialism. He shows how the works of Vishnu Krishna Chiplunkar (1850–82) in Marathi, Govardhanram Tripathi (1855–1907) in Gujarati and Bharatendu Harishchandra (1850–85) in Hindi betray an underlying tension born of an 'acute sense of subjection and a consequent urge for freedom, along with a feeling of grateful loyalty to British rule' (2014, 21). The schism in the public sphere was an external manifestation of a deeper malaise, a self-division that defied as well as deified the colonial/imperial discourse on modernity. The moment of prose and print in Indian literature, which is also our moment of modernity, is born of a deep-rooted anxiety about being Indian and a resolve to be modern – an impossible moment of irreconcilable contradictions when every choice was accompanied by its opposite.

Between consent and coercion, Indian languages had to find spaces of accommodation as well as assertion. In India, poetry had an uninterrupted oral tradition that reached back to the medieval era. This *kavya* tradition had not gone out of circulation but its appeal had worn thin. Print, in fact, made it possible to retrieve earlier texts; and it will be seen from the case of Tamil that the rediscovery of a native tradition was often an unintended effect of the colonial intervention in culture. But now print medium demanded a new format that could embody the new subjectivity informed by colonial consciousness. Western modernity was problematic as it lacked the intellectual resources to comprehend the cultural plurality of India. A complete rejection of the Western paradigms of modernity, as in Gandhi's *Hind Swaraj* (1909), would have meant a nativist assertion of civilisational proportions. Gandhi did appeal to a number of writers in Indian languages, but his ideological rejection of the West never found wide acceptance. This again shows how writers in Indian languages did not replicate reductive models of resistance. They were aware that 'the emerging fields of philology, geography and ethnology aimed to create a cognitive order that was a systematic empirical reconstruction of native ways' (Naregal 2001, 45), in order to contain them. Prose and the literature that emerged through prose took up this larger challenge of cognitive 'othering' inherent in the new discursive disciplines. If colonial consciousness was plagued by an ambivalence towards Enlightenment values, it was the literature produced in prose that embodied this consciousness. Since social sciences were, at this stage, deeply implicated in the Western discourses, they were incapable of developing a self-reflexive discourse that could both represent and critique that very representation. It is in modern Indian literatures produced in Indian languages (largely in prose and circulated through the new print medium) that emerged in the late nineteenth century that we can find a layered and complex representation of the deep-rooted schism of Indian modernity. That social sciences failed to grasp the ideological implications of Indian modernity is a fact that has not been highlighted sufficiently. This is the crisis that social sciences in India face today, and an increasing number of historians, political scientists and sociologists now turn to literatures in Indian languages to problematise the cognitive blocks that rendered their disciplines complicit with colonialism. As Gopal Guru and Sundar Sarukkai comment at the end of a debate concerning the incapacity of social sciences in India to confront the Indian experience, 'Indian social scientists have become consumers of the knowledge games of the Western academic world and are not seen as equal partners in the enterprise' (2013, 224). This process began in the nineteenth century itself. The language of experience has to be rooted in the complex web of indigenous imaginaries that question exclusionary categories produced in imperial cultures. The works of Bankim Chandra Chattopadhyay, Fakir Mohan Senapati, Potheri Kunjambu or Bharatendu Harishchandra enable us to reclaim an ethically informed discourse rooted in the contradictions of lived realities. In this sense, comparative literature in India can contribute towards bridging the gap between 'the epistemological with the emotional' in the service of a new ethical discourse rooted in the Indian experience (Guru and Sarukkai 2013, 45).

## 3

As has been pointed out above, print media brought about radical reorientations in our attitude towards literacy and the literary. A novel such as *Indulekha* clearly stages the contest between Sanskrit and English, and Malayalam seemingly aligns itself with the emergent colonial power structures in opposition to Sanskrit. But, at a deeper level, Malayalam itself is in a state of flux as it negotiates its internal contradictions. In that sense, the novelist uses the contest between two hegemonic structures to 'frame' Malayalam into modernity. This act of framing also inscribes Malayalam into a certain role within the emergent discourse of power within Malabar or North Kerala. This subtle shift is what makes the novel an ideological form, right from its inception. Comparative literature has to examine how new, emergent genres are deeply implicated in ideology. Our study of early novels often does not go beyond merely stating the obvious, never looking deeper into the form itself to decipher the unwritten. Much of nineteenth-century literature is like a palimpsest, requiring the ability to read what is not written. This is why literature now requires insights and methodologies provided by comparative literature. Texts cannot be now understood in terms of the literary alone, nor can they be understood only through the prior history of the language and society of the particular text. Comparative literature in the Indian context will have to revisit the moment in the ninteenth century when we moved into a new arena of the literary which demanded a new act of reading.

As the literary is reconstituted, the act of reading takes on a new character. The new education policy emphasised 'reading' as a means of shaping a new moral awareness and this could not be achieved by reading literature produced in regional languages. The colonial state put into practice new norms of discursive production while enforcing English as the language of 'knowledge'. Native languages needed to be co-opted into the project of modernity, and it is here that print played an important role. Translation of 'study materials' chosen by colonial administrators into native languages was to open up the world of the natives to the expanding frontiers of knowledge as seen by Europe. Obviously, Europeans could not come to terms with the complex plurality of Indian languages and their intractable inter-relationships in terms of aesthetic and linguistic traits. They deployed philology mainly to contain this proliferating plurality into manageable accounts. Languages came to be classified and the superficial affinities among them were now taken to mean deeper family resemblances. There were 'pure' languages of antiquity as opposed to 'hybrid' languages, which could not be placed easily. As is evident in the long history of translations from

Sanskrit into modern Indian languages, the hegemonic status of Sanskrit had become less intimidating to modern Indian languages, once their principal works became available to the local population in their own tongues. Indian languages had a way of negotiating hegemonic structures of power. However, in the colonial situation, these ways of negotiating power structures were put to test. Comparative Indian literature needs to enquire into the nature of these negotiations that contributed towards the reconstitution of Indian languages into 'modern' literary languages in the nineteenth century. Once Indian languages were 'essentialised' into a format that ensured their inferiority and backwardness, the only manner in which they could relate to their past was by either disowning it or by relegating it to a stage of 'folk expression' conditioned by orality before the advent of print. In this sense, the creation of a category called 'folk' was the result of the introduction of print. During the time *Indulekha* became a sensation in Kerala, the local legends and folktales were being collected and compiled into books. Here, the gaze into the future also occasions a backward gaze into the past – the moment of the modern alters the way we relate to the past. The novel belongs to the market place as well as the domestic privacy of the individual; it constitutes the individual reader as well as the consumer with desire.

There were also wide variations in the constructions of the modern across regions. The case of Hindi illustrates how a certain nationalisation of Hindu tradition accompanied the consolidation of a new Hindi accessible to the common people. Vasudha Dalmiya, in her path-breaking *Nationalization of Hindu Tradition,* shows how a number of social and political factors converged in the late nineteenth century to transform Banaras into the seat of a new Hindu culture and consolidated Bharatendu Harishchandra as a cultural hero whose endorsement of change was rooted in tradition. An ambivalence towards the very idea of the modern characterises Bharatendu's versatile cultural interventions as editor, poet, dramatist, essayist, fictionist and thinker. He used his organic links with a 'traditional' society to legitimate the creation of a public sphere that opened up new circuits of communication. That his *khadi-boli* Hindi excluded dialects spoken by the common people and also the words derived from Persian and Urdu, was an ideological shift that, in the process, created a popular medium for a new generation of English-educated Hindi speakers. Their nationalist aspirations were embodied in the new language which had the muscularity to become the language of modern knowledge. It is not easy to distinguish between Bharatendu's role as a conservative scholar and a modern thinker. He moved with ease among multiple worlds, which included those of business, commerce, education, printing and public debate (Dalmiya 2013, 117–43). But as we approach the twentieth century, we see him more as a moderniser who disrupted tradition even as he spoke its language with ease. As Dalmiya observes, 'the contradiction in Harishchandra's position allowed for a creative tension which enabled the wider authority that he exercised reach much beyond his own circles' (142). In forging a national literature, he went along with the canonisation of Hindu poets that equated 'Hindi' with 'Hindu'. It was the Sanskritised Hindi which now became the standard both in periodicals and in the classroom, as the new middle class identified with its ideological orientation (218–21).

The nationalisation of Hindu tradition, which characterised the evolution of a standard form of Hindi, is singularly absent in some of the other languages where the nationalist spirit took deep roots. Subramania Bharati (1882–1921) was a versatile Tamil poet eloquent in many forms, both traditional and modern, who wrote polemical prose as well as fictional works, besides editing a series of periodicals with explosive political content and reformist social themes. That Bharati spent a few years in Banaras at the turn of the twentieth century maybe relevant here, since he must have come to know of Bharatendu's works. For a long time, Bharati was forced to live in exile in Pondicherry (which was a French colony) as the British administration had registered cases against him for his political essays. In his study of the print history of Tamil, Venkatachalapathy finds Bharati a transitional figure in the shift from patronage to public (2012, 51–64). Like Bharatendu, he was a staunch nationalist and used the columns of his newspaper and periodicals to mobilise the common people for the political cause of resistance against imperialism. But Bharati remains largely an outsider in his own society, despite speaking on behalf of an emergent community of educated middle class. Though he had initially found some patrons to help with the publication of his books, much of his work remained unpublished at the time of his death. He had planned to bring out all his works in forty volumes, for which he required about thirty thousand rupees. The plan never took off and it was only after his death, when a new generation recognised his merit as a nationalist poet and 'rediscovered' him, that his works saw the light of day. Venkatachalapathy notes that the Tamil middle class consisting of English-educated Tamil people working as teachers, lawyers, clerks, petty traders, etc., had not yet come of age when a poet such as Bharati desperately appealed for their support. He observes,

> Over this period of transition, the Tamil middle class had not come of age, so to speak. It was in its nascent form, without possessing the clear consciousness of a class for itself. Consequently it did not heed the call of intellectuals who had emerged from within, people who were seeking to give this rising class a sense of homogeneity, and an awareness of its social function. (73)

Both Bharatendu and Bharati were harbingers of a popular idiom that was neither classical to the point of being opaque nor pedestrian to the point of being inane. Bharatendu is called the father of modern Hindi for his contribution in fashioning a language that could embody the new subjectivity that found flamboyant erudition and vulgar street parlance equally unacceptable. However, Bharati does not carry the burden of 'nationalising Hindu tradition'. Hindi was in the process of being standardised to take up the challenge of representing nationalist ethos, with increasing Sanskritisation accompanying its 'Hinduisation'. In both Tamil and Malayalam traditions we examined above, standardisation was a much more inclusive process, where the public sphere addressed the common people consisting of many castes and several religions. In her account of the standardisation of Marathi, Naregal shows how 'philology cleared the ground for the redefinition of linguistic identities mainly by setting up normalizing mechanisms through which the vernaculars acquired the modern forms' (2001, 48). The elites were aligned with colonial administrators in making claims on behalf of purity and noble descent. This attitude was well represented in Marathi. But it also had Jyotirao Phule (1827–90) whose *Gulamgiri* (Slavery, 1871) strongly contested the Aryan–brahminic point of view and drew a parallel between the condition of the lower castes in India under brahminic domination and the plight of the Blacks in America. Nemade has shown that in the process of standardisation, it was the Pune dialect of Marathi that was 'superposed on others' (2014, 98).

He notes that the standardisation of Marathi was greatly influenced by the urbanisation of western Maharashtra and the dominance of the upper castes in matters of culture: 'owing to its caste affiliation, standard Marathi had by the end of the century a puristic [sic] aura' (98). The emergence of Malayalam prose, on the other hand, was accompanied by a strong resistance to brahminic control exerted through its highly Sanskritised version. A similar critique of the hegemonic structures of caste system was available in Tamil as caste came to be increasingly problematised in the new novels and polemical writings.

'Region' is central to the national imaginary that is articulated in the late nineteenth and early twentieth century in India. In our cultural history much attention has been given to 'nation', but it is significant to see the 'region' as central to the production of culture in India. The works that are called 'literary' in a language are born of contestations and interrogations that go back a long way. Often this is deeply etched in the very language of the texts. The skill of close reading that comparative literature instills among its students demands attention to words and their echoes, the ability to sense subtle deviations of form and their symbolic implications. Literature is an echo-chamber where the resonances of words from the past come back to the present, modifying their meanings. The challenge is to retrieve the layers of meanings that are inherent in a text through an informed reading. Genres are received differently by each language. Various Indian languages and cultures have interpreted the novel or the essay or the short story from their different perspectives. Hence, it is necessary to see how the novel in Bangla differs from that in Marathi or Malayalam in its deep structure. Reception studies in India have to go beyond mere English-vs-Indian-language paradigm. For instance, Romantic poetry was received and its sensibility interpreted variously by different Indian languages. We are yet to study receptions across Indian languages with any degree of commitment to regional variations.

## 4

As may be clear from our discussion of the relations between prose, print and modernity, what happened in the nineteenth century in India was a massive reorganisation of our epistemological structures and a reorientation of imagination. We need to evaluate these paradigm shifts from our contemporary perspectives. The preceding decades have put on the agenda of contemporary criticism the need to resist hegemonic forces that legitimate homogenised world views. With the rise of disciplines such as postcolonial literature, gender studies and culture studies, ethical issues regarding representation have assumed urgency. Some of the assumptions held as sacred by comparative literature regarding texts and canons have been challenged by successive waves of theories, and these have resulted in new formulations regarding the literary, the role of the reader and literary history. A hermetic view of literary works and their canons informed by a linear approach to literary influences has given way to a complex awareness about the constitutive nature of ambivalence and polysemy in the production of literary texts. The view that literary texts are sites where a coherent view of cultural heritage can be defended is no more valid. Consequently, the 'concern for values and qualities' and 'a distant ideal of universal literary history and scholarship' that Rene Wellek mentions in the context of 'true criticism', in his essay on 'The Name and Nature of Comparative Literature' (1970, 36), appears increasingly problematic. The ethical turn in theory has opened up a context for realigning a discipline such as comparative literature with the social and political realities of the Global South.

In *Modernity at Large,* Arjun Appadurai argues that in a globalised world one cannot enforce a normative concept of modernity. He says, 'A central challenge for current anthropology is to study the cosmopolitan cultural forms of the contemporary world without logically or chronologically presupposing either the authority of Western experience or the models derived from that experience' (1996, 49). What Appadurai says in the context of ethnic studies is applicable to comparative literature as well. In redefining its field and methodology, comparative literature has to recognise that categories such as the text, the reader and the tradition are sets of relationships and not absolute entities with fixed essences. The nature of these relationships will vary from culture to culture. The idea of the text in a multilingual and multi-religious society with multiple cultural traditions will not be the same as that in a monolingual culture with a single language and religion. The field of comparative literature has to include studies of how these categories are constituted differently in different cultures. Reception theory and reader response criticism have contributed to the redefining of the field of textual production as a fluid interactive site that cannot be standardised. Discourses are forms of being in the world and, hence, articulate socially situated identities. The literary cannot be segregated from this subliminal layer of the social where language as discourse embodies identities, world views, attitudes and assumptions. In constructing the normative, discourses often marginalise certain experiences or subjects as the Other.

To understand this process of 'othering', one has to study the construction of mainstream canons with reference to their social and political frames of reference. As we have seen at the beginning of this chapter, in the foundational moment of modern Indian literature, colonial power structures created hierarchies and differences in Indian culture. The inherent ethnocentrism in colonial and imperial narratives, which parades as 'cosmopolitanism', needs to be tracked to their sources. In the binaries of the universal and the local, the international and the national/regional, and the univocal and the pluralistic, comparative literature studies need to resist the hegemonic tendencies inherent in the universal, international and univocal. Chinua Achebe puts it in unequivocal terms in the following statement: 'I should like to see the word "universal" banned altogether from discussion of African literature until such time as people cease to use it as a synonym for the narrow, self-serving parochialism of Europe, until their horizon extends to include all the world' (1988, 51–52)

By emphasising the social and the political in the construction of the literary, we demystify the very idea of literature. The shared world of ideas – the collective ways of seeing and world views – has a bearing on the material world we inhabit. Imagination cannot be conceived in individual terms alone. It is this constitutive and constructive role of imagination that is foregrounded by terms such as 'imagined communities', 'social imaginary', 'self-fashioning', 'white mythologies', 'imagining caste' or 'imagining desire', in recent critical discourse. Issues of representation, language, memory, experience and desire are inherent in probing the nature of the relation between subject-formation and collective experience. Appadurai suggests that the moment of globalisation has affected imagination as it 'has broken out of the special expressive space of art, myth and ritual and has now become part of the quotidian mental work of ordinary people in many societies' (1996, 5). There is no denying the fact that the relation between art and life has altered in a fundamental sense that invalidates several universalist discourses and assumptions. The formalist schools of criticism tended to attribute all imaginative functions solely to individual acts of creativity. A larger participatory space of inter-subjective communication can be located in society in the manner in which literary forms emerge or decline, literary texts are received and internalised by society, language functions as a site of legitimating creative acts of sublimation or subversion, or in the way in which social/political movements capture the imagination of an entire generation.

Literature is the site where 'social imaginaries' manifest themselves. The history of literary movements, literary forms and the production and reception of literary texts will have to be examined to see how social imaginaries inform and shape their trajectories. However, at present, comparative studies of literature hardly emphasise the constitutive and constructive role of social imagination in the shaping of literary texts. Moving away from an individual-centred view of the text towards a community-centred view of literature will liberate the very idea of comparative literature in India. In her preface to the translation of the Bangla classic *Dhorai charit manas* by Satinath Bhaduri, Ipshita Chanda comments that the narrative inhabits multiple worlds that lie beyond Bangla. She says, 'It appears that the claim that *Dhorai Charit Manas* can lay to being an "Indian" novel, apart from the obvious fact of its geographical location and language, is due to its multiplicity of registers harboured within the same language' (2013, xxi–xxii). She further says that this kind of hybridity is akin to 'the diversity of a pan-Indian movement like bhakti' (xxii). In modern Indian languages, the boundaries of language and culture are crossed constantly. For instance, a recent novel in Malayalam titled *Aarachar* (The hangwoman, 2015) by K. R. Meera, ably translated by J. Devika into English, sets the entire narrative in Kolkata of an earlier period. In the Malayalam novels of VKN (Vadakkke Koottala Narayanankutty Nair), M. Mukundan, Kovilan and Anand, the stories are seldom set in Kerala, thus creating routes of mobility between the region and the nation. Indigenous imaginaries are not about bounded spaces, but crossing borders and speaking from contact zones of culture.

This moment of the discovery of 'social imaginary' affords an opportunity for non-Western cultures which never subscribed to the tenets of individualism in the first instance and had imagined their modernity in alternative ways. This will mean focusing on 'the ways people imagine their social existence, how they fit together with others, how things go on between them and their fellows, the expectations that are normally met, and the deeper normative notions and images that underlie these expectations' (Taylor 2007, 23). The globalisation currently underway across the world, after the collapse of the Soviet Union and the emergence of a unipolar world, demands new strategies of analysis and evaluation in the wake of cultural products entering the market of commodities. This does not mean we have to position 'Indian literature' in the commodified market of international culture, but we have to recognise that 'Indian' cannot be conceived merely in terms of the nation or the nation state. Texts produced in India would also include texts produced by people who inhabit an imagined India by 'crossing borders', as mentioned by Gayatri Chakravorty Spivak in her *Death of a Discipline.* In a way, our task would be to discover how India is being imagined in countless ways across boundaries of cultures and nations. This also means that we will have to rewrite our literary histories. As Stephen Greenblatt mentions in his essay, 'A Mobility Studies Manifesto', we should take note of 'movements of peoples, objects, images, texts, ideas' across man-made boundaries. Further, 'contact zones where cultural goods are exchanged' need to be identified and analysed (2010, 250–51). Goethe spoke of 'world literature' giving rise to the idea of 'comparative literature', when he read a Chinese novel in translation and heard that his play had been staged in translation in another country (Greenblatt 2010, 17). Jyotirao Phule's *Gulamgiri* was inspired by the resistance to slavery in America. In an essay on how Germans read narratives of American slavery, Heike Paul has argued that American slavery and its critique have repeatedly served as blueprints for political empowerment far beyond America's borders (Greenblatt 2010, 122–72). One of the earliest Malayalam novels, written in the nineteenth century, was modelled on *Uncle Tom's Cabin* (Ramakrishnan 2011, 159–67). It is important to study cultural mobility to understand how cultures are locally rooted. To quote Greenblatt one last time, 'A study of cultural mobility that ignores the allure (and, on occasion, the entrapment) of the firmly rooted simply misses the point' (252–53).

## 5

Citing the example of the critical realism expounded by Fakir Mohan Senapati in his novel *Six Acres and a Third* (1897–99), S. P. Mohanty says, 'Modernity is thus a layered and a complex phenomenon, according to such writers as Senapati, and analysis of traditional culture needs to be nuanced and contextually sensitive' (2011, 3). In recent comparative criticism, there has been much talk of 'alternative modernities', but they tend to replicate European modernity in reverse. More nuanced cultural analyses of Indian texts will demonstrate how '"alternative" or "indigenous modernity" points to a project of historical retrieval and imaginative philosophical reconstruction' (Mohanty 2011, 3). Comparative literary studies could be the site for this retrieval and reconstruction since as a discipline, its provenance is the study of textual traditions and their intertextual/interdisciplinary relations to the making of culture. The critical interpretation of the ideologies of colonialism and imperialism is a precondition for the creative evolution of such a discourse of comparative literature. If a totalising impulse is at the back of the universal as a category, we need to critically examine the contents of comparative frameworks that endorse such hegemonic positions. We need to conceive of literary texts in broader terms to include cultural productions from different templates of time and space. Texts can be non-canonical and representative at the same time. An author considered 'minor' may reveal much more about a culture than its supposedly 'major' authors. The substance and worth of the comparative approach will depend on the treatment and the range and depth of concerns we bring to our reading. When comparative literature functions as a mode of apprehending the transactions among the literary, the cultural and the political in all their multivalent ways, it would bring about a paradigm shift in its practice.

Modernity was interpreted and understood in much of the colonial period on terms that privileged European hegemony. This is the reason why a unitary view of 'Indian literature' as a monolithic category gained currency in this period. Orientalist legacy has further complicated this picture. The larger question about forging an alternative view of 'modernity' can become a viable project only if we can reclaim 'region' as a site of plurality of Indian literary traditions. We need to recover counter-narratives that questioned essentialist ways of defining 'Indian' and 'literature'. We need to recognise that at the regional level, 'bhasha' literatures are highly plural and multiple. Indian languages are multiple at their very local level. Comparative studies of Indian literatures seem to assume that the literature of each language is a unified category. The oppositional tradition in each of the literary traditions has largely been forgotten in our eagerness to homogenise regional literatures into 'Indian literature'. The conflict between the cosmopolitan and the indigenous is evident in each bhasha literary tradition. A defining feature of Indian modernity has been this internal dialogic structure of bhasha literatures. Oppositional world views that call hegemonic structures of power into question did not originate in our encounter with colonial modernity. This is why comparative literature in India needs to go beyond texts to the sub-texts that inform texts. We need to evolve a discourse that can bring out these socio-political sub-texts. For instance, the fragmentary and chaotic nature of oral speech permits Vaikom Muhammad Basheer to challenge the hegemonic power structure that dictates absolutist views about identity. In his long stories, Basheer is able to bring out the moral evasions in the enactment of a nationalist discourse that embodies a linear view of modernity. His world of small-time crooks, pickpockets, gamblers and petty thieves defies the normative of the nationalist paradigm that legislates identities into standard, stipulated formats. What is oppositional in Basheer opens up not only ways of resisting authoritarian points of views but possibilities of community formation. This is where the carnivalesque and the double-voiced need to be seen as products of alternative paradigms of modernity.

It is time the comparatists in India understood the possibilities inherent in the textual material available in the traditions of modern Indian languages. We need to choose texts such as Fakir Mohan Senapati's *Six Acres and a Third* that provides 'a unique vantage point from which to analyse the relationship between literature and the shifting meanings of modernity, both colonial and traditional' (Mohanty 2011, 8). While comparing Senapati's novel with the Telugu play *Kanyashulkam,* Velcheru Narayana Rao argues that both these texts exemplify 'an indigenous modernity, distinct from colonial modernity' (2007, 135). As argued above, the contradictions of modernity, as it evolved in India in the nineteenth century, can be understood only by a close reading of texts from regional languages. Such a project needs to be addressed with all the intellectual resources at our disposal, from the vantage points of major writers of regional literary traditions who have contributed towards shaping our ideas of the modern, the Indian and the literary. An ethically responsible way of reading Indian texts in a context-sensitive way will be a starting point for evolving an Indian school of comparative literature. Such readings will fragment and pluralise our perspectives and alter our relations with the past and the future.

## References

Appadurai, Arjun. 1996. *Modernity at large: Cultural dimensions of globalisation.* Minneapolis and London: U of Minnesota P.

Achebe, Chinua. 1988. Colonialist criticism. In *Hopes and impediments.* London: Heinemenn-International.

Apparao, Gurajada. 2007. *Girls for sale: A play from colonial India* [*Kanyashulkam*]. Tr. Velcheru Narayana Rao. Bloomington: Indiana UP.

Arunima, G. 2006. Imagining communities—differently: Print, language and the 'public sphere' in colonial Kerala. *The Indian Economic and Social History Review* 43.1: 63–76.

Chanda, Ipshita, trans. 2013. *Dhorai charit manas.* New Delhi: Sahitya Akademi.

Chandra, Sudhir. 2014. *The oppressive present: Literature and social consciousness in colonial India.* London: Routledge.

Dalmia, Vasudha. 2013. *The nationalization of Hindu tradition: Bharatendu Harishchandra and nineteenth-century Banaras.* New Delhi: Permanent Black.

Foucault, Michel. 1994. *The order of things: An archaeology of the human sciences.* Vintage Book Edition.

Gangadharan, Thikkurissi. 1984. *Kerala varmayum malayala gadyavum* [Kerala Varma and Malayalam prose]. Kottayam: National Book Stall.

Govi, K. M. 1998. *Aadimudranam: Bharatathilum keralathilum* [History of printing in India and Kerala]. Thrissur: Kerala Sahitya Akademi.

Greenblatt, Stephen. 2010. *Cultural mobility: A manifesto.* New York: Cambridge UP.

Guru, Gopal, and Sundar Sarukkai. 2013. *The cracked mirror: An Indian debate on experience and theory.* New Delhi: Oxford UP.

Mohanty, Satya P. 2011. *Colonialism, modernity, literature: A view from India.* New Delhi: Orient BlackSwan.

Morrison, Toni. 1992. *Playing in the dark: Whiteness and the literary imagination.* New York: Random House.

Narayana Rao, Velcheru, David Dean Shulman, and Sanjay Subrahmanyam. 2003. *Textures of time: Writing history in South India.* New York: Other Press.

Naregal, Veena. 2001. *Language politics, elites and the public sphere.* New Delhi: Permanent Black.

Nemade, Bhalchandra. 2014. *The influence of English on Marathi: A sociolinguistic and stylistic study.* Mumbai: Popular Prakashan. (Orig. Pub. 1990.)

Rajagopal, Aravind, ed. 2009. *The Indian public sphere: Readings in media history.* New Delhi: Oxford UP.

Ramakrishnan, E.V. 2011. *Locating Indian literature: Texts, traditions, translations.* Hyderabad: Orient BlackSwan.

———. 2012. *Achatiyum aadhunikatayum* [Print and modernity]. In *Anubhavangale aarkkanu peti?* [Who is afraid of experiences?] Kottayam: D. C. Books.

Ramanujan, A. K. 1999. *The collected essays of A. K. Ramanujan.* Ed. Vinay Dharwadker. New Delhi: Oxford UP.

Said, Edward. 1995. *Orientalism: Western conceptions of the orient.* London: Penguin Books.

Spivak, Gayatri Chakravorty. 2003. *Death of a discipline.* New Delhi/Calcutta: Seagull Books.

Taylor, Charles. 2007. *Modern social imaginaries.* Durham: Duke UP.

Venkatachalapathy, A. R. 2012. *The province of the book: Scholars, scribes and scribblers in colonial Tamil Nadu.* New Delhi: Permanent Black.

Wellek, Rene. 1970. *Discriminations: Further concepts of criticism.* New Haven: Yale UP.

## Chapter Two

# Beyond the Orientalist and Postcolonial Constructs: The Telos of Translation Studies from the Perspective of Comparative Indian Literature

Translation studies has not received the attention it deserves in comparative literature studies in India. This chapter discusses the two major moments of transition in the history of modern Indian languages – the first in the first half of the second millennium; and the second in the nineteenth century, during the colonial encounter with English. In the first phase, which may be seen as a foundational moment, translation was the means by which modern Indian languages moved away from the hegemonic hold of Sanskrit. Sheldon Pollock's idea of 'vernacularisation' is critiqued here, for its inability to acknowledge the agency of modern Indian languages as revealed through translations. Indologists and orientalists tend to freeze India into a timeless zone where everything that is valuable belongs to a classical past. The cultural ferment of the colonial phase involved major negotiations with the imperial authority of English through translations. This is illustrated with reference to the emergence of missionary prose in Malayalam, which effectively became the medium for the new public sphere. Comparatists in India have their task cut out, as these cultural transitions and transactions can only be understood comparatively, through the study of translation as negotiations of power in a hierarchically stratified society.

During the last three decades, there has been a perceptible change in the way translation is viewed in India. As a student, I hardly came across any reference to 'translation' in English literature classrooms or in literary criticism in Malayalam where translations were taken for granted. We read the works of Dostoevsky, Brecht, Chekhov, Kafka, Camus, Sartre, Ionesco, Pirandello and Neruda, not to mention those of Tagore, Premchand, Bankim Chandra, Sarat Chandra and Tulsidas, in Malayalam, without ever bothering to find out who translated them or how they *functioned* as translations. However, today, in India, translations of Indian literature are being produced and marketed by major publishers; and there is increased visibility for translators – they are now invited to major literary festivals and are counted among 'writers'. The emergence of translation studies in the West has had its impact in India but, as an interdisciplinary field of study, translation studies is yet to make its presence felt. Social scientists and culture theorists assume that translation need not be taken into account in the production of knowledge about any society. The comparatists, on the other hand, have not paid any attention to the fact that in a multilingual society, categories such as 'literature', 'text' and 'reader' need to be configured differently from what they are in a monolingual, monocultural society. There is hardly any worthwhile research undertaken in the field, and the volumes of conference proceedings that one occasionally comes across hardly break any new ground. This chapter will explore the complex dimensions of translation studies in India, which is yet largely an unchartered area. To map the field comprehensively in its entirety would be a colossal task – it would take intensive teamwork by scholars from around the country and decades of hard work. If such a prodigious task is ever undertaken, it will enable us to reconceive comparative Indian literature as a field with its own protocol and pedagogy. Comparative Indian literature and translation studies overlap repeatedly as we consider issues in literary history, reception aesthetic, thematology, genology or the emergence of the book in Indian languages. Hence, both these disciplines have a bonding that is too intricate and symbiotic to ignore. The foundational moments of modern Indian languages are deeply implicated in translation as even a cursory look at texts in Indian languages would reveal.

In India, language is a site where, very often, social, cultural and political battles are fought. Alternatively, one may say that socio-political conflicts invariably acquire cultural and linguistic overtones, necessitating negotiations with, and through, languages. Some of these fault lines that cause fissures and ruptures run deep, and will have to be factored in the discussion of the shifts within our cultural terrains. Here, it would be instructive to recall how, in the first place, modern Indian languages came into being around the beginning of the second millennium, overthrowing the hegemony of Sanskrit, a language which had reigned as the sole preserve of intellectual and literary expression over a thousand years. Equally instructive is the way modern Indian languages shifted gear in the wake of the colonial encounter, assimilating and resisting elements in the 'superior' external literary traditions without losing their own ground. The fact that within a period of less than a century, modern Indian languages brought into their creative expression forms such as the novel, the short story, the autobiography, the personal and reflective essay, the modern drama and literary critical discourse is no mean achievement. Translation played a significant role in these engagements with the Other; but this has not received the attention it merits. The foundational moment of modern Indian languages, and their coming of age as major world literary languages in the context of colonial/imperial assault – these two contexts cannot be comprehended without exploring the role of translation as a creative mode of intellectual negotiation and political assertion.

## I

As Sheldon Pollock argues, the decline of Sanskrit and its replacement by regional languages as the medium of intellectual discourse and literary composition was one of the major shifts that took place in India or throughout South Asia from (roughly) 900 AD. Sanskrit lost its monopolistic status as the pan-Indian language of high culture. This was accompanied by the assertion of regional forms of articulation, both within the court and outside. Pollock uses the term 'vernacularisation' to describe this linguistic and cultural shift (2011, 330–38). I would prefer to use the term 'regionalisation' as 'vernacular' carries an unpalatable cultural baggage. Pollock offers a working definition of 'vernacularisation' in these words: 'Vernacularization is here understood not *a priori* or stipulatively, but from tendencies visible in the empirical record – as the historical process of choosing to create a written literature, along with its complement, a political discourse, in local languages according to models supplied by a superordinate, usually, cosmopolitan, literary culture' (23). This shift towards modern Indian languages took place in Kannada in the ninth century, in Telugu around the tenth century, in Marathi around the thirteenth century, in Gujarati around the twelfth century and in Malayalam around the fifteenth century, and in Assamese,

Bangla and Oriya around the fifteenth and sixteenth centuries. In his discussion of the Kannada scene, Pollock identifies certain features of the process of 'regionalisation', two of which may be relevant to our discussion. He finds a correlation between the 'vernacular innovation and a reconfiguration of the culture-power order' (336). As a new political discourse rooted in the region gained ascendancy and consolidated its position, Sanskrit yielded its place as a cosmopolitan language. The identification of the region and its people with its language marks a moment of transition when the regional language begins to function 'as the primary code of political communication' (337). As Pollock puts it, this is the moment when the 'aesthetics of vernacular power' began to produce 'a new power of vernacular aesthetics' (338).

Pollock's central argument regarding a transfer of power from Sanskrit to modern Indian languages assumes the unequal power relations between them as a cultural given, without going into their content. Pollock never discusses problems of caste in the context of the production of knowledge in India. He is eager to point out that Sanskrit was not monopolised by brahmins. However, it remains a mystery how and why the 'language of gods' remained out of bounds for large sections of lower-caste people and women in India. In his eagerness to incorporate the cultural shifts in India into a universal model that is dictated by the paradigms of European Reformation, Pollock erases the differences among the regions within India with reference to their modes of adopting and shaping new literary cultures centred around regional languages. The plurality of the Indian situation, marked by a deep heteroglossia, is not reflected in his argument. For instance, the trajectories of Malayalam and Kannada are not the same as far as their negotiations with Sanskrit are concerned. It has been argued that after the rise of regional languages into separate, independent languages, Sanskrit occupied a cultural space within many of these regional discourses, largely through its preeminence as the language of knowledge and its rich traditions of poetics. In her study of the evolution of the Marathi language and culture, *Language Politics, Elites and the Public Sphere,* Veena Naregal cautions against the adoption of categories derived from the European Reformation, and says, 'The literarisation of the vernaculars here did not lead to a redefinition of aesthetic norms and ideas of cultivation or notions of collectivity, as happened through Renaissance' (2001, 41). She further argues that in the case of Marathi, the rise of 'vernacular' textuality was mediated through the 'high' textual traditions of Sanskrit. But this is not entirely borne out by facts. In *Religion and Public Memory: A Cultural History of Saint Namdev in India*, Christian Lee Novetzke shows how public memory plays a crucial role in the creation of Namdev's image as a saint-poet in Maharashtra. The oral performance of *kirtan*, to which the common masses could relate emotionally, laid the foundation for his subsequent fame and reception. Novetzke observes that 'Namdeo is a key figure in Maharashtra as well as central, western, and northern India, and virtually ubiquitous in the Hindu and Sikh religious-literary traditions of these regions from the fifteenth century to the present, a period spanning Sultanate, Mughal, Maratha, and British rule as well as post-independence India' (2008, 1). This popular domain is absent in Pollock's discussion of 'vernacularisation' in India. He also fails to note that even the regions from where modern Indian languages emerged were multilingual to the core. The ninth-century Kannada text *Kavirajamarga*, which Pollock discusses at length, states that *desi* traditions are plural to the core, and not even the thousand-headed Vasuki can describe all the poetic styles that are available in Kannada (Ramakrishnan 2011, 27).

That Sanskrit was never the language of the masses is an accepted fact. In the large number of translations of the epics, the *Ramayana* and the *Mahabharata*, local literary traditions enter into the narrative creating a dialogic relation between the *marga* and the *desi*. For instance, the Oriya version of the *Mahabharata*, translated by the fifteenth-century poet and scholar Sarala Das, omits the Bhagavat Gita from the narrative. The situation for rendering the Gita is retained in the text, but Das chose to exclude the great statement that the Gita makes from his narrative (Patnaik 2012, 48). There are several such instances in Das's *Mahabharata* where the regional version does not follow the original. This is how the native reader, who lives her or his everyday in the life-world of the region, is incorporated into the text. That translations from Sanskrit routinely deviated from the canon has to be seen from the perspective of assimilating the 'region' into the narrative. This does not make the translation inferior. In fact, all the major renderings of the *Ramayana* and the *Mahabharata* deviate from the canonical Sanskrit texts in several ways, largely because of the ethical burden these poets carried as translators. Their primary responsibility was to the living speech community of which they were a part. They spoke in the present tense even when the stories they told belonged to the past. Their language was the common heritage the people had created over centuries, and they now sensed the great responsibility of investing it with a literary text that would give a separate identity to the people. The complete identification of these poets with their regions and its people gives their texts a new poetics. Paula Richman, in her introduction to *Ramayana Stories in Modern South India,* mentions how the retelling of Ramakatha in regional languages 'incorporate local practices into the story'. She elaborates, 'For example, when the wedding of Rama and Sita is described, the account might include nuptial rituals particular to that region' (2008, 10). To say that regional writers were merely reproducing the *kavya* tradition from Sanskrit is to reduce the project in which they were engaged, to mere copyediting of an already written text. They were producing new texts for a contemporary society, because the creative impulse in that society had matured to a stage where Sanskrit would not satisfy their needs of creative expression. Orientalists wanted to freeze India into a timeless frame where everything durable in India came from its classical past. Pollock's argument seems to subscribe to the same ideology, though it is packaged in a contemporary idiom.

Each of the modern Indian languages produced translations of the great Indian epics during the period from the tenth to the sixteenth century. This should alert us to the churning that was happening across India during this creative upsurge of translations. The distribution of the *Ramayana* across modern Indian languages will help us understand this complex trajectory: Assamese (fourteenth century, translated by Madhav Kandali); Bengali (fifteenth century, Krittivasa); Gujarati (seventeenth century, Premananda); Hindi (sixteenth century, Tulsidas); Kannada (twelfth century, Nagacandra or Abhinava Pampa); Kashmiri (eighteenth century, Prakasha Bhatta); Malayalam (seventeenth century, Thunchaththu Ezhuthachan); Marathi (sixteenth century, Ekanatha); Oriya (sixteenth century, Balrama Dasa); Tamil (tenth century, Kambar); Telugu (sixteenth century, Molla). The cognitive grid that produced these translations attests to the presence of a domain of social imagination deeply grounded in the cultural practices of the people dating back to around 500–800 AD when modern languages began to emerge in their rudimentary forms. Pollock fails to trace this domain of social imagination that has shaped the modern Indian sensibility across its several languages, strongly resisting the hermetic aesthetic of a hegemonic language such as Sanskrit. It is significant that Pollock does not mention the word 'translation', not even once in his massive tome on Sanskrit. This cognitive blockage is derived from an Orientalist mindset – anything worthwhile in India has to be in Sanskrit and at least a thousand years old.

The gap between the 'high' culture of Sanskrit and the 'common' practices of the masses has always been apparent to the discerning scholars of regional languages. It is true that this gap was not theorised until modern print cultures altered the power relations between the traditional *kavya*-centred literary tradition and the modern print-centred prose tradition in the nineteenth century. The large number of prose-based literary forms – such as the travelogue, the short story, the biography, the autobiography and the novel – that emerged in the nineteenth century did not subscribe to the paradigms of Sanskrit aesthetics. Bhakti poetry, which constituted the initial impulse for the translations that inaugurated modern Indian literary traditions, marked a shift away from Sanskrit poetics as it used forms such as *vachana* and *abhang*[1] for literary composition, to address the elite as well as the masses.

The defiance of the hierarchy institutionalised in the caste system and the assertion of collective aspirations of the people towards a shared experiential world characterise much of the Bhakti poetry in regional languages. The rise of *manipravalam*[2] in Malayalam points to the emergence of a participatory cultural space where the cosmopolitan and the local interpenetrate, enabling Sanskrit to retain its legitimacy within a regional cultural framework. Though *manipravalam* existed in varying degrees in all South Indian languages, only in Malayalam did it become the standard medium of composing poetry. This is because Malayalam, in its development towards an independent language, had to confront the hegemonic structures of both Tamil and Sanskrit. And the form of *manipravalam* enabled the native speech community to retain a regional cosmopolis without being subservient to the dominating power of Sanskrit or Tamil.

U. R. Ananthamurthy has argued that modern Indian languages have successfully negotiated the hegemonic status of Sanskrit through translation. He comments,

> The philosophers say that there is a little fire somewhere in the *atma* (soul) which can digest anything; this is known in Sanskrit as the *Jeernagni*, the digestive fire. I consider the Indian *bhashas* the great *Jeernagnis* of India, because they digested Sanskrit at one time, as they digest Europe now. They have been transacting with different languages in this manner all through their history. (2014, 87)

Ananthamurthy points to the direction in which translation studies in India should move. Modern Indian languages have internalised the epistemological structures of Sanskrit, along with those of other similarly placed languages of antiquity, to such an extent that they could confidently confront the challenges of colonial modernity embodied by English. Postcolonial theorists in Brazil have advanced a theory of translation as 'cannibalism', in the context of their colonialist ruptures. One of its leading proponents, Else Vieira, in 'Liberating Calibans', remarks,

> Cannibalism is a metaphor actually drawn from the natives' ritual whereby feeding someone or drinking someone's blood, as they did to their totemic 'tapir,' was a means of absorbing the other's strength, a pointer to the very project of Anthropophagy group: not to deny foreign influences or nourishment, but to absorb and transform them by the addition of autochtonous input. Initially using the metaphor as an irreverent verbal weapon, the *Manifesto Antropofago* stresses the repressive nature of colonialism. (1999, 98–99)

What is significant here, as well as in Ananthamurthy's view, is the perception of a deeper process at work in the process of translation in societies such as India and Brazil. It is concerned with ideology and epistemology. Indian languages have never forgotten the fact that translation is a way of producing knowledge. Translation studies in India needs to recover this teleology grounded in knowledge production. This will be possible only if we view the two moments – the one that marks the beginning of modern Indian languages, during the first half of the second millennium, moving away from the hegemonic structures of Sanskrit and similar languages; and the other moment during the nineteenth century, of confronting the equally dominant colonial structures of epistemology – not as isolated events but as part of the larger matrix of the history of knowledge production in the country through translations that took place within Indian languages.

No theory can emerge based on our experience of translating Indian texts into English. These English translations only fulfil a larger need of the globalised world. That is why the project of translating Indian classics into English undertaken by the Murty Classical Library, under the general editorship of Pollock, has to be seen as part of an Orientalist project. In his general editor's note (featured on the website of the Murty Classical Library), titled 'Why a Classical Library of India?', Pollock states that books written before 1800 alone will be chosen for translation by the Library. He pays rich tribute to the multilingualism of India but finds its great tradition 'ruptured' by colonialism. For him, 'knowledge' means what is contained in ancient Indian classics. In fact, in a lecture titled 'What is Indian Knowledge Good for?', Pollock argued that with the passing away of languages such as Pali and Prakrit, everything valuable in Indian tradition will be erased. For him, the decline of Sanskrit is the biggest crisis that India has experienced in its history (Pollock 2013). Pollock fails to see that Indian languages, being dynamic entities, are required to negotiate political structures of power by producing new types of knowledge. If they have developed new genres and have taken to print culture, which enabled them to recover their past for a new literate audience, the question of 'rupture' needs to be reconsidered. A. R. Venkatachalapathy, in his scholarly analysis of the emergence of print in Tamil literary culture (2012), shows how the process was deeply implicated in several other narratives such as those of patronage, emergence of the public sphere, production of textbooks, rise of the popular novel, birth of the woman reader, and so on. If India had stayed with its ancient classics, without moving on to these new phases of cultural history, it would have become an exotic museum of ancient relics.

## 2

In the northern part of India, the shift from Sanskrit to regional languages took place at a time when Persian and Arabic emerged as languages of authority, with the consolidation of political power by the Mughal empire. The spheres of influence exerted by Sanskrit, on the one hand, and Persian and Arabic on the other, remained mutually exclusive as their power and authority were derived from different traditions and sources. In this context, the shift towards modern Indian languages assumes visibility in the textual traditions of Bhakti, and the enabling role played by Persian and Arabic in this process needs to be noted. Sufi poetry and the Islamic world view played a crucial role in shaping the poetic discourse of Bhakti. Arabic and Persian were languages of intellectual discourse, and not merely those of the civic authority. By the thirteenth century, Persian and Arabic had helped constitute South Asia as a cultural domain of great intellectual rigour. In her introduction to *Poetics and Politics of Sufism and Bhakti,* Kavita Panjabi comments, 'The influence of Sufism permeated the whole of Islamic world from Persian right upto the borders in Bengal, combining Arabic and Persian influences with indigenous languages, literatures and folk cultures, and drawing the latter into the wide open Persio-Arabic network, even as it transformed Indian literatures and society in significant ways' (2011, 6). This evidently shows that the literary world of India during the period from the thirteenth to the eighteenth century was characterised by a deeply resonant multilingualism which writers like Pollock refuse to acknowledge. A poet such as Amir Khusru (d. 1325) wrote in Persian, Hindawi and Brajbhasha, and was fluent in Turkish and Arabic. As mentioned above, Namdev's poetry cuts across many languages in western and northern India. This deep-rooted and widespread multilingualism transcended political boundaries and opened up social spaces. The lexical influence of Persian and Arabic can be seen even in the works of Eknath (roughly 1270–1350) who composed poetry in Marathi in the fourteenth century (Naregal 2001, 16/23n). Raja Ram Mohan Roy, one of the key reformers of the nineteenth century, was well versed in Persian and Arabic, besides Sanskrit, which shows that this multilingual tradition continued well into the nineteenth century. Roy's first book was a treatise, *Tuhfat-ul-Muwahiddin* (A gift from the monotheists, 1805), in Persian with an introduction in Arabic. In the treatise, he underlined the need for a 'rational approach to religions and religious experience' and drew attention to the 'achievement of monotheism throughout the world' (Tagore 2009, 10–11). Obviously, a rational approach could be derived from Persian and Arabic as well.

This multilingualism also led to an intellectual ferment in medieval India, leading to dialogues among different ideologies and philosophies.

Jonardon Ganeri, in the essay 'Intellectual India: Reason, Identity, Dissent', comments, 'India in the 17th century, the century after Akbar, was a place of great intellectual excitement. Muslim, Hindu and Jaina intellectuals produced works of tremendous interest, ideas circulated around India, through the Persianate and Arabic worlds, and also between India and Europe' (2009, 258). In 1656, the year in which Dara Shikoh's (1615–59) grand project of translating fifty-two Upanishads from Sanskrit into Persian was achieved, Francois Bernier (1620–88), the French physician and philosopher, was in India and he translated the works of Descartes and the empiricist Gassendi into Persian. Thus, much before the advent of colonial education, the ideas of the Enlightenment were available to the elites of India through Persian. It was through the translation of Bernier's *Travels in the Mughal Empire* into English that Dryden got the material for his play *Aurangzeb* (1675). Ganeri asks, 'With Gassendi's work translated into Persian even before it was available in French, and the monotheistic pantheism of the Upanishads and Dara Shukoh already in France and England years before Spinoza's *Ethics* were published, what more dramatic evidence could there be of the rapid global circulation of ideas in the 1660s and 70s?' (260).

Arabic and Persian were not merely languages of the court and administration, but the medium of intellectual discourses that impacted the world view of discerning Indians. Their liberating influences provided a powerful impetus for the bhashas to question and subvert the hegemony of the Sanskrit cosmopolis. This also means that before the arrival of English, India had already been in dialogue with the West and had contributed towards the rise of modernity in the West through its own dialogic traditions. This intellectual history was effectively erased from public memory with the forcible evacuation of Persian and its traditions from all over India. This also meant a shift from the multilingualism of medieval India to the bilingualism of the nineteenth century where English became the language of the intellect and Indian languages its inferior Other.

In Kerala, Malayalam emerged as a literary language at a time of political turmoil in the hundred years between 1650 and 1750, when the Portuguese and the Dutch were engaged in a war for supremacy on the western coast. The Portuguese had made their presence felt in

Cochin (Kochi) and the Arabs were entrenched in Calicut (Kozhikode) under the patronage of the Samoodiris. By the end of the seventeenth century, 1660 to be precise, the Portuguese commercial empire in Indian waters gave way to the Dutch, who were in turn displaced by the British in another wave of attacks and counter-attacks. The presence of Portuguese missionaries in Kerala contributed to the development of prose through the translations of the Bible and publications of grammars and dictionaries. Malayalam was deficient in prose, though there was a certain tradition of writing in royal proclamations and courtly documentation. The new 'missionary Malayalam' obviously followed a trajectory that was different from the highly Sanskritised Malayalam or the earlier variety of Malayalam derived from Tamil. Many varieties of Malayalam, such as Arabi Malayalam and Jewish Malayalam, had evolved during the long periods of Kerala's contacts with various communities from around the world. Malayalam contains a large number of words from Persian, Arabic, Portuguese, Dutch and many other European languages. It was through this hybridisation that Malayalam evolved into a 'modern' language capable of dealing with the larger project of modernity. To say that its 'cosmopolitan' tradition was an imprint of the Sanskritic model is to falsify history.

Languages such as Malayalam used translation as a mode to negotiate the multiple life worlds they inhabited. It must be remembered that Sanskrit rarely translated other texts and that its resources were not openly accessible to most of the people in India. One of the reasons why colonial administrators patronised Sanskrit was this 'purity' that made it the ideal medium to recover an 'Aryan' antiquity. Max Mueller says, 'But what is far more important than its merely chronological antiquity is the antique state of preservation in which that Aryan language has been handed down to us' (2000, xvii). Orientalists as well as Anglicists refused to engage with the multilingual ethos of regional languages and their cosmopolitan traditions. William Carey (1761–1834), one of the reputed Serampore missionaries who translated the *Ramayana* into Bangla in 1802 and a scholar of Marathi, Telugu and Hindustani, comments, 'If any language could be adopted as the universal medium of communication with all the different Indian nations it would be Sanskrita, which is indeed not only the key to all Indian literature, but also the parent of every language spoken throughout India' (quoted in

Ranganathan 2009, 73–74). While the Orientalists translated 'classical India' into modern European languages to construct a grand narrative of its Aryan past, the Anglicists harped on the lack of rational discourses and scientific temper in modern Indian languages. Charles Grant (1746–1823), one of the first Anglicists to spell out the 'white man's burden', finds print as an effective vehicle for dominating the native consciousness. He writes,

> The art of printing would enable us to disseminate our writings in a way the Persians never could have done, though their compositions had been as numerous as ours. Hence the Hindoos would see the great use we make of reason on all subjects, and in all affairs, they also would learn to reason, *they would become acquainted with their own species, the past and present state of the world;* their affections would gradually become interested by varying engaging works, composed to recommend virtue, and to defer from vice; the general mass of their opinion would be rectified, and above all, *they would use a better system of principals and morals.* (Ranganathan 2009, 83; emphasis added)

'Reason' becomes an organising principle for recovering one's past as well as knowing one's place in the world. Indian languages are now required to conform to this paradigm which is derived from the discourses of Enlightenment rationality. The 'othering' of Indian languages is achieved though the deployment of a moral economy where they are banished to the realm of the 'irrational'. They are repeatedly referred to as 'dialects' incapable of transmitting 'modern' knowledge. Macaulay's infamous minute states, 'All parties seem to be agreed on one point, that the dialects commonly spoken among the natives of this part of India contain neither literary nor scientific information, and are moreover so poor and rude that, until they are enriched from some other quarter, it will not be easy to translate any valuable work into them' (Ranganathan 2009, 85). Thus, the intense multilingualism and the shared metaphoric universe sustained by Indian languages were disputed by the hegemonic structures of colonial power.

The fuzzy nature of the pre-colonial society enabled communities to relate to the pan-Indian Sanskrit cosmopolis on their own terms, but the colonial authority had a hegemonic hold on all their faculties including imagination, necessitating a reworking of all their resources and discourses. The conceptual grid of colonialism has at its disposal the elaborate cognitive apparatus of rationality as an organising principle.

This is why the introduction of English, along with the advent of print, set in motion an unprecedented process of standardisation from which no Indian language could escape without risking extinction. English occupied the space marked by modernity, appropriating for itself the power of arbitration regarding the nature and content of modernity. Sanskrit fell from its pedestal to the status of an archaic language. The process of modernisation that was now underway demanded that regional languages have to internalise the logic of rationality and empiricism that had already been initiated by print. The internal economy of regional languages became differentiated, acquiring an elitist 'high' form that equipped them with features of English and Sanskrit. Many varieties of modern Indian languages now came to be relegated to the level of 'dialects', while those closer to the elite variety gained greater currency and value.

In the colonial context, modernity manifests itself in the political–cultural discourse of nation and nationalism. The Orientalists and the Anglicists, seemingly opponents in their authentication of Sanskrit and English (both pan-Indian languages) respectively, effectively meet in the narrative of the nation that has to reconcile the requirement of an uninterrupted history of unitary discourses with a present where a univocal rationality could be embodied in a homogenised contemporary idiom. Regional linguistic traditions become the Other in this scheme of a past that is imagined as future. Instead of designating the nation as a work in progress, in all its imperfect visions and revisions and complex living heteroglossia, the nation was bestowed an imagined unity in its Sanskritic high tradition; and this constructed homogeneity was consecrated and canonised through a pact with discourses of universality and objectivity under the façade of a false modernity. In this enactment of culture–power conjunction, region becomes a fragment, a 'lack' that is forever suspect and incomplete. The earlier confidence with which Indian languages had asserted against Sanskrit and developed their own independent literary styles could not be recovered in their encounter with English, largely because of the political power of the hegemonic colonial apparatus.

In the nineteenth century, Persian was progressively replaced by English throughout India: in 1832 in Bombay and Madras Presidencies, and in 1837 in Bengal Presidency. This set in motion a process which gradually resulted in the Sanskritsation of Indian languages under state patronage. The fracturing of the shared composite culture of Hindi/ Urdu is a case in point, and reflects the disastrous consequences of the cleavage that developed in North India. The founding moment of the linguistic divide that finally deepened into a communal divide and the two-nation theory, is an order issued by Antony MacDonnell, Lieutenant Governor of United Provinces of Agra and Oudh, on 18 April 1900, allowing permissive use of Devanagari in the courts of the province (Rai 2000, 17). This subtle move, in effect, put the colonial stamp of approval on the legitimacy of Sanskritised Hindi as against Persianised Urdu which was perceived as a threat by the Hindi elite. In the 1870s and 80s, Hindustani in the Persian script gave way to Hindi in the Nagari script. The pedants of Fort William College and the missionaries of Serampore contributed in their separate ways to the institutionalisation of Sanskritised Hindi. This was also the time when print media played a crucial role in shaping the subjectivities of various communities. To quote Alok Rai, 'The rough beast of cultural differentiation—of amputation and self-mutilation leading eventually to civil war and partition—was formed in new parallel nurseries which were the innocent and certainly unintended consequence of colonial education policy' (32). The subjectivities legitimated by a centralised nation state demands allegiance to the *langue* of the elite discourse and not the *parole* of the popular multilingual heteroglossia. Here then is the fault line that animates the conflictual terrain of regional Indian languages. The contestations that have accompanied the formation of the public sphere in regional speech communities have repeatedly problematised the elitist positions embodied in nationalist narratives.

## 3

I will conclude this chapter with a brief note on the role of missionary Malayalam in shaping modern Malayalam prose. As was pointed out above, the mainstream literary tradition of Malayalam, till the eighteenth century, was made up of poetry and had not developed a viable form of prose for articulating ideas, feelings and attitudes. This began to change with the arrival of European missionaries in the sixteenth century. Here we need to remember that the missionaries had an impact on Indian languages as a whole. Reverend Robert Caldwell – in a lecture titled 'Languages of India in their Relation to Missionary Work', delivered on 28 April 1875 on the occasion of the Annual meeting of the Society for the Propagation of the Gospel – outlined the nature of the contributions made by missionaries to even 'minor' tribal languages, besides the major languages of India. Towards the end of his lecture, he remarks that Christian ideas are being taught in about twenty-three languages of India, and expresses the wish that the time will come 'when every dialect and language in India will be consecrated to Christ' (587).

Missionaries did not turn to traditional forms of prose but to the ordinary speech of the common people, for their models of writing; and this revolutionised the manner in which Malayalam prose was written. Scholars of Malayalam have been reluctant to recognise the role of missionaries in the development of Malayalam prose. For instance, S. Guptan Nair, a veteran scholar of Malayalam, in his introduction to a book on missionary Malayalam by P. J. Francis, harps on the proselytising role of the missionaries, which, according to him, prompted them to opt for the common speech current in society (Francis 2006, 7). While this is true, the fact remains that they saw language from the outside and transformed it to suit the demands of writing discursive prose where ideas and feelings could be communicated. The first travelogue written in Malayalam, *Vartamanapustakam* (1780) by Paremmakkal Thoma Kathanar, is remarkable for its detailed account of the social conditions of Kerala Christians in the eighteenth century, apart from references to the problems faced by Christian sects in Kerala. P. K. Parameswaran Nair, the eminent literary historian, observes that 'many qualities rare in Malayalam prose of those times, such as the systematic presentation of ideas, division into paragraphs and rational ordering of sentences, could be traced here' (Parameswaran Nair Smaraka Trust 2000, 150).

Many historians of Malayalam prose tend to argue that, given the conditions of transformation in the eighteenth and nineteenth centuries, the Sanskritised prose of the seventeenth century would have developed into its modern form, even without the intervention of the missionaries. For instance, Prabhakara Varier, an eminent historian of the language, says, 'If we examine the development of prose from the seventeenth to nineteenth centuries, it can be seen that a new clear prose is gradually emerging. Missionary prose has not played any role in this process' (2004, 104). But this contradicts the facts we are confronted with. The intervention of print, translations of the Bible, and the publication of dictionaries, among others, constitute an important stage of colonial modernity that redefined the direction taken by the Malayalam language. Benjamin Bailey (1791–1871) – a protestant priest from Dewsbury, Yorkshire, England – not only translated the Bible into Malayalam and produced a monumental Malayalam–English dictionary that took twenty-eight years of labour, but also designed the types for printing in Malayalam, setting a standard form of the alphabet and altering the manner in which the language was written. As the first principal of the Kottayam College established by the Church Mission Society (CMS), he was the first to introduce English into the curriculum for college education in Kerala. The round and shapely Malayalam type he introduced in place of the square-type letters went on to become the standard type for writing and printing Malayalam, making him the first typographer of the language. In translating the Bible into Malayalam (first published in 1829), he used an idiom that incorporated colloquial words and common usages, thus moving away from the high Sanskritic style. The first Malayalam book to be printed in Kerala, *Stories Translated from English for the Benefit of Small Children*, was printed in the modern Malayalam type developed by Bailey and was published in 1824. What is central to the present argument is that the imprint of colonial modernity can be seen in all the projects initiated by Bailey: the translation of the Bible, production of Malayalam types, introduction of English and the establishment of the Malayalam printing press. He effectively laid the foundation for a new Malayalam prose that led to the rejuvenation of literature in the modern phase. What displaced the Sanskrit-centred high tradition was a combination of the projects of modernity that brought about changes in the dissemination of literature, educational curriculum and modes of relating to the society. The new literary forms such as the novel, the short story and the autobiography did not develop from the earlier prose forms but under the impact of the new prose which had internalised the logic of the new print. However, it has to be noted that the new hierarchy – with English occupying a superior status both as the administrative and intellectual medium, and Malayalam as the medium of the masses – further created a schism in the world of culture that has deepened into a major fault line in our socio-cultural domain. Here we need to see the complex linguistic and cultural scene in a single Indian language, Malayalam, which defies easy generalisations. This is why we have to be wary of postcolonial constructs in the area of translation, since they tend to see India as a single unit. Postcolonial theory is concerned with only those issues that touch upon the Anglo-American academy. It fails to go deep into issues that originate in the multilingual regions of India. One of the basic responsibilities of Indian comparatists is to be ethically responsive to the linguistic and cultural realities in India as embedded in texts produced in Indian languages. An Indian comparatist cannot work with translations alone; she or he has to return to the original languages of the subcontinent. That there is hardly anything in postcolonial critical tradition which can help explore the ground reality in India makes the Indian comparatist a lonely figure; but loneliness is the price you pay for the ethical commitment to the cause of the Other.

It is significant that at a crucial stage in the development of its prose, Malayalam internalised the syntactical features of English. By the time *Vartamanapustakam* was written in 1785, missionary Malayalam had begun developing a new prose style capable of expressing a range of ideas about society, religion, art, architecture and moral values. Another book written during this period was *Jnanamuthumala* (A garland made of the pearls of wisdom) that appeared in 1784. C. L. Antony, an eminent linguist of the last century, in his analysis of this text demonstrates how it marks a significant advancement in the development of Malayalam prose by incorporating the colloquial language of central Kerala (1989). It carries the stamp of its times in several of its syntactical and grammatical features, but there is no denying the fact that modern Malayalam prose developed from this kind of missionary prose. Antony argues that the foundation of modern prose in Malayalam was laid in the works of missionary prose. The first Malayalam book to be published (in 1811) was the New Testament, printed in Courier Press in Bombay (Mumbai). Bailey's Malayalam–English dictionary appeared in 1846, and it continues to be a standard lexicon. It was titled 'A Dictionary of High and Colloquial Malayalam and English' and included a large number of words of everyday usage from all communities from the south of Kerala.

Thus, the impetus for the transformation of Malayalam into a modern language came not from Sanskrit but its encounter with European languages and its incorporation of the local and everyday speech of the living community. This is where it parted company with the Sanskritic tradition which had fossilised Malayalam into a language with very little expressive power. This process, strangely enough, secularised Malayalam, giving it the capacity to address the common people collectively, through various periodicals that began to appear from 1847 onwards. The translations of Shakespeare that became available in the latter part of the nineteenth century, and the early novels such as *Ghatakavadham* (The slayer slain, 1877), were all written in the language that developed from missionary Malayalam, which leaned heavily on the spoken varieties of the language. In an editorial written in *Malayala Manorama* on 11 February 1893, the editor states that of the seventeen periodicals published in Kerala, six appeared every week, one thrice a month, four twice a month, and the remaining six once a month (Ramakrishnan 2011, 25). This testifies to the emergence of a popular Malayalam which spoke to the common people irrespective of their religion or caste. G. Aunima, in 'Print, Language, and the Public Sphere in Colonial Kerala', while discussing two religious tracts – *Mohammad charitam* (The history of Muhammad) and *Muhammado isaanabiyo aru valiyavan* (Muhammad and Jesus compared), both published in the mid-nineteenth century – suggests that they show 'a recognizably modern prose style' (67). Curiously, these tracts, which were meant to distinguish between communities along religious lines, address them collectively through a modern written idiom that renders the presence of the public sphere tangible. Arunima points out that words derived from Sanskrit such as *veda pustakam* (religious tract) as well as everyday words such as *padachavan* (god) and *valiyavan* (the superior figure) figured in these tracts, suggesting the presence of 'a shared Malayalam that cut across linguistic roots and communal boundaries' (67). One has to acknowledge the role of missionary Malayalam in shaping this standard Malayalam. At the turn of the century, there were debates on the 'purification' of Malayalam. However, this did not mean a return to Sanskrit roots but the reclamation of the language's Dravidian kinship (70). Obviously, the new public sphere was characterised by its resistance to elitist notion of culture.

The example of the emergence of standard Malayalam shows that modern Indian languages used the emancipatory potential of colonial modernity as embodied in English to turn away from the hegemonic hold of Sanskrit during the period between the eighteenth and twentieth centuries. As discussed earlier, in their foundational moment, modern Indian languages had relied on the creative potential of the popular domain to confront the hegemony of Sanskrit. What is at work in both these confrontations with hegemonic power structures is the dynamics of a multilingual culture that is deeply ingrained in the very structure of these languages, enabling them to view with suspicion categories that seek closure and finality. They also demonstrate the social imagination of the people in employing languages to invent new genres and accomplishing greater fluency of expression, internalising new standards of enunciation and metaphorical vitality. Translation functioned on the cusps of these transitions, as a creative force directing the linguistic and literary acts of reclamation and renovation, mediating between the inner and the outer, the real and the imagined, and the intelligible and the inarticulate. As in the case of Sanskrit, the presence of English has created a new hierarchy where modern Indian languages are required to approximate themselves to the epistemological models set by English with its professed rationality. As a result of this false hierarchy, the symbiotic relations among Indian languages have come to be viewed with suspicion and distrust, as languages have come to feel increasingly insecure in their competition with English. Modern Indian languages have also distanced themselves from their oral resources that have been relegated to the 'irrational' pre-modern domain. The Other of modern languages is now located within themselves and this accounts for the embattled state of their present being. The task of the comparatist is to recover this Other and articulate its being in an attempt to negotiate the otherness in favour of an emergent dialogic relation between Indian languages and literatures, as embodied in the monumental projects of translation accomplished in the past. This is how a society re-imagines itself. This has implications for the future of our democratic and cultural institutions, as the limits of our languages also mark the frontiers of our thoughts.

## Notes

1. Literally, '*abhang*' means 'absolute', 'eternal', 'immutable', 'ceaseless', 'unbroken', 'impeccable', etc. It refers to a Marathi metre which all Varkari poets have used since the thirteenth century. It consists of four lines and each line contains three to eight syllables. Unlike Sanskrit-based metres, it is highly flexible and musical, and closer to the speech rhythms of Marathi. Poets such as Jnanadeva, Namdev and Tukaram used it widely and gave it a classical status in Marathi poetry (Chitre 1991, 207). *Vachana,* according to A. K. Ramanujan is 'a religious lyric in Kannada free verse'; '*vachana*' means, literally, 'saying' or 'thing said'. In contrast to the Sanskrit tradition, *vachana* refers to 'what is uttered here and now' (Ramanujan 1979, 11, 37).
2. *Manipravalam* refers to a hybridised poetic style where Sanskrit words combined with local languages such as Malayalam, Tamil and Kannada. It played an important role in localising Sanskrit in both political discourse and literature. According to Sujit Mukherjee, it was used for 'exposition and commentary first, later for literary composition' (1999, 225)

## References

Ananthamurthy, U. R. 2014. *Rujuvathu* [Selected essays edited with an introduction by N. Manu Chakravarthy]. Bengaluru: Prism Books.

Antony, C. L. 1989. *Bhashapathanangal* [Language studies]. Thrissur: Kerala Sahitya Akademi.

Arunima, G. 2006. Imagining communities – differently: Print, language and the public sphere in Kerala. *Indian Economic and Social History Review* 43.1: 63–76.

Caldwell, Robert. 2007. The languages of India in their relation to missionary work. *TAPASAM* II. 3–4: 574–88.

Francis, P. J. 2006. *Pathiri Malayalam: Oruvichintanam* [Missionary Malayalam: A reconsideration]. Kottayam: Current Books.

Ganeri, Jonardon. 2009. Intellectual India: Reason, identity and dissent. *New Literary History* 40. 2 (Spring 2009): 247–63.

Max Muller, Friedrich. 2000. *India: What it can teach us?* New Delhi: Penguin.

Mukherjee, Sujit. 1999. *A dictionary of Indian literature I: Beginnings to 1850.* London: Sangam Books.

Naregal, Veena. 2001. *Language politics, elites and the public sphere.* New Delhi: Permanent Black.

Novetzke, Christian Lee. 2008. *Religion and public memory: A cultural history of Saint Namdev in India.* Columbia: Columbia UP.

Panjabi, Kavita. 2011. *Poetics and politics of Sufism and Bhakti in South Asia: Love, loss and liberation.* Hyderabad: Orient BlackSwan.

Parameswaran Nair Smaraka Trust. 2001. *Malayala sahitya charitram pathinezhum pathinettum nootantukalil* [The history of Malayalam literature in the seventeenth and eighteenth centuries]. Kottayam: Current Books.

Patnaik, Bibudhendra N. 2012. *Introducing Saaralaa Mahaabhaarata.* Mysore: Central Institute of Indian Languages.

Pollock, Sheldon. 2011. *The language of the gods in the world of men.* New Delhi: Permanent Black.

———. 2013. What is Indian knowledge good for? First Balvant Parekh Memorial Lecture. Baroda: Balvant Parekh Centre for General Semantics and Other Human Sciences.

Rai, Alok. 2000. *Hindi nationalism.* Hyderabad: Orient BlackSwan.

Ramakrishnan, E. V. 2011. *Locating Indian literature: Texts, traditions, translations.* New Delhi: Orient BlackSwan.

Ramanujan, A. K. 1979. *Speaking of Siva.* Harmondsworth: Penguin Classics.

Ranganathan, Balaji. 2009. *Orientalism and India.* New Delhi: Creative Books.

Richman, Paula, ed. 2008. *Ramayana stories in modern South India: An anthology.* Bloomington and Indianapolis: Indiana UP.

Tagore, Saumyendranath. 2009. *Raja Rammohun Roy.* Makers of Indian Literature. New Delhi: Sahitya Akademi.

Varier, K. M. Prabhakara. 2004. *Malayalam: Mattavum valarchayum* [Malayalam: Change and development]. Trichur: Vallathol Vidyapeetham, Sukapuram, and Current Books.

Venkatachalapathy, A. R. 2012. *The province of the book: Scholars, scribes, and scribblers in colonial Tamil Nadu.* Ranikhet: Permanent Black.

Vieira, E. 1999. Liberating Calibans: Readings of antropofagia and Haroldo de Campos' poetics of transcreation. In *Postcolonial translation: Theory and practice,* ed. S. Bassnett and H. Trivedi. London and New York: Routledge.

**CHAPTER THREE**

# Dialogics of Dissent in Indian Literature: From Bhakti Tradition to Dalit Literature

The categories we use to interpret our social and cultural phenomena are often derived from cosmologies that are alien to our experiential worlds. This leads to the erasure of the singularity of lived experiences. The term 'dissent' is used here to suggest an alternative paradigm of interpretative apparatus that will question the universalist models current in knowledge production. Ideas from Mikhail Bakhtin and B. R. Ambedkar are used here primarily to critique hegemonic systems centred around European rationality and Indian caste system. The gulf between theory and experience is a fact we confront in the study of Bhakti and Dalit literatures which contest hierarchical power structures rooted in exclusions of various kinds. This chapter analyses a numbers of texts and authors including *Therigatha,* Bulleh Shah, Tukaram and modern Dalit poetry and fiction written in the second half of the twentieth century, to demonstrate how they resist assimilation into hegemonic discourses by embodying new moral imaginaries. Literary utterances constitute an act of dissent when they acquire subversive and self-reflexive dimensions, creating a social space of critical consciousness. These readings provide models for a 'comparative humanities' which is yet to take shape in our institutional environment.

## I

Of late, there has been some talk of 'critical humanities', as 'mainstream humanities' is increasingly seen as trapped in the legacy of Euro-American categories of epistemology. In the name of 'Indian knowledge', we have translated India into European terms and this has led to a crisis in our ability to represent Indian society to ourselves and to the world. The categories we employ in analysing social and cultural phenomena are not derived from our encounters with our eco-system or experiential cosmology. What is lacking in the interpretative discourse practised in the humanities and social sciences is an awareness of the dynamics of this transfer and the appropriations and approximations that characterise our narratives. There is also a larger question of the ethics of translation involved here, and this points to a sense of incommensurability between the languages, cultures or peoples involved in the process of dialogic exchange called translation. Words are deeply embedded in social practices and through their embodied nature, in local history. In theorising translation, we move away from the particular, from 'local habitations' of words and their inherited meanings, and uproot them from their embedded and embodied formations. Fiction, poetry, autobiography or such imaginative forms of writing take us back to the incommensurable in the 'singular' before a 'universalist' paradigm is imagined. In approximating the singular to a European episteme, which constitutes an overarching self informing and regulating all production of 'modernity', a certain erasure of the particular is involved. This chapter uses the word 'dissent' to seek out an alternative paradigm to contest the erasures involved in the construction of a hegemonic 'universalist' paradigm.

A brief annotation of the term 'dialogics' is in order. Mikhail Bakhtin has persuasively argued in his study on Fyodor Dostoevsky that the latter's novels contain a 'plurality of unmerged consciousnesses', that the perspectives of characters are not subordinated to authorial intentions. Dostoevsky's great achievements were in finding an adequate form for the dialogic impulse in the social world. Bakhtin writes,

> Dostoevsky, like Goethe's Prometheus, creates not voiceless slaves (as does Zeus), but free people, capable of standing alongside their creator, capable of not agreeing with him and even of rebelling against him. A plurality of independent and unmerged voices and consciousnesses, a genuine polyphony of fully valid voices is in fact the chief characteristic of Dostoevsky's novels. (Bakhtin 1984, 6)

Language, by its very nature, is a discourse that inhabits a domain of answerability, where words are filled with voices, intentions and desires. Thus, dialogism is inherent in the very act of communication where the social constitutes the verbal sphere. 'Monologism' implies a social world where diversity of thought and action is curbed by a hegemonic, unified consciousness that controls all values and meanings. In an appendix to the book on Dostoevsky, in its 1963 edition, Bakhtin explained:

'Monologue is finalized and deaf to the other's response, does not expect it and does not acknowledge in it any decisive force. Monologue manages without the other, and therefore to some degree materializes all reality. Monologue pretends to be the ultimate word. It closes down the represented world and represented persons' (1984, 293). In Indian traditions, for instance, the monologic nature of the Vedic tradition in Sanskrit was challenged by the dialogic organisation of poetic language in Bhakti poetry. The poets of the Bhakti traditions spoke from within the domain of lived experience. They spoke in the 'vernacular' languages of the masses, not in Sanskrit. This 'oral poetic' also enabled them to reach out to the people who shared the idiom and also to the material practices that informed the texts with their performative dimension.

Culture is a contested field where monologic forces of authoritarian regimes, religious orthodoxies and feudal social organisation try to curb the inherent dialogic nature of the word. Hence, what is dialogic also questions the prevailing ideologies of power. It is in this sense that we will look at the nature of dialogics in Bhakti and Dalit literatures.

In *The Cracked Mirror* (2013), Gopal Guru suggests translation of theory as a test of its ability to address living subjects. He feels that Dalits should test the tenacity of their theory 'on the basis of how much influence these theoretical formulations enjoy in the popular mentality' (28). This is not merely a question of translating 'theoretical content into an ordinary idiom or common speech', but of recovering an ethical principle in the very structuring of experience. As Sundar Sarukkai points out in the same volume, 'Lived experience should be seen as the experience of being a subject and not an experience by a subject about a subject' (37). If theory remains purely empirical, it cannot incorporate lived experience; and if experience remains a universal category without a localised subject, its truth value becomes suspect. The only way to break out of this impasse is to 'demand that ethics be integrated to the act of theorizing. If this is allowed, then lived experience becomes the ground for such ethical intertwinement with theory' (37). This is where the confrontation with the incommensurable mentioned above becomes an essential condition of 'comparative humanities' which seeks to recover the ethical dimension in comprehending lived experience. As Sudipta Kaviraj argues in his response to *The Cracked Mirror,* 'the Dalit experience should be regarded as central in our understanding of the moral imaginary of the Indian democratic society, not just by Dalits, but by all' (2013, 388).

The philosophy of B. R. Ambedkar, who had an acute sense of the role of language and dialogue in the making of a society, is relevant to the present discussion. In words reminiscent of Bakhtin, he suggests in his famous essay, 'The Annihilation of Caste': 'The strength of a society depends upon the presence of points of contact, possibilities of interaction between different groups which exist in it. These are what Carlyle calls "organic filaments", i.e., the elastic threads which help to bring the disintegrating elements together and to reunite them' (2002, 285). Dissenting voices restore the communicative thrust to those who are excluded from the dialogue. Their experiences, thus, find a way back into the mainstream of voices in that society. Hence, 'dissent' is integral to the project of locating and recovering lived experience. The Bhakti and Dalit writings that are discussed in this chapter have to be seen against the hegemonic narratives in circulation in their cultures. The self/other dichotomy we noticed in the context of the European episteme has been endemic to Indian cultural production from the pre-Christian era, when a well-entrenched brahminic discourse had a hegemonic hold on the interpretative apparatus of the worldly phenomena. Here we need to underline the dialogic nature of the production of a social consciousness – a prerequisite in contesting hegemonies. Ambedkar clearly elucidates this point in 'The Annihilation of Caste':

> And the only way by which men can come to possess things in common with one another is by being in communication with one another. This is merely another way of saying that society continues to exist by communication, indeed in communication. To make it concrete, it is not enough if men act in a way which agrees with the acts of others. Parallel activity is not sufficient to bind men into a society. . . . The caste system prevents common activity and by preventing common activity it has prevented the Hindus from becoming a society with a unified life and a consciousness of its own being. (268)

Meanings are always socially constructed in a society. Words are accented with the desires, intentions, attitudes, assumptions, preferences and prejudices inherent in speech communities. Consciousness can transform itself into self-consciousness only in the context of the Other, by confronting it. In the process of becoming a society, it will confront the Other and also move beyond the self. In an act of dissent, it is the self-conscious who is in communication with the Other, creating a frame of reference that is beyond the self. This is why dissenting speech remains singular and refuses to be assimilated into the hegemonic discourse. This act of disavowal may gesture towards the universal – in an attempt to situate the local and the vernacular in a communicative, dialogic context – but the universal has no legitimating authority here. It has to be granted that a text that constitutes an act of dissent has a critical relation with the very language it speaks in. It uses a mode that both interrogates and exceeds its immediate purpose. In every act of dissent, the mode of utterance has a subversive, self-reflexive dimension. It deconstructs the speaker as much as it deconstructs its listener, by drawing attention to the manner in which they are constituted, in the first place, as social beings. This self-reflexive element in the texts of Bhakti or Dalit literature has not been sufficiently understood in the context of the epistemological crisis we mentioned at the beginning of this chapter.

The moulds of shaping experiences, given by a discourse, also plot the self and its utterance in a certain way. To break the mould is to disrupt the cultural lexicon of experience. In this sense, dissent tests the linguistic resources of a culture, as it has to find a new lexicon of experience to convey a radical view of the world.

## 2

The tradition of 'inspired utterance', which one comes across in both Bhakti poetry and Dalit literature, shows how narrating an experience often shapes an ethics by addressing and confronting the Other. This tradition goes back to *Therigatha,* the Buddhist scripture where songs of experience were considered '*udana*' or 'spoken in a moment of insight'. 'Theris' were enlightened Buddhist nuns who led an ascetic life. In many of their poems, they look back on their former selves in the light of the self-knowledge they have gained. Their poems are rooted in the personal and address the existential and the everyday, without mystifying the world and its ways. In one of the poems, Uttama speaks of how she was taught by a nun to tame her heart:

I listened to what she taught,
did exactly as she said,

for seven days I sat in one position, legs crossed,
given over to joy and happiness.
On the eighth day I stretched out my feet,
after splitting open the mass of mental darkness. (Hallisey 2015, 33)

In one of the poems by a nun called Punnika, we come across a dialogue between the nun and a brahmin who is going to a river, shivering in the cold, to take bath. He tells Punnika,

Anyone who does an evil act
whether old or young,
is freed from the fruits of the evil act
by washing off in water.

And the nun replies,

Who told you that,
like a know-nothing speaking to a know-nothing,
that one is freed from the fruits of an evil act
by washing off in water?
Is it that frogs and turtles
will all go to heaven,
and so will water monitors and crocodiles,
and anything that lives in water,
As will killers of sheep and killers of pigs,
fishermen and animal trappers, thieves and executioners,
everyone who habitually does evil?
. . . . . . . . . . . . . . . . . . . . . . . . . . . .
But these rivers might carry away all the good done too,
you'll be besides yourself about that
Aren't you afraid of that, Brahman, each time you go into the water? (125)

Subsequently, Punnika reminds him that if he has done evil, there is no escape from suffering. And at the end of the poem, we see the brahmin moving away from his initial position and ready to accept the Buddhist dhamma.

*Therigatha* poems stand witness to a lived reality; and in telling them, the Budhist nuns constitute their own selves. This self-fashioning gives the poems a dynamics of movement in time. Their openness to the experience of suffering and their revelations about their own imperfect selves, plagued by erotic and evil thoughts, create an eco-system of shared worlds. They describe the transformation in terms of everyday experiences which are within the grasp of their illiterate listeners. Sumangala's mother, addressing her son, says that she was reminded of 'the sound of bamboo being split' (21) when she destroyed the anger and the passion for sex within her. Ubbiri speaks of her transformation in terms of removing an arrow that is stuck in her body: 'He pulled out the arrow that was hard for me to see / the one that I nourished in my heart' (39). Siha speaks of an experience in such a way that her poem sounds almost like a confessional poem by a modern woman poet. She says that she was 'pained by distracted attention and by desire for sex' and that she 'was always disturbed, without any control over [her] thoughts' (53). She wanders for seven years; but this does not give her peace of mind. Then she decides to commit suicide and goes to the forest:

> Taking a rope, I went to the forest, thinking
> It is better to hang than to live this low life.
> I made the noose strong and tied it to a branch
> but just as I looped it around my neck, my mind was set free. (53)

Dissent is about setting oneself free, seeing the world afresh through a different discursive frame, when the hegemonic power formation can no more disable or constrain you. *Therigatha* poems narrate such moments when a paradigm shift enables one to step into a new self. These poems stage the transformative moment of epiphany when the waking subject asserts one's right to reject a master narrative that structurally and ideologically overdetermines one's location and identity. It opens up an alternative value system that is not based on exclusion and hierarchy. The nun–poets of *Therigatha* do what Bhakti poetry attempted subsequently – to question the authority of sacred texts that legislated the caste system.

## 3

There have been many exchanges between Bhakti and Sufi traditions in the northern parts of India. This may be illustrated with reference to Bulleh Shah (1680–1757) who wrote in Punjabi. Like the great Sufi saint Mansur al-Hallaj (c.858–922) whose proclamation, 'Anal Haq' ('I am the Truth'), resulted in his martyrdom, Shah repeatedly proclaims his direct apprehension of the world without the burden of the mediating structures of religious thought. He also emphasises his own ignorance and simplicity, as in this poem:

> Reading and reading, you become
> a mullah, then a quazi, but God
> is content without all this learning. (Shackle 2015, 39)

He adds,

> Bullha is neither a shiah nor a sunni,
> neither a learned scholar nor a magician or philosopher.
> He has studied only that inspirational knowledge
> in which *alif* and *mim* alone are needed. (69)

The addressivity of this kind of utterance goes beyond the sectarian divisions of society. That is how it creates a dialogic domain of critical consciousness that enables a community to view its own nature and functions from an alternative perspective.

This tradition of subversive speech derives part of its intellectual robustness from the philosophy of Lokayata, which proclaimed a materialistic vision of the world rooted in the reality of physical perceptions. Lokayatas were the first to challenge the brahminic knowledge system in the subcontinent and most of their writings, mentioned by Patanjali and several Buddhist scholars, have disappeared without a trace. Lokayatas rejected notions about the 'other world', the concepts of *atma, narak, swarg, moksha*, etc., and all rituals connected with Hinduism. They strongly argued in favour of a secular world view centred around justice and physical reality. By reconstituting the world after their own ideology, Lokayatas spoke from the centre of their discursive terrain, which was not reactive or the Other of a dominant discourse. This is the reason why the Lokayata tradition became the everyday consciousness of the common people, particularly from the lower castes.

We come across the continuation of this cosmos in the poetry of Bhakti and also in the thoughts of Ambedkar. Ambedkar asserts unambiguously, 'You must not only discard the *Shastras,* you must deny their authority, as did Buddha and Nanak' (2002, 290). Bhakti poetry denies authority to a scriptural view of the world, and turns away from other-worldly themes. They are secular in the sense that they firmly resist ideas of heaven, hell, salvation and afterlife, while retaining a sense of the material world as a finite reality that cannot be transcended. Their insistence on bearing testimony to the lived reality of their lives transforms their poems into a quest for alternative systems of belief that can collectively transform society. This shift from the individual to the collective is a significant aspect of Bhakti poetry. While commenting on Tukaram, the seventeenth-century Bhakti poet, Nemade says that 'to him, literature was part of his faith in life' (1991, 41). Tukaram faithfully records the various stages of his journey towards faith and surrender to God. In one of his poems, he comments, 'I have sinned more / Than most' (Chitre 1991, 33). He emphasises the need for experience to transcend the limits of worldly life: 'Tuka says, everything will be a waste, / Without experience' (Nemade 1991, 55). Lived experience becomes the means of knowing and transforming oneself in Bhakti literature. While translating Tukaram, Dilip Chitre titles a section in the volume as 'Being Human', where one can hear Tukaram's existential struggle to make both ends meet, his helplessness in confronting caste prejudices and his sense of utter despair at his inability to find any refuge in the land of his birth:

> I am tired.
> You are my last stop.
> My final place of rest. (Chitre 1991, 56)

Tukaram questions the authority of the upper castes to interpret sacred texts. In a well-known *abhang*, he says, 'We alone know the real meaning of the Vedas, / Others only carry it on their shoulders like a burden' (Nemade 1991, 31). Tukaram wrote many poems on the caste system, where he spoke of his low birth as a kunbi and condemned the hierarchy of the *varnashram*. As Nemade points out, 'He condemned the paraphernalia of brahminism: notions of high birth, blind beliefs, chanting of the Vedas, orthodox standards, ritualism, verbalism and bookish learning. He recognized only individual morality, because it was by the core of the individual morality that a man was truly tested' (53). His poems are replete with references to famines and rural poverty. His helplessness and isolation are vividly described in many of these poems:

> Where shall I go now?
> What shall I eat?
> With whose backing shall I live in this village? (Chitre 1991, 39)

The poems invoke such images of the world to authorise a personal point of view. One can easily draw many more such examples of Bhakti poems from Kabir, Basavanna, Allama Prabhu, Mahadeviyakka and many others. The nature of their dialogic imagination is distinctively visible in Tukaram's poems discussed above.

The emancipatory potential of Bhakti poetry kept the spirit of resistance alive in India, creating a space of dissent. The poetics and politics of Bhakti have enabled intellectual negotiations with institutionalised religions, particularly with the priestly hegemony. This dissent structures a deeper interior realm of desire and aspiration in the subcontinental social history. The emphasis on the contingency and transience of worldly phenomena, as represented by the Bhakti poets, shape an idiom of resistance to the essentialist notions of otherworldly narratives. That the Buddhist nuns spoke in Prakrit and the Bhakti poets spoke in regional languages, further complicate our discussion on the idea of dissent as an ethical act of disavowing exclusionary, hierarchical and essentialist notions of self and society. As Sundar Sarukkai observes, 'Asymmetries of representation are an ethical problem and have direct consequence, on pedagogy, on making sense of oneself and one's community, and even on social policies' (Guru and Sarukkai 2013, 155).

As against the uncritical celebration of Western theory, we need a responsible enquiry into what Sarukkai describes as 'the meaning-bearing capacity of concepts' (Guru and Sarukkai 2013, 155). For instance, Tukaram's ironical tone in '*bar jhale deha, nikhale divale / bara ya dushkale peeda keli*' ('Well done, O God, I became bankrupt / Well done, this famine has tormented me'; Nemade 1991, 19), communicates a heightened sense of self-consciousness. The poem exceeds its context, by questioning the common sense born of complete surrender to providence. The irony opens up a self-reflexive space of textual memory, recalling into its ambit the otherworldly fatalism that circulates in the grand narratives of the sacred language. This clears a critical space of dissent that defies theorisation in terms of borrowed concepts. In Bhakti, Sufi and Dalit poetry, the speaking subject positions herself at a point of liminality where multiple worlds are brought into critical relations.

## 4

This critical space of dissent is also seen in the poetry of Namdeo Dhasal (1949–2014), whose Marathi is a mixture of Bombay (Mumbai) Hindi and many other languages such as Urdu, Telugu and Tamil, spoken in the shady world of Mumbai in and around Kamatipura, thus underlying the polyphony of a modern city. In one of his poems, he addresses the elites of the society in these words:

Their Orthodox Pity (*Thyanchi sanatan daya*)

Their orthodox pity is no taller than a Falkland Road pimp
It's true, they haven't raised any ceremonial tent for us in the sky
After all, they are the feudal lords; they have locked all light in their vault. (2007, 47)

The poem ironically captures not only the denial of humanity to Dalits but the upper castes' refusal to give them light or even a view of the sky. The ghettoisation of Dalits is seen as a direct consequence of the hegemony of the upper castes.

We can't find even dust to fill up our scorched bowels
The rising day of justice, like a bribed person, favours only them
While we are being slaughtered, not even a sigh escapes their generous hands. (47)

The last line above is an exact translation of the original line, '*Apali katal ghadtana tyancha sadhal hatatun niswashi dhalat nahim*'. This heightened awareness is an important attribute of Dhasal's poetry, as he speaks from a crowded underworld of emaciated figures struggling to find an exit from their dark tunnel. His articulation bristles with restlessness and rage, as in the following poem, 'Man, you should explode':

Launch a campaign for not growing food, kill people all and sundry by starving them to death
Kill oneself too, let disease thrive, make all trees leafless
Take care that no bird ever sings, man, one should plan to die groaning and screaming in pain
Let all this grow into a tumour to fill the universe, balloon up
And burst at a nameless time to shrink
After this all those who survive should stop robbing anyone, or making others their slaves
After this they should stop calling one another names—white or black,
Brahmin, kshatriya, vaishya or shudra. (36)

Dhasal's poetry in Chitre's English translation reminds one of the American poetry of counter-culture of the 1960s, particularly that of Allen Ginsberg and Black American poets. This is poetry as performance where the powerful speaking subject mobilises the community to confront its depravity through evocations and invocations, speaking from within the crowd and from outside. The poem's intertextual relation with a larger narrative of subversive political movements adds a strong sense of self-reflexive element to his tone and texture. While his orality is derived from the lived reality of the local, Dhasal's poems, with their verbal energy, enact a movement towards breaking the barriers of the ghetto he is trapped in. The oral is also derived from the dissenting voices of Bhakti we discussed above. Dalit poetry is richly intertextual, seeking its resources from both the oral/local and the universal/transnational and from the political/performative. Dhasal is deeply aware of the polluted nature of the space he inhabits and packs its destructive potential in the profane, everyday idioms, calling into question all notions of elitist nationhood. In the poem 'Water', he realises something of its flowing torrential eloquence in the very dynamics of the verbal structure of the poem. In 'An Ode to Ambedkar', we once again confront the performative aspects of Dalit poetry, where the poetic voice goes through many shades of emotions ranging from lyrical invocation to rage and unbearable torment. The ethical plane of Dalit poetry has to be located at this level of performative dialogism, where it rises above the individual voice to the collective, and questions and confronts issues of power and authority. Dissent here transforms itself from a critical and reflective attitude towards a revolutionary consciousness that calls into question the very nature of institutional authority that constitutes the Dalit subject.

## 5

One of the paradoxes of the discourse of dissent is that it can very easily turn into a mirror image of what it resists. When the disabling discourses that transform human beings into victims become the very means of voicing dissent, we have a situation of cognitive blockage. Very often, our emancipatory aspirations are framed in the language of domination. Toni Morrison, in *Playing in the Dark: Whiteness and*

*Literary Imagination*, shows how Euro-centric knowledge about Afro-Americans marginalise and disable every act of representing Black experience. She comments, 'American Afrikanism makes it possible to say and not say, to inscribe and erase, to escape and engage, to act out and act on, to historicize and render timeless' (1993, 7).

Morrison's comment may help us understand how imperial gaze infiltrated our colonial modernity to inscribe and erase, at the same time, what was local, intimate, personal and contingent. The homogenising monumentality of the elitist nationalist narrative had built in blockages that plotted India into a narrative that was authored in the West. It is against this cognitive blockage that we need to look at Dalit autobiography. A monolithic view of modular modernity that anticipates all its mutations has come to inform our own narratives of evolutionary history. Social realism has come to gain a hegemonic authority in fictional writing in the twentieth century. However, Dalit autobiography constructs the self differently as it subscribes to a different sense of the self. The notion of the self as a discrete rational entity constituted by the trajectory of its triumphs over its environment, a narrative convention derived from the positivist tradition of the nineteenth century, is rejected by Dalit narratives. Dalit autobiographies problematise the relation between the self and society. It also questions the consensus that informs various narratives of modernity. Dalit autobiographies can be read as testimonies that stand witness to our critique of modernity. The idea of the human or humanist, as encoded in the elitist narrative of the nation, is subjected to an intense scrutiny by the Dalit autobiographer.

Dalit autobiographies mark a shift from the Romantic idea of the self with a unique interiority to a collective self of the community. Thus, in such narratives, memories enact a social space of collective resistance, questioning the hegemonic constructions of the self. What they recover is the continuity between memory and history, rendered invisible by the mystique of the evolutionary logic of history. Dalit autobiographies make it possible to speak of a 'life-script' as a cultural model, giving individuals a sense of their self that they are not able to derive from their disjunctions of time and space. It is here that 'writing' (graphy) becomes central to Dalit self-narratives, as they construct life (bios) from the fragments of the self (auto).

The secular modern world also drains the autobiography of various forms of history which are intangible. It was American Black writing which tapped the resources of collective memory, often the memories confronting that which is unspeakable, in both autobiography and fiction. Traumatic experiences of slavery cannot be narrated unless the American English assumes the contours of a Black American vernacular. The orality of the narrative in Dalit autobiography points to its ethical dimension recovering a deeper domain of the social, making it a 'thick' description of the lived reality.

The traumatic past of the Dalit conceals horrors of slavery which are often pushed to the collective unconscious. It is this awareness that forces Ambedkar to ask the question, 'Can it be said that Mr Gandhi has recovered the title deeds to humanity, which the untouchables have lost?' (2002, 171), in the essay 'What Congress and Gandhi have Done to the Untouchables?'. In a seminal passage from the essay, highlighting the *living death* of the Dalits, Ambedkar comments,

> The system of Untouchability had been a gold mine to the Hindus. In it the 240 million Hindus have 60 million of Untouchables to serve as their retinues to enable the Hindus to maintain pomp and ceremony, and to cultivate a feeling of pride and dignity, befitting a master class beneath it, which cannot be sustained and fostered, unless there is a servile class to look down upon. (315)

In the fictional narratives of C. Ayyappan in Malayalam, and those of Devanura Mahadeva in Kannada, we see a complex movement towards realising the potential of this collective memory in the telling of stories.

Ayyappan's short stories are peopled with the dead, ghosts who possess the living and dictate them to follow their unfulfilled desires. In many of his stories, he creates the haunting atmosphere of unnatural deaths, nightmares from where the speakers cannot find an exit route, and evil spirits that punish the living for unknown reasons. He captures a liminal world, where the past and the present, the living and the dead, and the memory and what is forgotten, cannot be distinguished. Ayyappan's stories are an attempt to exorcise the unconscious guilt and the collective anxiety bred by a traumatic past. He relies heavily on the social practices and beliefs of the pulaya community in central Kerala. Betrayals, ruthless murders of lovers, victimisations by landlords, ritualistic murders of slaves, are all part of the collective memory of the Dalit castes of Kerala.

They are yet to be confronted in the domain of imaginative fiction. But in the reworking of the folk realm of experiences into fictional narratives, Ayyappan has mapped a world of haunting history that cannot be narrated in the social realist mode. In the story *Kavalbhootam* (The guardian spirit), we find two local goddesses who are sisters. The elder sister possesses a fierce gaze that can kill anyone on whom she trains her eyes, while the younger sister is a benevolent goddess who pulls her elder sister down to protect the passerby. Whenever someone passes by, the elder sister will enquire with the younger one, 'Who is passing by?', and the latter will reply and also not allow her sister's gaze to fall on the human being. But, sometimes, out of exasperation, the younger goddess would just say, 'Why don't you find out yourself?', and then the unfortunate passerby has to confront the curse of the elder sister's gaze. In the story, a young man goes to the shrine in the dead of night to confront the evil goddess; but what he sees is a naked woman and two local ruffians. The man flees in panic as the woman embraces him. But he returns to the shrine, this time to commit suicide. He plans to stand on the stone goddesses and put a noose around his neck. He hopes to become a fierce spirit with many evil spirits at his command, so that he can torment all his enemies. Ayyappan's enchanted world is peopled with such characters whose desires continue to haunt them even after death. By turning the act of committing suicide into a transformative act of empowerment, Ayyappan questions the logic of the prevailing politics of emancipation.

The struggles of the Dalits in Kerala have been largely contained by symbolic acts such as temple entry movements and shared eating (*misrabhojanam*) and, in some rare cases, by inter-caste marriages. This tokenism never emancipated Dalits from their caste subjectivities. That modern Indian Dalit literature portrays the Dalit as a victim who is at the mercy of the caste system allows only limited positions for the Dalit narrative to confront their entrapment in the caste body. By invoking an underworld of traumatic anxieties that are peopled with magical moments of confrontations, Ayyappan creates a liminal world, where Dalits return to life after their *durmaranangal* (evil-deaths) to complete their tasks. He invokes a deep layer of collective memories that has never been narrated in Malayalam fiction. In his essay on Ayyappan, Udaya Kumar comments,

> Ayyappan's engagement with beliefs, practices, and histories of his community should not be seen as aimed at the valorization and restoration of a tradition. The uses to which Ayyappan's work puts elements of a Dalit mythography are distinctively modern. These mythographic elements work as props for the staging of modern scenes of subjection and desubjection. (2010, 187)

Ayyappan's rejection of the social realist representation has to be seen against the fact that it has been complicit with the hegemonic structures of the nation state in narrating a paradigm of liberation and development for the downtrodden. He consciously shapes a world of magical acts and surreal images so that they cannot be read as 'national allegories'. This defiance can also be seen in the two novellas of Devanura Mahadeva, an accomplished Kannada writer.

Mahadeva also revisits folk memories to tap their rich resources. In recovering the experiential images and symbols embodied in the collective experience of the community, he asserts an ethical position that is unique in contemporary Indian literature. The narrative mode he has used in both the narratives, particularly in *Kusumabale*, effects a breakthrough in the very structuring of the story. He departs from the Western style of narration, defying the logic of modernity, and creates an enchanted world peopled with spirits from the nether world, in close proximity to the human world. Vivek Shanbhag, in his introduction to the English translation of the novel, comments that 'the Dalit world Mahadeva has created was intrinsically connected with the other units of society' (Mahadeva 2015, xxii). The central event of the novel is the murder of a Dalit youth, Channa, who had mysteriously disappeared. In the course of the novel, it becomes clear that people of all castes are responsible for this murder. The binary of Dalit/upper-caste is carefully deconstructed when *jothammas*, lamp-spirits from all the houses in the village, assemble in the middle of the village after midnight and narrate the stories of these houses. There is a *jothamma* which has returned to the village after a period of twelve years and from her narration it becomes clear that Channa was in love with Kusumabale who belonged to another caste. Kusuma's husband did not even see the child born to her. Now Kusuma has lost her vivacity and beauty; she has become anaemic and drained. The entire story of Kusuma's family, through three generations, is narrated in the novel through fragmentary episodes. This is how we come to know the stories of Somappa, Yada and Akkamma. Yada was the son born to a servant and hence Akkamma was excommunicated from the village. They settled just outside the village, where Yada set up a tea-shop, and through his entrepreneurship, became rich. Just like *jothammas*, each house also has its own spirit. They also narrate stories. Amasa and Garesiddha live on the fringes of society, often breaking the law. When Garesiddha is caught stealing coconuts and is taken prisoner by upper-caste people, Amasa brings the Dalit Sangh leaders to the village and they intervene in the matter. This is the beginning of the Dalit Sangh in the village. The village is changing. Much after the death of Channa is reported, he appears in a scene where he talks with the brahmin teacher, Madhavacharya. The teacher is looking for a match for his daughter. He also thinks Channa should not have been born a Dalit. Madhavacharya's daughter lusts after Amasa. In the novel, sexuality becomes a source of transgressive emotions, breaking the caste barrier. When the Dalit Sangh has its meeting, one of the *jothammas* possesses a Dalit called Kuriahaih who speaks many unpleasant truths about Dalits and their attitudes. Devanura Mahadeva is also present in the meeting of the Dalit Sangh, sitting in a corner, smoking a *beedi*. When the Dalit march begins, Channa's father wishes his son were there. In fact, he is under the belief that his son is in Mumbai, flourishing in the house of its king. Kusuma is now being treated by black magicians from Kerala. As she is beaten, she speaks in French, 'I want to go to my home'. Many chapters in the novel are in the form of lyric poems. In a chapter titled 'Life returns to the bodies of Akkammadevi and Yaada', we come across the following lines:

> And back there
> darkness falling,
> and life slowly getting back to the half dead-bodies
> of Akkamahadevi and Yaada that Siddura
> flung on the grazing grounds,
> Akkammadevi sat up,
> the tears streaming from her eyes
> flowing up to the pond. (32)

The narratives move among the dead and the living, between the past and the present, bringing different spaces and times into a participatory dialogic plane where the binaries of modernity break down. Mahadeva creates a magical realist text, which is also a 'folk epic', out of the collective memories of the community. He carnivalises and subverts the ruthless logic of caste violence that includes lynching, as was practised in America when slavery was legal. Mahadeva has been able to embody the narrative perspective of *Bahitshkrut Bharat* (the Other India), where the resources of the language create cultural capital for the Dalit community.

As Ambedkar pointed out, in 'The Annihilatios n of Caste', the 'pomp and ceremony' of the upper castes is sustained by creating a 'servile class to look down upon' (see quote above). The vision that makes a new paradigm possible comes from a Dalit critique of the social structure. The tradition we have examined has created an alternate source of conceptual apparatus, questioning the cognitive block engendered by the distorted cosmos of a hegemonic system of caste discrimination. The achievements of the traditions illustrated above are central to any democratic idea of India, and its differences and diversities.

Ambedkar was aware of a deep moral asymmetry between the Western concept of individuality, modernity and civil/human rights that inform the ideology of nationalism, and its incapacity to represent the traditionally disenfranchised sections of the Indian society. His strong dissenting voice is creatively transformed into an artistic mode of narration in Dhasal, Ayyappan and Mahadeva, based on an ethical imperative that questions the universality of Euro-centric concepts and endorses the specificity of the everyday experience of social exclusion.

## References

Ambedkar, B. R. 2002. *The essential writings of B. R. Ambedkar.* Ed. Valerian Rodrigues. New Delhi: Oxford UP.

Bakhtin, Mikhail. 1984. *Problems of Dostoevsky's poetics.* Ed. and tr. Caryl Emerson. Theory and History of Literature (Volume 8). Manchester: Manchester UP.

Chitre, Dilip, ed. and trans. 1991. *Says Tuka: Selected poetry of Tukaram.* New Delhi: Penguin Classics.

Dhasal, Namdeo. 2007. *Namdeo Dhasal: Poet of the underworld. Poems 1972–2006.* Trans. Dilip Chitre. New Delhi: Navayana.

Guru, Gopal, and Sundar Sarukkai. 2013. *The cracked mirror: An Indian debate on experience and theory.* New Delhi: Oxford UP.

Hallisey, Charles, trans. 2015. *Therigatha: Poems of the first Buddhist women.* New Delhi: Murty Classical Library of India, Harvard UP.

Kaviraj, Sudipta. 2013. Why is the mirror cracked? *Comparative Studies of the South Asia, Africa and the Middle East* 33. 3: 380–91.

Kumar, Udaya. 2010. The strange homeliness of the night: Spectral speech and the Dalit present in C. Ayyappan's writings. *Studies in Humanities and Social Sciences* XVII: 1 & 2: 177–91.

Mahadeva, Devanura. 2015. *Kusumabale.* Trans. Susan Daniel. New Delhi: Oxford UP.

Morrison, Toni. 1993. *Playing in the dark: Whiteness and the literary imagination.* New York: Vintage Books.

Nemade, Bhalchandra. 1991. *Tukaram.* Makers of Indian Literature Series. New Delhi: Sahitya Akademi.

Shackle, Christopher, trans. 2015. *Bulleh Shah: Sufi lyrics.* New Delhi: Murty Classical Library of India, Harvard UP.

**Chapter Four**

# Globalisation, Resistance and Social Imagination: The Work of Art in the Market Place

Globalisation and the changes unleashed by the predatory nature of multinational capital have had an unsettling effect on much of the world. Can culture cope with the challenges of globalisation's hegemonic hold on the forces of homogenisation? The nightmarish underbelly of the globalised world is invisible, set against the glitter of the bazaar. In the absence of a coherent critical apparatus that can resist its allure of desires, societies are likely to withdraw into nativism and cultural nationalism. The symbolic value of a cultural text loses its power of resistance when it becomes an exhibit in the universal market place. Multiculturalism of the First World is unwilling to engage or understand the Other, and forces migrants to assimilate into its cultural habitat, alienating them from the resources of community and memory. Hence, it becomes imperative to preserve cultural diversity and local knowledge, as outlined by Alice Walker or Kallen Pokkudan, to resist the levelling impact of globalism.

## I

> To articulate the past does not mean to recognize it 'the way it really was'. It means to seize hold of a memory as it flashes up at a moment of danger. . . . In every era the attempt must be made anew to wrest tradition away from a conformism that is about to overpower it.
>
> Walter Benjamin, 'Theses on the Philosophy of History'

Globalisation, one may argue, is a moment in history which has few parallels in our recorded past. It is not easy to 'periodise' globalisation with any degree of finality. The world has been progressively globalised from the fifteenth century onwards, when expeditions in search of new continents got underway. While some argue that it is an advanced stage of modernity which began in the nineteenth century, others view it as an entirely new stage in history with its own distinctive features. Marx and Engels had rightly diagnosed the basic feature of the 'bourgeois epoch': 'Constant revolutionizing of production, uninterrupted disturbance of all social conditions, everlasting uncertainty and agitation distinguish the bourgeois epoch from all earlier ones' (Marx 1983, 207). Globalisation marks a stage where these tendencies have accelerated to such a degree that they have begun affecting the life of common people across the globe. After the fall of the Soviet Union, these changes assumed menacing proportions, as a unipolar world controlled by the United States of America became a distinct possibility. The structural adjustment programmes dictated by the World Bank and the International Monetary Fund (IMF) envisaged a market-driven world of free exchange with a minimal role for the state. This context of globalisation raises an important question: would countries like India be able to resist the homogenising impulse of globalisation in matters of culture and knowledge?

T. K. Oommen has argued that 'globalisation which prescribes universal norms and which pursues cultural homogenisation cannot have inclusion as its value orientation' (2007, 41). Transnational communities, which claim 'exclusive status' in a borderless world, do not consider the nation state as sacrosanct, and this implies a reorganisation of cultures with their roots in the national past.

In seeing globalisation as a North Atlantic phenomenon, and more specifically as an American phenomenon, we forget that the rest of the world has also gone through far-reaching economic transitions at several levels. It has been argued that if large-scale migrations are any indication, the non-European world is strongly implicated in the processes that constitute a globalised world. As Adam McKeown says,

> . . . a quick review of published contemporary statistics shows that northern and southeastern Asia should be ranked with the Americas as the world's three great frontiers. Absolute and per capita emigration rates across Asia were as large as the transatlantic migrations and followed similar cycles of ebb and flow. Manchurian soy fields, Malayan tin mines, African palm oil plantations and Siamese rice paddies were as much a part of the expanding world economy as Manchester factories and North American wheat. (2009, 226)

This implies that globalisation needs to be seen also from the perspective of those from the former Third World. The hegemonic nature of

American culture has rendered this perspective unavailable and invisible for obvious reasons.

Migration is a phenomenon determined by the nature of capital. Liberalisation and privatisation that accompany globalisation ensure easy mobility of labour by removing the legal protection which is essential for its security and survival. The fact is that large sections of the employees of the globalised modern world are not part of an articulate diaspora capable of representing themselves.

## 2

'Culture' equips one with the basic resources for defining and articulating one's identity. In the dark underbelly of the globalised world, the everyday world of physical or mental work – whether it is in the air-conditioned 'call centres', in the mechanised factories, or the desert farms where shepherds do not have any human contact for months together – often turns 'Kafkan', with individuals cut off from the nourishing sources of community. The migrant labourer, who barely manages to survive each day, forms the backbone of globalised production. However, they do not have any say in matters that shape their destinies. In Los Angeles, for instance, garment factories will close down if 'illegal' Mexican migrants are deported. Hence, the US government will keep threatening them with deportation while paying them low wages to keep these factories running. They have no access to legal remedies. In Surat, Gujarat, where I lived for more than two decades, textile mills will grind to a halt if the migrant labour from Orissa and Uttar Pradesh return home. But they live in dehumanised conditions, exploited by contractors who have absolute authority over their bodies. Confronted by the squalor and deprivation under which they live, one is reminded of the Dickensian industrial city of nineteenth-century English novels. They are cut off from meaningful relationships with their communities and live in a state of extreme alienation, without any social support systems. Since the bulk of these labourers belong to the informal sector, they have no means of articulating their grievances. As Aijaz Ahmad points out, 'what globalization does want is a nation state that is *weak* in relation to labour but *strong* on behalf of capital' (2004, 103). Globalisation, thus, has its impact on people who do not receive its dividends. The tribal who is evicted from his or her forest land, the traditional artisan whose place in the productivity chain is displaced by cheap, imported goods, and the roadside vegetable vendor deprived of his or her daily earnings by multinational chain stores, are also victims of globalisation, though we do not always see the connection.

What are the implications of this state of affairs for 'culture'? If we are to resist the predatory impulse of multinational capital inherent in globalisation, we need to grasp its working in our society. The upwardly mobile middle class in India is fascinated by the advantages of aligning with a globalised world. Moreover, no political party in India has been able to articulate a coherent response to the onslaught of globalisation in terms of programmes and policies. The rise of primordial identities related to religion, region and ethnicity to the centre stage may be one of the ways in which a society, driven to walls, responds to the pressures of globalisation. The insecurity that nags our middle class makes them fall prey to such regressive ideologies. It is significant that states which boast of high per capita income and substantial foreign direct investment, such as Gujarat and Karnataka, have now become breeding grounds for disruptive ideologies which threaten the social fabric of the nation. This also questions our ability to negotiate the impact of globalisation on our society and culture. We may be entering a stage of history where the ability of our culture to negotiate the alien traditions of a globalised world would be severely tested.

## 3

Indian culture has negotiated alien traditions of various linguistic and national origins, both during the pre-colonial and colonial periods, mainly through the agency of Indian literatures. In such inter-textual dialogues, the indigenous and the native constitute the larger frame of reference. This is to say that the hegemonic elements in the alien tradition could be domesticated and brought into a critical relation with the local and the regional. The hegemonic makes a claim to the universal and to that extent, shifts the frame of reference to an intangible, immanent principle that would evade definition in terms of the lived reality of the received cultures. The wilful and total surrender to the dominant tradition, described as 'mimicry' by some theorists, has raised fundamental questions regarding the legitimacy of discourses which look elsewhere for validation. The dark underbelly of the globalised world, mentioned above, is a reminder that culture has to find ways to contest and resist the predatory impulses that have become endemic to the process of globalisation.

The debates we had on 'nativism' during the 1970s and 80s did touch upon certain issues of modernity and modernisation. Nativism was a response to the rootless cosmopolitanism of metropolitan traditions which were incapable of entering into a dialogue with native perspectives. Globalisation tends to reinforce cultural nationalism as its double, as the repressed native discourses can return only as the Other of the secular modern whose space is equated with the metropolitan. The crisis we face is existential as well as political. To recover the secular modern in native traditions, we need to 'seize hold of a memory as it flashes up at a moment of danger', as Walter Benjamin suggests (1968, 255). We need to know how the contingent and fragmental 'in-forms' us. In the past, it was this ability to confront the contingent that enabled us to confidently negotiate alien traditions from our standpoint. One can cite the origin of the novel in India, or the constitution of the nationalist-romantic and modernist traditions in fiction, poetry and drama, as moments of such confrontations which made a difference to the indigenous ways of making sense of the changing nature of reality, without conceding space to the hegemonic thrust of alien world views.

But there are reasons to believe that globalisation is a stage of multinational capitalism which will destabilise the norms of negotiation that inward-looking cultures have perfected over centuries. The norms of evaluating art works have undergone changes in a globalised world. The works of modern Indian painters such as Tyeb Mehta (1925–2009), Francis Newton Souza (1924–2002) and M. F. Husain (1915–2011) have acquired a cult following in the domain of international art. The 'market' is in a position to consecrate symbolic goods and ensure their circulation as well as currency. Bourdieu (1994) has argued that the field of cultural production is structured by an opposition between the field of restricted production and the field of large-scale production. 'High art' or 'serious literature' acquires symbolic value by distancing itself from commercial value and economic profit. This is why a cultural field is a universe of belief. Literary texts are anchored in a complex system of cultural relationships determined by institutions and social forces. Indian literatures, rooted in their separate linguistic traditions, can be seen as well-defined literary fields constituted by a network of institutions, agencies and patronage that operate within contexts of centrifugal and centripetal cultural forces. Their inner dynamics can only be understood with reference to the aesthetic norms, and rules of receptions and rejections that have gone into the making of their ideological structures. For instance, the modernist movements in Indian literatures had a liberating effect on the literary fields in several Indian languages, because the terms on which the alien tradition was received were set by the inner dynamics of these literary traditions. In other words, they did not surrender their cultural autonomy in negotiating the alien tradition.

Globalisation tends to destabilise the nature of the mediations that the field of cultural production has emphasised and facilitated as a means of resolving social conflicts from within. In Bourdieu's (1994) opinion, the mass or popular culture cannot stake claim to a higher symbolic value as it is subjected to the demands of commercial production. The symbolic value of a cultural text is determined within the literary field of a society; and in this sense, it partakes of the larger social and political processes that constitute the collective identity of the people or community. This endorses a relational view of identity formation and cultural production. The collective social life of the people impacts the direction of culture in such a context. It is as culturally embedded beings that people participate in the production of values in a society. Literature is one of the sites where this process takes place. Here, it is instructive to remember that the Progressive phase in Indian literatures produced texts in all major literary forms, in response to the complex social situation in India in the 1930s and 40s. Social realism was an enabling fictional mode because it allowed Indian writers to discover the social contradictions which had not been articulated earlier. Here, an alien cultural product is assimilated into the native socio-literary contexts, on terms decided by our society.

The cultural forces unleashed by globalisation can destabilise the process of constituting symbolic capital in societies which have no means of resisting the onslaught of alien cultural products. This does not refer to the creative appropriations involved in artistic practices. Art or literature has always borrowed idioms, vocabularies, styles or modes from alien cultures. A case in point is Pablo Picasso's use of African art, or Thomas Mann's use of an Indian myth in his novella *Die vertauschten kopfe* (the myth which Girish Karnad later used differently in *Hayavadana*). There is another kind of appropriation which reduces a mode of seeing to a commodity, without reference to its context of origin. Picasso was not using African art commercially to make his art more 'marketable'. He was working in the avant-garde mode which questioned all established ways of representation in Western art. On the other hand, the 'montage', a mode of cinematography perfected by Sergei Eisenstein, came to be used by commercial films and filmmakers for entirely different ends. In *Battleship Potemkin* (1925), Eisenstein uses tonal montage in the famous fog scene. The dialectic of black, white and grey, as well as light and movement, communicates not only grief but a stubborn will to resist. It is essentially an ethical statement that creates a social space of representation. However, commercial films have used tonal montage largely to celebrate erotic passions and violence, thus eroding the social content Eisenstein had incorporated into the narrative of his films.

In the context of literature, this can happen differently. Cultural products that have evolved over long periods of time, such as folk songs or myths, metaphors or even dialects, may lose their symbolic significance if they are removed from their contexts and reduced to 'fetishised' exotica. One is reminded of Peter Brook's staging of the *Mahabharata* with actors from across the world. The compulsion to conform to a universal system of values, in effect, neutralises the subversive force of the text, which the *Mahabharata* retained through its innumerable rewritings against local and regional contexts. Ratan Thiyam's *Chakravyooha* and Heisnam Kanhailal's *Karna,* both in Manipuri, are examples of statements of dissent made through aesthetic experiments, without losing their universal dimensions.

Aijaz Ahmad has shown how globalisation has come to substitute 'exchange value' for the 'use value' of cultural products. Citing Samir Amin, he says that culture is a domain where 'use values are produced and shared *as use* values cooperatively and non-coercively' (2004, 104; emphasis in original). But in the context of globalisation, art gets caught 'in circuits of exchange, market pricing, advertising and so on' (105). The dawn of modernity had liberated artists from the bondage of patrons. However, now the market has enslaved artists and authors. If, earlier, the local was largely independent of market forces, now it has been penetrated by the market, as evidenced by the popularity of 'ethnic' products in the global market. The market is a domain of desire which continuously incites the mind with images, and creates a continuous state of anxiety and restlessness.

In this context, I would briefly mention two Malayalam novels, both of which have won wide acclaim, though for different reasons. Benyamin's *Aadujeevitham* (2008; translated into English as *Goat Days* in 2012) dealt with the dark underbelly of the life of migrants from Kerala in the Gulf. T. D. Ramakrishnan's *Francis Itty Cora* (2009) was sensational in its involved plotting of several genres ranging from the mystery novel to science fiction, the story moving across time and space. Benyamin describes the life of Najeeb Muhammad in a goat farm in interior Arabia, where he is forced to work by a rich Arab. His traumatic life among goats gradually reduces him to an animal-like creature, as he is now a slave without any hope of returning to the world outside. The style is stark and the narrative invokes the desert in all its myriad manifestations, alluring as well as terrifying. When the dreams of globalisation turn into a nightmare, you are utterly alone without any support systems in the host country. This novel has sold more than a lakh copies in Malayalam largely because this was the first novel to speak of the terrors of globalisation. Its critical tone forces us to reconsider the glitter of globalisation from a humanist point of shared suffering. On the other hand, Ramakrishnan's *Francis Itty Cora* is breathtakingly inventive and moves between countries and time zones in such a way that it strains our imagination. The dark rituals of Christians in central Kerala, cannibalism in New York, the Italian Renaissance, the history of Kerala mathematics, international fleshtrade run by women academics – the novel opens up an endless world of desire, erasing the boundaries between the virtual and the real, making the real appear fantastic and vice versa. Globalisation is endorsed and celebrated here in a triumphant tone, reducing questions of evil and exploitation to mere fictions. As the epigraph of the novel says, 'There is no history. It's just a story spiced up with lies, anecdotes and yarns'. The moral economy of globalisation is transformed into a phantasmagoria of moving images that float across the pages without adding up to any coherent vision. That globalisation can allure and entrap one in its triumphal discourse is an intimidating possibility. Malayalam has a long critical tradition and it has produced novels far superior to *The Da Vinci Code* in which Ramakrishnan seems to have found a model to emulate. But the situation may be changing even in Kerala. In the postmodern landscape of Kerala, malls and temples alike wear festive looks – the material and the otherworldly are often confused, as literature increasingly becomes part of 'festivals' to be celebrated mindlessly.

## 4

Identities and texts are socially fluid because they are contested from within, against the changing contexts of social reality. The fundamental dialogical character of the literary text is a possibility that can be realised only in a concrete social context, through responsive interactions. This is what is repressed in the globalised context of dehistoricised reception which becomes a celebration of the alien tradition's triumphant universalism. In the psychic fantasy of globalisation, the narrative of the developed society (where 'whiteness' is an important marker) becomes a diffuse value system, which can signify a variety of values such as individualism, mobility, equality, freedom, modernity, goodness and competence. 'Freemarket' becomes a supreme good and sets itself up as the universal system against which the rest of the world is seen and studied. What is distressing about this process is the transaction between repressed desires and the triumphalism of the market. The subjectivity constituted within such transactions is characterised by amnesia (loss of memory) and aphasia (loss of speech). The paralysis bred by the market is cleverly concealed in the illusion of freedom created by the continuous flow of 'brands' in the market. A work of art becomes a brand to be promoted through orchestrated salesmanship. An author becomes an accomplice in the conquest of markets.

In her *Playing in the Dark,* Toni Morrison has argued that the noble ideals of American democracy were outlined in relation to the slave's black body. Slavery as an economic institution was at the core of colonial and imperial projects which shaped the rhetoric of freedom, equality and universality. The rhetoric of multiculturalism enacts the social contract of globalisation. This rhetoric does not interrogate the historical legacy of racial inequality inherent in the economic and political asymmetries that define the present. Christopher Clausen, in his *Faded Mosaic: The Emergence of Post-Cultural America*, argues that true multiculturalism would demand an immersion in the alien cultures that are radically different from one's own.

If Americans are tolerant of the Indian caste system while believing in the legacy of Renaissance individualism and Enlightenment social contract, they would not be true to themselves. It creates a false sense of kinship with non-Western cultures without entering into their world views. Clausen uses the term 'post-cultural' to suggest that for large sections of people in North America, cultural moorings have lost their political relevance in daily lives where technology and mobility have done away with the need for an active public sphere where literature becomes a participatory space of shared values. In societies like that of India, literature has not completely lost its ability to set the social agenda. With the advent of a globalised culture, we stand to lose the participatory public sphere which can intervene actively in the political domain. Literature, at some deeper level, is political, because it is about choices. It is about memory and history.

Culture is memory, and in living societies, it determines the nature of relations between the past and the present. In the absence of an active public sphere, culture would become entertainment, a leisure activity with no social significance. The hegemony of globalisation reduces culture to a bazaar of exotica with no deeper history. For large sections of diasporic writers, the compulsion to conform to the hegemonic structures of globalisation has already meant progressive states of cultural amnesia. There are voices in literature which illustrate this phenomenon and plead for greater involvement in history. Denise Nico Leto, an Italian–American poet, in her 'The Mary Morelle Show', speaks of the manner in which her family names were 'Americanised':

> The United States
> took their own
> Italian names
> and spit them out
> in shortened versions.
> Giovanni became Jonny became Jon
> Cavacini became Cacini became Caci (Casey)

> The pressure to assimilate performed
> miraculous mutations.
> Alfonsina became Alfy became Al
> Letinoni became Letino became Leto (lido)
> What was Italian became no one
> what was American became everyone.
> To be both was to be someone else.
> Brief, clipped endings
> were survival. (Gillan and Gilan 1994, 167)

These lines suggest the continuous pressure to assimilate into the American society. The rhetoric of multiculturalism is a facade to conceal the hegemonic aspects of the American will to subjugate and domesticate.

Liberal and communitarian arguments regarding the limits of the acceptability of the Other have a long history in the West; for constraints of space, we cannot go into their merits. As Charles Taylor has convincingly shown, identities are dialogically constructed. The contradictions between the idea of equality and the demand for 'recognition' in a society have to be addressed politically by engaging the cultural difference. This is what literary works achieve when they render historical processes visible. This function of the written word is displaced by the markets' invasion and celebration of the domain of literature. Taylor says,

> But merely on the human level, one could argue that it is reasonable to suppose that cultures that have provided the horizon of meaning for large numbers of human beings, of diverse characters and temperaments, over a long period of time—that have, in other words, articulated their sense of good, the holy, the admirable—are almost certain to have something that deserves our admiration and respect, even if it is accompanied by much that we have to abhor and reject. Perhaps one could put it another way: it would take a supreme arrogance to discount this possibility *a priori.* (1992, 72–73)

This means that hegemonic constructions of culture are 'supremely arrogant'. The hegemonic nature of the globalised culture will not allow the fusion of cultural horizons originating in separate worlds. It follows that the extreme alienation of large sections of people, which we discussed in the second section of this chapter, will deepen in the years to come.

Against such a backdrop of deepening alienation, memory becomes a crucial agent of retrieving the cultural past. One reason why ideologies of hatred have found an easy acceptability among the articulate middle class is the perception of an erosion of their self-identity. In the context of globalisation, capital becomes invisible and its manifestations cannot be explained in rational terms. Selective readings of the past appeal to such sections of society which feel alienated but cannot see how and why. It is necessary to retrieve alternative visions of the past that are creative and constructive in resisting this alienation. For instance, in the novel *Now is the Time to Open Your Heart,* Alice Walker talks about the need to retrieve memories we are not even aware of. The novel narrates the spiritual journey of Kate, a writer, along the Mississippi. She is part of a group of women who undertake this long journey to understand others through their narratives of love, loss, conflicts and tragedies. One of the characters mentions an aboriginal Indian who came every year to worship 'bones' on a farm. The farm is now owned by a white man who thinks that the Indian's claim is a big joke. Every year, he used to turn up on a particular day and would go to a tree which, according to him, marked the site of his ancestors' bones. Once he came with his son whom he wanted to initiate into this annual rite of memory. His son seemed to be disinterested. Later, he came with his grandson, to show him the location of the ancestral bones. Meanwhile, a mining company had bought the entire land and had begun excavating the area. When they drained a lake nearby and began digging the lake bed, they discovered a huge heap of bones buried kilometres deep. They estimated that the bones must be at least 30,000 years old. This means that the aboriginal Indian is carrying a memory which went back several epochs of evolution. It is as if his body had registered that memory in its cells and nerves. He resists the transient world of virtual images through his memory, which is deeper than the mineral deposits under a lake. Walker reminds us of a dimension of the mnemonic retrieval we are unaccustomed to.

The aboriginal Indian's mode of resistance works because his is a living memory which is unavailable to us. Our cultures still retain such resources in their oral forms, if we have the time to search for them. As a performative act of totalisation, globalisation can numb our senses and cripple our capacity for metaphors. It erodes the social imagination that may increasingly surrender its polyphonic diversity to a monistic perspective. To possess an identity is to be situated in history and culture. This state of being 'embedded' is what literature tries to capture and communicate. From proverbs and dialects, folksongs, rituals and customs, stories narrated and remembered, and memories of tragedies and traumas overcome, a society creates metaphors and meanings that are constitutive of its identity and culture. If globalisation means the erosion of the ground beneath their feet, entire societies will end up as driftwood on the flood waters of virtual images that drown them in their invisible waves.

We will end this discussion with a reference to another text – an autobiographical piece by Kallen Pokkudan, an illiterate social activist in a remote rural area in northern Kerala. He has single-handedly reclaimed a huge mangrove forest against stiff opposition from vested interest groups that included leftist politicians. In his self-effacing fragmentary narrative, *Kandal kadukalkidayail ente jeevitam* (My life among the mangroves, 1998), Pokkudan hardly speaks of himself but takes a stern position against the world of 'progress' and 'development'. That he had no means even to support himself when he was engaged in this 'greening' of the mangrove forest may be beside the point, but it poses moral problems for the self-obsessed consumerist society of Kerala. In an epiphanic moment in his autobiographical narrative, Pokkudan describes a single mangrove plant that shelters a whole ecosystem of water insects, fungi, fish and such beings. It is a complete world view which refreshes our ways of seeing. In a chapter in his new extended autobiography *Ente jeevitham* (My life, 2010), titled *Dalitarum kandal vanamekhalayum* (Dalits and the mangrove forest region), Pokkudan describes how Dalits subsisted on the fish and fowls in the mangroves. Being bonded labourers, they were confined to the locality and lived in shacks adjoining mangroves and paddy fields. He lists twenty-two varieties of mangroves and more than forty varieties of fish, all from memory. Pokkudan says, 'Dalits, fish and the mangroves lived in their own world, unaware of the world outside' (170). Dalits had an intimate knowledge of the ecosystem constituted by the water bodies, birds, insects, fish, plants and the mangroves. His intimate knowledge of the interdependence between humans and the mangroves prompted

Pokkudan to turn to nature in search of answers for questions that had plagued him as a political activist. His effort to plant mangroves in areas where they were facing extinction are blocked by political leaders who wanted to reclaim the land for building roads and other civic amenities. However, Pokkudan succeeds in his mission through a long struggle involving grass-root-level activists, environmentalists, media and the judiciary. His autobiography shows how local knowledge is central to survival in a globalised world (2010, 157–65).

Pokkudan remembers what we have been trained to forget. He demonstrates that one can acquire a vision by being oneself, by not surrendering one's ways of seeing. Such visions can emerge only from those sections of society which have not internalised the logic of globalised discourses. Pokkudan enables us to see the source of violations in our contemporary world. His example demonstrates that alternative paradigms of development are possible, if we are able to break out of our narcissistic cocoons of blinded selves.

## References

Ahmad, Aijaz. 2004. *On communalism and globalization: Offensives of the far right*. New Delhi: Essays Collective.

Benjamin, Walter. 1968. *Illuminations.* Ed. Hannah Arendt. Trans. Harry Zohn. New York: Schocken Books.

Benyamin. 2008. *Aadujeevitham.* Kottayam: Green Publications.

———. 2012. *Goat days.* Trans. Joseph Koyippally. New Delhi: Penguin Books.

Bourdieu, Pierre. 1994. *The field of cultural production.* Cambridge: Polity Press.

Clausen, Christopher. 2002. *Faded mosaic: The emergence of post-cultural America*. Maryland: Ivan R. Dee.

Gillan, Maria Mazziotti, and Jennifer Gilan, ed. 1994. *Unsettling America: An anthology of contemporary multicultural poetry.* New York: Penguin Books.

Marx, Karl. 1983. *The portable Karl Marx.* Ed. Eugene Kamenka. New York: Penguin Books.

McKeown, Adam. 2009. Periodizing globalization. *History-Workshop Journal.* http:// muse. jhu. edu/jounals/history-workshop journal/063/63. (accessed November 15, 2009).

Morrison, Toni. 1992. *Playing in the dark: Whiteness and literary imagination.* Cambridge: Harvard UP.

Oommen, T. K. 2007. Social exclusion and the strategy of empowerment. Unpublished key-note address delivered at a seminar held at the Department of Sociology, Veer Narmad South Gujarat University, Surat.

Pokkudan, Kallen. 1998. *Kandal kadukalkidayail ente jeevitam* [My life among the mangroves]. Thrissur: Green Books.

———. 2010. *Ente jeevitham* [My life]. Kottayam: D. C. Books.

Ramakrishnan, T. D. 2009. *Francis Itty Cora.* Kottayam: D. C. Books.

———. 2014. *Francis Itty Cora.* Trans. Priya K. Nair. New Delhi: Three Rivers Publications.

Taylor, Charles. 1992. *Multiculturalism: Examining the politics of recognition.* Ed. Amy Gutmann. New Jersey: Princeton UP.

Walker, Alice. 2003. *Now is the time to open your heart.* London: Random House.

**CHAPTER 5**

# Redefining the Secular and the Modern: The Politics of Identity and the Minority Discourse in Contemporary India

In modern societies, religion has not only survived but has become a major source of conflict. This chapter attempts to examine the contradictions inherent in the secular modern as a category rooted in Enlightenment rationality. Secularisation has had different trajectories across the world. The process of minority formation has to be seen as a historical response to the coercive aspects of modern secularisation. This historical process is examined with reference to the formation of a region-specific minority identity among the Muslims of Kerala. The 'othering' of Muslim social identity has rendered their material reality unrepresentable. This crisis of representation is brought out through close readings of a major fictional work by Vaikom Muhammad Basheer and some of the recent short stories by a new generation of Muslim writers from Kerala. The stories written in the wake of the Babri Masjid demolition articulate the anxieties of the community regarding the cognitive violence inherent in the stereotypical images that circulate in the public sphere, alienating them further from the national mainstream.

## I

With the advance of modernity, religion has not disappeared from the contemporary world. The emergence of modern institutions has redefined the social significance of religion. We tend to associate religious practices with pre-modern world views, but secularisation has not rendered religious practices and ideas redundant. Carl Schmitt has observed that 'all significant concepts of the modern theory of the state are secularized theological concepts' (1985, 36). As an ideology, secularism reconstitutes the self in relation to a new set of paradigms derived from Enlightenment rationality. However, secularisation has taken different trajectories in different countries. The formation of the secular is not always accompanied by the shifting of the religious from the public to the private domain. In the United Kingdom, for instance, one can identify close links between the state and the church, but the people tend to be secular in their views; while in the United States, the federal state is strictly secular even as the population professes their religious faith openly (Asad 2003, 190–91). In India, despite a strong narrative of the secular articulated by the Constitution that sanctifies the state, the nation, as represented through symbols and images, is mediated through a refined Hinduism that has clear elitist associations. Talal Asad argues that 'the secular' should not be conceived as 'the space in which *real* human life gradually emancipates itself from the controlling power of *religion* and thus achieves the latter's relocation' (190–91, emphasis in original). This also explains the deep sense of ambivalence that surrounds terms such as 'minority' and 'minority experience' in contemporary discussions of the secular nature of Indian society.

The ambivalence built into the minority discourse in India has become more intractable in the last two decades. Even among those who subscribe to the secular modern, there is a great deal of ambiguity when it comes to recognising the 'minority' as a historical category. It is important to recognise that the process of 'minoritisation' among different communities did not take place in the same way; and even among religious minorities, their relation with the majority community is not shaped in the same manner in every part of India. For instance, the minoritisation of the Muslim community and that of the Dalit community have followed different trajectories. Following D. R. Nagaraj, I would argue that Dalit movement articulated a Dalit identity through the mode of 'self-minoritisation and self-closure' (Nagaraj 2010, 115). Ambedkar had stated before the Simon Commission: 'We claim that we must be treated as a distinct community, separate from the Hindu community, our minority character has been hitherto concealed by our inclusion in the Hindu community, but as a matter of fact, there is really no link between the Depressed classes and the Hindu Community' (qtd. in Nagaraj 2010, 117). Nagaraj argues that Ambedkar created a new identity for Dalits, 'by treating them as an embodied mass of humiliation' (118): 'Self-minoritization in this case meant the removal of spiritual, or ideational, link with other forms of protest, ignoring the idea of a common historical fate that binds Dalits with other subaltern producers' (118). Ambedkar's strategy of limiting the Dalit identity to those communities and castes that had a common history and shared memory created a self-definition that cleared a social space of resistance, but this did not open up a larger unity among the similarly oppressed minorities.

Unlike the Dalit movement's conscious strategy of minoritisation to negotiate with colonial modernity, the Muslims in India did not have a vantage point to engage with the same historical situation. Partha Chatterjee observes that 'the tendencies of religious reform with the minority communities were blocked by the fears that reform would mean capitulation to majoritarian homogenisation and the loss of identity' (2010, 3). For instance, legal reform of Muslim personal law has remained a particularly intractable problem, because the way the secular modern was defined by the imagined community of late-nineteenth-century India left no space to accommodate the self-definition of the dominant religious minority of Muslims. Asad has observed that secularisation (which, according to Max Weber, is the dominant feature of modernity) is a coercive process even in the West. The religious minority's ability to represent itself becomes seriously compromised when the experience of religion is confined to the private, domestic sphere. The subjectivities born of the 'private'/'domestic' religious experience cannot find articulation in the public sphere without seriously disputing the dominant feature of the secular modern as inscribed in the narratives of the nation and the nation state. This means that the secular modern needs to be redefined to address the anxieties and compulsions of the minoritarian discourse.

The everyday world of the minority community is unable to relate to the secular ideal since it denies its members an affective anchoring in lived experience. Terry Eagleton, in his *Culture and the Death of God*, has argued that the instrumental rationality of the Enlightenment was unable to see the human society as a socially-rooted organic whole and this prevented people from relating themselves to its abstract ideals. He observes,

> In its universalism and cosmopolitanism, it [the Enlightenment] paid too little heed to the fact that local customs, pieties and affections are the places where power must embed itself if it is to flourish. Otherwise

> it will prove too abstract and remote to be assured of its subjects' allegiance. There can be no effective sovereignty without a foundation in lived experience, which is one reason why Reason feels the need for a kind of supplement or prosthesis known as the aesthetic. (2014, 32–33)

In the readings of select fictional works from Malayalam, presented in the following sections, the lived reality of the minority community will be seen in conflict with the coercive aspects of the secular modern as an abstract and absolute norm of the modern nation state.

## 2

This chapter will focus on Kerala and Malayalam fiction, since the only way to historicise minoritarian discourse is to regionalise it. It is not possible to posit a monolithic Muslim identity for India. Even within Kerala, North Kerala, or Malabar, presents a distinctively different experiential site, when compared to the rest of the state in historical terms. The Muslims in the interiors of Malabar are largely converts from the lower castes, unlike the rich Muslims in coastal areas. Malabar witnessed a series of conflicts in the nineteenth and early twentieth centuries between Muslim peasants and Hindu landlords, which culminated in the Mappila Rebellion of 1921, during which large parts of South Malabar were 'liberated' by Muslim rebels who ran a parallel government till the British army brutally suppressed the armed rebellion and banished or hanged all its leaders. As Shahid Amin points out in his study of the Chouri Choura incident, nationalist and regional narratives often contradict each other when the same facts are deployed differently in their formulation (1995, 35–41). The root cause of the Mappila Rebellion was the intervention of the colonial government in the revenue system, empowering landlords to evict tenants for failing to pay taxes. The protest by the tenants, who were mostly Muslims, often resulted in violence against the landlords. Between 1836 and 1919, there were twenty-nine episodes of rebellion. The protest assumed communal overtones when it found patronage from the religious leaders of this sub-region. As M. T. Ansari shows, in his essay in *Subaltern Studies XII*, the figure of the fanatic Muslim is articulated in the colonial discourse during this phase. This figure gains currency in the popular imagination and circulates in the literary discourse throughout the twentieth century, erasing the Muslim's material life and excluding him from the nationalist discourse of the secular modern. This framing of the Muslim into a fanatic dehistoricises him, metamorphoses him into an illiterate, irrational savage who has to be feared and tamed. For evidence from literary discourses, one may point to *Duravasthha* (The tragic plight, 1922) by Kumaran Asan (1873–1924), a long poem on the inter-caste marriage between a Dalit youth and a brahmin woman, set against the background of the Rebellion; and a novel by Uroob (1915–79), *Sundarikalum sundaranmarum* (The women and men of beauty, 1958), which refer to the 'cruel Muhammadan' who is marked as the Other.

This 'othering' of the Muslim in mainstream culture and popular imagination has rendered his material reality unrepresentable. As opposed to the 'savage' Muslim in the writings of the mainstream, we also come across, in popular narratives (in fiction, films and plays), the figure of the 'good Muslim' who is always shown wearing a skullcap, a beard and a belt, and as eager to help his Hindu neighbours. This crisis of representation has found articulation in the fictional works of Vaikom Muhammad Basheer (1908–94). Basheer, who was inspired by the Progressive movement, was a nationalist and valorised the secular modern as a desirable ideal; but he finds the assimilation of the Muslim community into its logic as leading to the loss of its difference, without which the community cannot sustain a viable mode of belonging to the society. We will briefly discuss the novel *Ntuppuppakkoranendarnnu* (*Me Grandad 'ad an Elephant*, 1951; hereafter mentioned as *Me Grandad*), which brings out the implications of the project of modernity for the minority Muslim community in Kerala.

Written in 1951, *Me Grandad* addresses the question of reforms in the Muslim community with a sense of urgency. In the course of negotiating the question of modernity, Basheer has to face some of the basic paradoxes implied by modernity. *Me Grandad* may be read as a critique of the project of modernity embodied in the nationalist discourse. The central character in the novel is Kunjupathumma, who moves out of her minority 'subculture' into the 'national' culture through a series of encounters and decisions. Brought up in Muslim culture, Kunjupathumma shares the 'common sense' typical of the members of the community who are illiterate and pious to a fault. With characteristic irony, Basheer writes,

> In the world there are only two classes, Muslim and Kafir. Whether they are men or women, after death all kafirs will go to hell. They are all fallen ones. If Muslims imitate them they will become lost souls worthy of hell. The kafirs Kunjupathumma saw were school mistresses. Although they are kafirs, they smell nice. They all wear saris. They all have those small kuppayams known as blouses. Underneath the blouse they have a thin, tight bodice. What is more, they wear flowers on their head. (Basheer 1980, 54–55)

The Muslim and Christian communities in Kerala, in the first part of the twentieth century, had their own distinctive ways of dressing. Joining the mainstream meant moving away from these culture-specific markers of identity. The novel portrays the reforms that were sweeping the Muslim community. These reforms emphasised education, standardisation and integration into the mainstream community. The formation of the linguistic state of Kerala in 1956, unifying the regions of Malabar, Kochi and Travancore, also set in motion a process of standardisation in educational curriculum and linguistic usage. Caste markers came to be associated with regressive world views. A communist government came to power in 1957, and this accelerated several progressive legislations that dismantled the feudal power structure. That Kunjupathumma's mother always invokes the family's feudal past as a lost paradise, long after they have been reduced to penury, indicates the underlying conflict in the novel.

Nisar Ahmad and his sister Ayesha represent the progressive Muslims in the novel. They take it upon themselves to 'reform' Kunjupathumma, the illiterate, orthodox girl who speaks the Muslim dialect to their utter shock. But Basheer portrays the fables and myths that inform the world of Kunjupathumma, bestowing on her a unique power of imagination which one does not associate with the world of modern rationality. Nisar Ahmad and Ayesha 'teach' Kunjupathumma to speak 'proper' Malayalam which is closer to the written 'standard' Malayalam. Kunjupathumma can traverse this distance between the dialect and the standard speech only through a cultural assimilation. She has to transform herself into a national subject, partaking of the larger process of modernity that has no space for her 'differences'. At one point, Kunjupathumma asks Ayesha, 'If you learn to read and write. . . . And if you are well informed, it is not possible to live like a Muslim? Is it true?' This question has a greater significance than the context seems to imply. Can the Muslim retain his/

her unique community-specific markers of identity and still enter into the domain of modernity? Does membership in the world of modernity imply a loss of all that specifically contribute towards their collective identity? Kunjupathumma's assimilation into a standard 'national' identity alienates her from the larger bonds of community. One needs the specific culture of a local, living community to relate oneself to a larger 'national' identity. The local and communal are not negative sources of identity but affirmative modes of belonging to a larger collectivity. Basheer demonstrates how the local is constituted in terms of specific modes of knowing and experiencing the world. Subcultures have their collective wisdom and their native ways of perceiving the world. Such cosmologies inform the larger narrative of the nation. Though Basheer takes sides with the progressive Muslim and endorses Kunjupathumma's assimilation into secular modernity, he is aware of an uneasy resolution here, since this assimilation does violence to the process of belonging to a culture-specific identity.

A minority discourse becomes possible only if the members of the group can operate as meaningful collectivities with their specific experiences rooted in separate social contexts. A minority discourse, in this sense, is an 'ethical-political' discourse which, in the view of Jürgen Habermas, would pertain to a group or collective identity and enable members of a community to see themselves as inhabitants of a specific region, as heirs to a specific culture, allowing them to decide how they want to deal with their historical destiny, with one another or with nature. Plamen Makariev, commenting on Habermas's views on minority discourse, writes,

> Habermas regards ethical political discourse as being twofold in character. On the one hand, they can be self-reflexive to a certain extent insofar as they are not based upon a fundamentalist mentality. As such they enable groups to critically appropriate their own traditions. On the other hand, however, they cannot be completely dissociated from the respective domain of the lifeworld. (2013, 24)

Minority discourse, as an ethical-political discourse, provides a means of explicating and articulating a shared value orientation. The secular modern, as a normative hegemonic source of validation of collective needs and self-understandings, affects the manner in which a minority discourse projects the self-understanding of a community. The larger framework of citizenship will form the foundation for this negotiation between the particular demands of a community and the collective will of the society. As Habermas points out, 'Reason and will reciprocally determine each other in ethical discourses, for these discourses remain embedded in the context they thematize' (1996, 167).

In the context of Kerala, the Marxian discourse of emancipation has subscribed to the rationalist ideal of the secular modern, complicating the legitimacy of the marginalised minorities as a separate group. The Marxists have strongly disputed the claims made on behalf of the politics of identity. The appeal to the authenticity of the self, derived from the daily experiences of exclusion or violence, calls into question the claims made on behalf of the class struggle. What is disputed is the claim that class transcends all divisions based on markers such as gender, caste, religion, region and race. In the last three years, the organs of the Marxist Party in Kerala have found it necessary to refute the claims of the politics of identity as conspiracies of capitalism. Prakash Karat, in an essay on the politics of identity, observes that 'the impetus to globalization provided by capitalism and the setbacks suffered by socialism were primarily responsible for the legitimacy gained by the politics of identity' (Master 2010, 12). However, the arguments put forward by the party ideologues betray the inability to engage with the anxieties and insecurities of Muslims in the post-Ayodhya Kerala. K. N. Panikkar, in his essay in the same volume, argues that traditionally, organisations based on caste and religion have played a dual role, both constructive and regressive, in the social formation of India (33). Since all societies have multiple identities, it is natural that identities based on region, caste, religion and ethnicity tend to assume significance in a society that is yet to develop class consciousness. Citing Gramsci, Panikkar argues that 'man-in-mass' is bound to have a 'contradictory state of consciousness' that will result in an ambivalent attitude towards questions of social change (34). Citing the example of Muslims in Kerala, he says that large sections of the community are extremely poor. The assertive attitude of majoritarian forces, particularly in the wake of the communal incidents after the demolition of the Babri Masjid in Ayodhya, makes them vulnerable. Hence, the Muslims in Kerala find themselves in a double bind. Without the larger support of the community they cannot shape an ethical-political discourse on their culture-specific identity. However, the community is economically and socially divided, creating a conflict of interests regarding the larger commitment to the well-being of the community, particularly of its most vulnerable sections.

## 3

In the post-Ayodhya situation, the Muslims in Kerala are increasingly seen as part of a pan-Indian or international Islamic community, though such a perspective falsifies their life-world constituted by the Malayalam language and their immersion in local realities. The culture-specific nature of their identity is erased when they confront the challenges of fundamentalism. Here, it may be interesting to discuss a few short stories from a volume titled *Ariku* (Margins, 2012), edited by Samad Kunnakkavu with an introduction by this writer in Malayalam, which showcased issues of communal and cultural identity in the context of the minorities in Kerala. The stories in the volume show how the secular modern legitimates only certain kinds of identities as 'modern'. This process of 'othering' is a major theme in these stories.

In the story *Aligadhil oru pashu* (A cow in Aligarh) (Kunnakkavu 2012, 110–23), by Anwar Abdullah, the narrator speaks of a harrowing time he had in Tiruchirappalli, when preventive arrests were made in connection with the visit of the union home minister to Coimbatore. The authorities find that fearing arrest, almost all male members of the minority families in the area have disappeared. Anis, one of the members of this group, narrates an episode from his life in Aligarh, from the time he was a student there. The incident occurred in 1993. After the widespread communal riots in Bombay (Mumbai) and other parts of the country, the students on the campus were filled with anxiety and fear, though they found the place fairly secure. Then, suddenly, the dead body of a cow was discovered on the campus, and the needle of suspicion was pointed at the students of the zoology department. Anis, one of the zoology students, was among those who were threatened with dire consequences. For the first time in his life, he felt as if he were a proclaimed victim. There were rallies and processions demanding action against the culprits. The district magistrate ordered a post-mortem examination of the dead body. The night before the post-mortem, the district authorities shifted all the students under suspicion to a railway station where they were kept under guard. Anis describes the trauma he went through, and his fear that they could be attacked any moment. His classmates too went through the same harrowing experience. Even when they were allowed to leave for their home towns, nobody had the courage to step out of the room alone. Then, the station master brought a newspaper which had reported that the post-mortem examination proved that the cow had died of natural causes. As the story clearly shows, the incident changed Anis forever – he became a drifter; he felt vulnerable and unsure of his own identity in a free India.

In another story in the same collection, *Badusha enna kalnadakkaran* (The pedestrian called Badusha) (95–101), Unni R. describes the plight of an elderly Muslim man who is fond of taking long walks, enjoying the landscape and the sights and sounds of nature. His wife cautions him when he goes out to the beach in the dead of night, asking him, 'Are you mad to go for a walk at this time of night?' He is picked up by the police and brutally beaten up. For the police, the very fact of his appearance, his bearded face, is enough to confirm his identity as a 'criminal'. Something similar happens to a lunatic in the story *Matabhrandan* (The fanatic) (27–38) by Shihabuddin Poythumkadavu. Here a mentally unstable person is taken into custody by the police after a bomb goes off in the city. He was searching for food in a garbage heap, and his bearded visage, caught on a CCTV camera, becomes evidence against him. He was retrieving some leftovers, but, in the dimly lit footage, he is seen planting a packet. Since the bomb had gone off in the vicinity, his arrest is a 'breakthrough' the police can celebrate. He is framed as a hardened criminal, his incoherent answers confirming that he is a trained terrorist who has been taught to mislead the police.

In all these stories, the law-enforcing agencies frame the Muslim identity as potentially disruptive to the nation state. The majoritarian world view has come to be internalised by the nation state, which, as a republic, has to guarantee equality before the law for all its citizens. In this sense, these stories attest to the moral failure of the nation state. For instance, K. P. Ramanunni's story, *Chila matetara samsarangal* (A few secular conversations) (17–27), lampoons the hypocrisy of the elites who pose as secular but profess a deep-rooted hostility towards the minorities. One of the speakers in this story, who happens to be a professor at a university, is unable to stand the appearance of a Muslim,

Bavootty, who always wears traditional 'Mappila' clothes and sports a beard and a skullcap. Bavootty is a philanthropist who generously donates to the cause of education. But his manners and appearance mark him as an 'obscurantist'. It does not take long for his son to be arrested for alleged links to an extremist organisation. Bavootty is taken into custody for questioning, is beaten up for speaking in Arabic, and finally dies on the way to the hospital. The professor invites all his friends, including a 'moderate' Muslim, Aryankav who edits a progressive journal, *Navakeralam* (Modern Kerala), for a get-together to 'celebrate' Bavootty's persecution and death. The case of Aryankav also sums up the dilemma of the 'moderate', 'modern' Muslim. To become a member of the 'secular' society, he has to disown his own community. The title of his periodical clearly points to the democratic ideals once held dear by the progressive and reformist sections of Kerala society.

As shown above in the discussion of Basheer's novel, the Muslims in Kerala had clearly endorsed modernity through education and social reforms. But the global and national events after the 1990s have brought into focus a certain crisis of identity among the Muslim community in general, and the community in Kerala is caught in a nightmare of history, with the secular modern discourse offering no safe passage. We need to bring into the minority discourse a larger framework of citizenship, which is an indivisible and irrefutable right guaranteed by the Constitution, and that alone can bring legitimacy back to the representation of the minority subjectivity in our troubled times.

## References

Amin, Shahid. 1995. *Event, metaphor, memory: Chauri Chaura 1922–1992.* New Delhi: Oxford UP.

Ansari, M. T., and Deeptha Achar, ed. 2010. *Discourse, democracy and difference: Perspectives on community, politics and culture.* New Delhi: Sahitya Akademi.

Asad, Talal. 2003. *Formation of the secular: Christianity, Islam, modernity.* California: Stanford UP.

Basheer, Vaikom Muhammad. 1980. *Me grandad 'ad an elephant!* Trans. R. E. Asher and A. C. Chandrasekharan. New Delhi: Viking.

Chatterjee, Partha. 2010. Fasting for Laden: The politics of secularization in contemporary India. In Ansari and Achar 2010, 3–22.

Eagleton, Terry. 2014. *Culture and the death of God.* New Haven and London: Yale UP.

Habermas, J. 1996. *Between facts and norms.* Cambridge: MIT Press.

Kunnakkavu, Samad, ed. 2012. *Ariku: Orangalilakappettavarekurichulla kathakal* [Margin: Stories about the marginalised]. Kozhikode: Prateeksha Books.

Makariev, Plamen. 2013. Cultural rights and deliberative policy: Beyond Habermas' 'Between facts and norms'. *Journal of Public Deliberations* 9.1. Available at: http://www.public deliberation.net/jpd/vol9/iss1/art2.

Master, M. V. Govindan, ed. 2010. *Swathwarashtreeyathepatti* [Regarding identity politics]. Thiruvananthapuram: Chinta Publications.

Nagaraj, D. R. 2010. *The flaming feet and other essays.* New Delhi: Permanent Black.

Schmitt, Carl. 1985. *Political theology.* Cambridge: MIT Press.

# SECTION 2

# Reading as Recovery: The Textual Worlding of the Singular

**Chapter Six**

# Interrogating Modernity: The Social Imaginary in Tagore's Prose Works

Rabindranath Tagore shaped a critique of Euro-centric modernity through his deep engagement with the self-divisions and dichotomies of his generation, in the wake of the imperial project of transforming India. He recovered the oppositional content of multiple traditions of metaphysical enquiries and poetic articulations, to subvert the homogenising impulse of modernity. Both his prose and poetical works partake of the same social imaginary that problematises the normative function of modernity. In his fictional works, Tagore explores the contestations between the masculine and feminine to examine how the social discourse of the modern is shaped through various forms of power relations. The experiential content of his poetry embodies and enacts a communitarian voice, clearing an ethical space that can re-imagine self–world relations from the perspective of an inclusive humanity that defies forces of 'othering' and alienation.

## I

The context of Rabindranath Tagore has not disappeared from our society. His contemporaneity has to be located in his engagement with ideas of his times that have a bearing on the fashioning of a modern Indian self. Tagore's contributions as a writer, thinker, educationist and public intellectual have been seminal in shaping the modern consciousness in India. Along with Gandhi, he came to epitomise India's interpretation of modernity from an Indian perspective in the colonial context. His engagement with modernity shaped a critique of what was essentially a Euro-centric discourse and cleared a conceptual space for the quest for alternative models of modernity. While commenting on Tagore's views on rationality, in the context of his relations with Gandhi, Bhikhu Parekh comments,

> For Tagore, the intellect had no 'personal concern or basis'. It was primarily interested in power, in mastering its object by studying its formal and general features, and sought 'not reality, but law.' It inspired and lay at the basis of the modern Western civilization devoted to dominating its natural and social environment. The nation state, a uniquely modern institution, was a 'creation of the intellect' as was the capitalist economy, and both were causes of much violence and dehumanization. (2015, 66)

Tagore's works were attempts to rework and transform received ideas on a variety of subjects – from the role of the nation state to the relation between the private and the public domains in modern society, against the particular historical and social contexts of India at the turn of the twentieth century. His works reflect the divisions of a society caught in the hegemonic structures of colonial and imperial powers. But they were not circumscribed by the immediate context of imperialism as his moral concerns address the larger question of the role of art in shaping the relations between culture and power.

It is important to remember that the Indian intelligentsia in the late nineteenth and early twentieth century had to reinterpret the received European knowledge in the light of their own intellectual histories. The complexity of Tagore's situation can be understood better if he is placed against the larger Indian context at the turn of the twentieth century. Poets like Kumaran Asan (1873–1924) in Malayalam, Muhammad Iqbal (1877–1938) in Urdu, Keshavsut (1866–1905) in Marathi, Subramania Bharati (1882–1921) in Tamil, D. R. Bendre (1896–1981) in Kannada, Mahjoor (1885–1952) in Kashmiri, Bhai Vir Singh (1872–1957) in Punjabi and Bharatendu Harischandra (1850–85) in Hindi were also involved in defining the modern Indian subject and shared similar anxieties and self-doubts in their projects of countering the discourses of colonial modernity. It is true that their responses were conditioned by their distinct literary traditions. But they could not escape a schism in their very being in facing an alien tradition that was hegemonic in its totalising effect. The process of appropriating Western knowledge involved selective adaptation, translation, incorporation, sceptical interrogation or rejection. A certain melancholy, born of being torn between two worlds, was characteristic of these great poets, and this may be seen as a condition of the self becoming aware of itself.

To illustrate the Indian case further, a brief look at Kumaran Asan may be instructive. Asan was twenty-seven years old in 1900 when he returned to Kerala after three years in Bangalore and two years in Calcutta (now Kolkata). There is no reference to Tagore in his writings, but he did translate certain writings of Swami Vivekananda. Asan remains a towering figure in Malayalam poetry, dividing Malayalam literature between 'pre-Asan' and 'post-Asan' periods. One can identify at least five elements that link Asan to Tagore, against the larger issues addressed in this chapter. The first of these elements is Asan's activist role as a poet. As the secretary of the Sree Narayana Dharma Paripalana Yogam (SNDP), he was deeply engaged in the politics of the day. He was a member of the legislative assembly and regularly made speeches highlighting the problems of *avarna* communities. Asan's prose writings include editorials, speeches delivered on public forums, memorandums submitted to the government, letters on various issues to many public men, and book reviews and articles. Secondly, Asan's poetry does not deal with any of these public issues he dealt with directly. His major poems – *Veena poovu* (The fallen flower), *Nalini*, *Leela*, *Chinthavishtayaya Seetha* (Seetha lost in thoughts), *Chandala bhikshuki* and *Karuna*, all long narrative poems – revolve around female protagonists whose quest for love, or self, culminates in a moment of self-knowledge accompanied by the loss of the self. It is the interiority realised in the texture of his poetry that has given him a central place in Malayalam poetry. It was a poetry of profound tensions and tragic conflicts of the kind one had not encountered before. The dialectic between the inner and the outer, recovery and loss, acceptance and assertion, define the onward movement in these poems. Thirdly, this dialectic also reflects deeper conflicts such as those between the lover and the ascetic, the reformer and the revolutionary, and the artist and the activist. They have been central to Kerala's poetic scene in the last century. Fourthly, Asan's poetry, characterised by a high degree of interiority (as evidenced by the texture of his poems), embodies the social energy unleashed by a radical reform movement. Lastly, Asan had a lifelong fascination for Buddhism. Two of his major poems, *Chandala bhikshuki* and *Karuna*, are based on episodes related to the life and philosophy of the Buddha, which figure prominently in Tagore's works. Though there is no evidence that he had read Tagore's *Chandalika* or *Fruit-Gathering*, which tells the story of Vasavadatta and Upagupta, Asan's treatment of the same characters and themes reflects concerns that show a similarity of approach towards questions of emancipation. Asan's poems raise several issues of female sexuality and its relation to the emancipatory project of modernity.

At some risk of generalisation, it may be said that while confronting the discourse of modernity, the major poets of Indian languages at the turn of the twentieth century had to bargain hard to save their soul. They fashioned the self through an idiom of interiority that was deeply embedded in the shared experiential spaces of the community. Javed Majeed, in his essay on Muhammad Iqbal, shows how there are two defining tensions within his Persian and Urdu poetry: 'the first is between territorial nationalism and the global imaginings of religious identity, and the second is between the homogenizing imperatives of nationalism and the subjectivity of individual selfhood' (2010, 133). At the end of his long poem, *Javid nama* (1932), Iqbal says, 'Abandon the East, be not spellbound by the West / for all this ancient and the new is not worth one barleycorn' (qtd. in Majeed 2010, 147). At another point in the same poem, Iqbal says that the sun blazes and burns with inward fire when it is between the East and the West, though it is an easterner (148). Like Tagore, Iqbal sees the relationship between people and the nation as problematic. Nation as a politically defined territory becomes an 'impediment to self-realisation and to knowing the true nature of things' (148).

## 2

Tagore's writings were seen as emerging from a Westernised consciousness by many of his contemporaries. Dinesh Chandra Sen, for instance, commented that his works were 'European literature written in the Bengali language and they are the first of its kind' (Chakrabarty 2008, 158). Tagore was one of the first to use the short story form in Bangla. His use of the novel became progressively more complex as he began to use this characteristically Western form to debate issues of an Indian society caught in the turmoil of nationalist assertion. His lectures and essays addressed the question of violence implicit in imperialism. In the process, he shaped a new social imaginary that went beyond a prescriptive view of the modern. In his essay 'The Canker of

European Civilization', Tagore observes, 'The western nations, under the urge of their city-bred civilization, are dividing human society into two antithetical sections of light and darkness, not only at home but all over the globe' (Tagore 2008, 4:416). He was aware of the Benthamite dimension of industrial civilisation. The predatory element at its core unsettled him as he saw its potential to disrupt the moral fabric of societies like that of India. He saw in Japan a deepening disconnect between the people and the nation state. 'The hysteria in her politics' and the 'unscrupulous greed of her commerce' was at odds with the spirit of their inner being that carried the stamp of centuries of reflection and intimate contact with nature. In his essay on religious education, he observes, 'There are truths which are of the nature of information, that can be added to our stock of knowledge from the outside. But there are other truths, of the nature of inspiration, which cannot be used to swell the number of accomplishments' (Tagore 2008, 4:258).

The question of modernity is not seen here in terms of binaries that reduce the rest of the world as 'pre-modern' because only Europe can be 'modern'. The logic of modernity that Europeanises our paradigms renders our experiences invisible and unrepresentable. In the march of the modern Tagore sensed a relentless effort to approximate our apparatus of representation after the European models. This modular form of modernity recasts all history into the modern and the pre-modern, and reduces history to a linear path where the rest of the world can exist only in a state of desire and want. In an essay on religious education, Tagore quotes a poem by a Baul poet called Madan, 'whose courage to decry the conventional paths of the pious as leading to spiritual futility is made evident' in the song that Tagore quotes:

> Thy path, O Lord, is hidden by mosque and temple:
> I hear thine own call, but the guru stops the way.
> What gives peace to my mind, sets the world ablaze—
> The cult of the One dies in the conflict of the many.
> The door to it is closed by many a lock, of Koran, Puran and rosary.
> Even the way of renunciation is full of tribulation:
> Wherefore weeps Madan in despair. (Tagore 2008, 4:259)

This Baul song illustrates the oppositional content in a tradition which resists domestication and standardisation. This song interrogates all institutionalised sites of religion and demands a sensuous apprehension of the world. This language is inaccessible to modernity because it reduces the world into a regime of the normative. Such experiences are very often termed as anarchic or mystical. Is it possible to accommodate the sensuous world of the Baul singer in the idiom of the modern? What Tagore examines in much of his works is how the modern precludes and excludes the experiences of those who have been constituted as the Other of the modern in Indian society. His discussion of the question of nation and nationalism, which has been widely discussed, will illustrate this point further.

Tagore answers the question, 'What is Nation?', in the following words:

> It is the aspect of a whole people as an organized power. This organization incessantly keeps up the insistence of the population on becoming strong and efficient. But this strenuous effort after strength and efficiency drains man's energy from his higher nature where he is self-sacrificing and creative. For thereby man's power of sacrifice is diverted from his ultimate object, which is moral, to the maintenance of this organization, which is mechanical. (Tagore 2008, 4:458)

At various points in his discourse on the nation, Tagore uses the metaphors of the machine, the householder who becomes a drunkard, and the giraffe which turns the pastoral land into a desert. He finds 'the insistence of the population on becoming strong and efficient' a part of the domestication process implicit in the operations of modernity – from the organisation of the nation state to the constitution of the modern individual. However, he objects to the institutionalisation of instrumental reason to the exclusion of alternative points of view and denial of multiple modes of representation. Tagore's words remind us of the 'panopticon' elaborated upon by Michel Foucault in *Discipline and Punish*. Much later in the twentieth century, a critique of reason and Euro-centric modernity emerged from the very heart of Europe. Max Horkheimer says that 'the disease of reason' is that reason was born from the human urge to dominate nature and turn it into mere object: 'One might say that the collective madness that rages today, from the concentration camps to the seemingly most harmless mass-culture reactions, was already present in germ in primitive objectivization, in the first man's calculating contemplation of the world as prey' (1947, 176). Tagore's critique of modernity is directed against this objectivisation.

Bhikhu Parekh says that for Tagore, nationalism represented a 'double pathology': 'The state which was just one dimension and institution of society was abstracted from it and given a central guiding role. It was then hijacked and chartered in the service of a single goal determined by a dominant group seeking to shape society in its own image' (2015, 69–70).

This is reflected in the essay 'The Robbery of the Soil'. In words that remind us of Gandhi, Tagore says that modern civilisation is based on 'intemperance' and 'universal greed' that make victims of large sections of people, particularly in Asia and Africa (2006, 33–34). He mourns the disruption of community bonds due to the accumulation of private wealth and deepening of individualism: 'In a society where the greed of an individual or of a group is allowed to grow uncontrolled, and is encouraged or even applauded by the populace, democracy as it is termed in the West cannot be truly realized' (33–34). He could see the incompatibility between the 'capital' and the nation. Tagore also predicted that it would lead the European nations into a path of self-destruction. He says, 'Not merely the subject races, but you who live under the delusion that you are free are everyday sacrificing your freedom and humanity to this fetish of nationalism, living in the dense poisonous atmosphere of world-wide suspicion and greed and panic' (Tagore 2008, 2:427). This incompatibility resists narration, mainly because forms such as the novel appear to partake of the logic of modernity.

Tagore's critique of modernity takes on different forms in his novels and poetry. This has led critics to believe that his poetry is mystical while his fiction is realistic. It has been argued by Dipesh Chakrabarty that his novels and poems – his prose and poetry, to be more precise – have come to share 'a division of labour', since the fiction addressed issues of 'political' importance such as poverty, feudal oppression and communalism, while his poetry 'afforded the possibility of transcendence' for the Bengali middle class (2008, 153). To say that Tagore's prose located the political in historical time, while his poetry 'created a political' that resisted historicisation, is to subscribe to the binaries created by modernity. Amartya Sen comments on Tagore's consistent use of rationality (2005, 104), while Amit Chaudhuri believes that Tagore's 'profound engagement with history' lies in the 'reticent, self-repeating, half-lit world of his poems and his songs' (2008, 86). Both his prose and poetry partake of the same social imaginary that contests the normative function of modernity. They do it differently – but for this reason, one cannot say that his poetry is primary. The interiority he realised in his poetry was made possible by his involvement in the public sphere as an activist and critic of society. In poetry, Tagore had access to the resources of a longer pre-modern tradition dating back to the oral traditions of Bhakti poetry, Baul songs and Sufi tradition. Tagore's reworking of these traditions is informed by his encounter with colonial modernity and the tensions engendered by this encounter. What appears in his fictional narratives as conflicts of the opposites are not resolved in his poetry, but is realised in the texture of its radiant metaphorical discourse.

Three aspects of this social imaginary articulated in Tagore's works merit close attention. Firstly, Tagore explores in his novels the relation between the masculine and the feminine in the context of the modern, to investigate its symbolic investment in the constitution of the social. Secondly, he investigates the relation between culture and power in his prose writings as a whole, including his essays on nationalism. Nationalism is repeatedly discussed mainly because it involves a conjunction of power and culture. What Tagore explores is how culture can be retrieved as an experiential site outside the gaze of hegemonic discourses. Music becomes an analogy for this site where power is both present and absent. Thirdly, the experiential in his poetry enacts or performs the communitarian voice, clearing an ethical space within the contemporary literary discourse. It is important to realise that there is an ethical dimension to his poetic or aesthetic. These ethical dimensions were also realised and elaborated upon in his fictional works.

## 3

Tagore was quick to see the encoding of the masculine in the colonial/imperial discourse. As a response to imperialism, nationalism took on militant features that were articulated in the early Indian novel in the figure of the aggressive mendicant, as in *Anandamath* (1882). Texts such as the Bhagavat Gita were used to endorse the militant nationalism of this period. Tagore saw its implications for the constitution of the modern Indian subject. The grand narrative of the nation required a heroic past which took on masculine overtones. His novels also offer a critique of nationalism by foregrounding the regional and the local. In his novels, the narrative of the nation is cast against the lived life of the locality. The inability to transcend the historical and the political embedded in the local brings out the fraudulent nature of the nationalist discourse.

The protagonist of *Gora* (1910) is unable to acknowledge the presence of the woman in society as an agent of change, in his blind pursuit of an ideal that is both masculine and nationalist. When Binoy says, 'Because women remain out of sight, our country has remained only a half-truth to us,' Gora's answer is, 'in the natural state of society, woman is veiled like night—all her functions are private and unseen' (Tagore 2007, 107). As Meenakshi Mukherjee observed, for Gora, women exist largely as 'symbols of grace, purity and motherhood' (xv) and are to be confined in the domestic space. Tagore was highly critical of the deification of women as done by Bankim Chandra Chattopadhyay in his novels that denied women the reality of their being. As Mukherjee observes, 'Gora's humanization is simultaneously also a process of feminisation' as he moves away from 'an inflexible intolerance to a certain measure of self-doubt' (xviii/xv). Gora gradually begins to understand that women are individuals and not 'static icons of culture' (xv). Gora's realisation that the 'Bharatvarsha' he has imagined has no basis in the lived reality of sectarian divisions of caste, race and class also brings him the awareness that women are individuals and not symbols, and the brand of nationalism he had advocated is exclusivist. It is this awareness of the woman as the Other of the nationalist discourse that forced Tagore to take it up for further analysis in *The Home and the World* (*Ghare-baire*, 1916). In one of the chapters devoted to Sandip, in *The Home and World*, Tagore shows his 'masculine' world view:

> There are a handful of weak souls in the world who do not know how to seize, cannot hold on to what they have, their fists come loose at the drop of a hat—morality is the consolation prize for these souls. But those who can desire with all their heart, savour with all their soul, those who don't suffer from hesitation and reluctance, they are the favourite sons of Nature. It is for them that Nature has set forth all that's beautiful, all that's valuable. (Tagore 2005, 37)

Sandip equates the masculine with the power and will to rule and dominate which he sees as an amoral life-force. Tagore demonstrates its seductive charm through the character of Sandip. While Gora recognises that he was after false gods and is forced to confront the truth of things by circumstances, Sandip is incapable of self-criticism. It is this self-righteousness that has a compelling impact on Bimla. She is captivated by his rhetoric: 'Just as the nation suddenly woke up, looked ahead and said, Vande Mataram, my heart and soul and every nerve in my body today woke up to say "Vande" to some unknown, exotic—something that defied explanation!' (Tagore 2005, 98). She ceases to be herself, under the spell cast by Sandip. In one of the most emotional scenes of the novel – where, finally, Nikhil asks Sandip to leave his estate, due to the mounting communal tensions in the village – Sandip quotes Browning in Bangla and also a song in Bhairavi, in his conversation with Bimla. The derivative nature of nationalism, also its inability to embody the local and the regional, becomes apparent here. Even when she suspects that there is something amiss in his amoral world view, Bimla is unable to resist Sandip's charms. At one point, Bimla says, 'I understand it all, but magic can't be kept at bay' (186). The seductive charm of Sandip is what disrupts and destroys the world of Nikhilesh, and Bimla is inseparable from his exclusivist nationalism that puts women on a pedestal to turn them into instruments of a larger project. It does not allow women to choose and assert their own world view.

Tagore was also troubled by the way the discourse of the Hindu religion was co-opted in the service of nationalism. The novel *Four Chapters* (*Char adhyay*, 1934) shows how the Bhagavat Gita is used to justify violence. Indranath, in this novel, says, 'We have ceremonially immersed all traces of kindness—I would have despised myself otherwise for being sentimental. This is the very truth that Sri Krishna had explained to Arjuna: Do not be wanting in compassion, but be unflinching in the call of duty' (Tagore 2002, 13). The Gita was used to legitimise surrender to an organisation and its discipline, in the name of sacrifice and dispossession of the self, and it was framed as a master-text to legitimate violence. In this process, what was metaphorical became literal. Indranath tells Ela who refuses to be driven by this impersonal ideology:

> At the very heart of power is the cultivation of cruelty; forgiveness may come in the end. . . . What is more important is that you are the very manifestation of primaeval female energy, of *shakti.* This you can prove only by leaving behind the quagmire of kindness and sympathy and moving on to firmer shores. Give us power. Give strength to men. (6)

The irony is that Ela walked out of her own house as she felt that 'girls were made ready for marriage through a process that completely crippled their self-respect and stifled all individual notions of right and wrong' (xv). Indranath wants women to be instruments of change and this requires them to be 'unwoman-like'. This was also the position of Gora in his early stage.

In the second chapter of *Four Chapters*, the discussion between Ela and Atin (Atindranath) veers around to the comparative merits of *prakriti* and *purusha.* Atin wants her to 'delude him and take him to that space' that is her own universe, her own right. He feels that his life's flow is choked and muddied running against the 'concrete road of government duty' (Tagore 2002, 47). This is how he describes the *swadeshi* movement which he compares to the chariot of Jagannath pulled blindly by thousands of young men. Atin argues that human beings cannot be reduced to puppets: 'It is closer to the truth to regard him as being infinitely varied—a creature of spiritual strength' (48). Atin, a man possessed by words, realises that a simple human relation with Ela is possible only at the cost of their self-destruction. He finds patriotism a pack of lies that traps their selves: 'Deception, pettiness, mutual suspicions, conspiracies for power and spying will one day pull them down into cesspools. . . . In the ugly world, inside the pit, the poisonous air engulfs them by day and night. They will never be able to defend the *paurush* in themselves, without which no great work is ever achieved in this world' (7). Atin realises that there is no path of return for him to shape a more human response to the call of history. He says that he has murdered his *swabhav,* 'my yet unrealized self' (92). Having killed his real self, he turns into a monster. He says, 'There is nothing that I am incapable of doing. I have fallen into the very bottom of the abyss" (98). Tagore shows how single-minded surrender to an ideology corrupts the very core of the self – a theme reminiscent of Dostoevsky's in *Crime and Punishment.* This also provides a critique of the discourse of modernity in general. While Atin resorts to violence as he has completely lost touch with his interior self, Ela still preserves it through her passion for him and her refusal to be an instrument in service of the mechanical organisation of power. What Tagore critiques is the conjunction of culture and power in the ideology of nationalism and its deployment as a means of instrumental rationality to subjugate and domesticate. All his major novels grapple with this process to fashion a counter-narrative to this process which is at work at the core of modernity. This is not confined to nationalism and the nation state alone, but characterises the very process in which the world is organised in the context of modernity.

In his 'The Robbery of the Soil', Tagore observes that 'villages are like women. In their keep is the cradle of the race' (Tagore 2006, 36). In his novels, Tagore's women are mute or unable to articulate their points of view. Characters like Gora, Sandip and Atin are endowed with great powers of articulation as they come to internalise the discourse of the modern. However, the women – like Sucharita, Bimla and Ela – remain inarticulate and even mute, since they inhabit a liminal world which cannot be fully comprehended in the discursive prose of the novel. This is because they cannot be fully contained by the discourse of modernity. They enable the transition from the closed world of the secular modern to a humanised and inclusive space of experience. There are also others like them who refuse to internalise the logic of Euro-centric modernity. In one section of *The Home and the World*, Nikhil speaks of his teacher, Chandranathababu. Everything about him is simple and he refuses to be lured by money or power. He enables Nikhil to come to terms with truth without losing his humanity. He now understands that, 'When we see truth as formless we can be free' (Tagore 2005, 93). This moment is expressed through a couplet from Vidyapati, the Maithili poet. This is part of an inner realisation that cannot be articulated through the form of the novel.

Tagore increasingly realised the inadequacy of the novel as a literary form, as it appears to be complicit with modernity. His major political novels – *Gora* and *The Home and the World* – were written in the early part of his life. In his later stage, as Ashis Nandy says, Tagore moved from 'the prose form of the conventional novel to a poeticized form more suited to allegorical tales of the kind which were to appear on the English and French literary scenes much later' (1994, 18). However, in his later novels, there is 'a sort of thinning', as suggested by D. R. Shashidhar who cites Niharanjan Ray's comment: 'Why are the novels of the period so poor, so sterile, and to use a word that associates with Tagore, so sobbing?' (qtd. in Miri 2016, 95).

The form of the novel allowed Tagore to explore the process through which Western modernity organises the world of the self and reconstitutes the relation between the self and the world. The moral universe represented by his women characters can be best understood by the subjectivity projected through his poetry. They help us elaborate on his 'social imaginary' – a set of assumptions that go into the making of a shared world. Tagore's novels, through the projection of the feminine, strain to project the moral universe of the inarticulate. It is in the representation of the essentially local/regional that this moral universe attains a shape and a form.

There are two underlying tensions in his treatment of the theme of the modern in general and the idea of the nation in particular. The awareness of a certain inviolate space of selfhood informs his representation of the conflict between the masculine and feminine. The territorial idea of the nation is seen as violating the inner cohesiveness of the local/regional as an experiential space. This is what often assumes the nature of the conflict between impersonal masculine forces and the woman. The other tension is between the homogenising impulse of nationalism and the inviolability of individual selfhood, which he embodies in the texture of his most intimate poems. Tagore shows how the impulse to homogenise and 'masculinise' leads to violation and desecration. This has something to do with the processes of 'enchantment' and 'disenchantment'. As Charles Taylor observes, 'One of the central features of Western modernity is the progress of disenchantment' (2007, 49). This is a process of disembedding from the collective world of the social, as 'in early religion, we primarily relate to God as a society' (53). To live in an 'enchanted' world is not to live in the world of spirits or magic but to relate to the world in an organic manner without violating its order of things. Tagore's novels are about the violation involved in disenchantment, while his poetry enacts the embeddedness of the self in the social and the communitarian order of things. This partakes of the local and the regional without homogenising it or subjecting it to the will of the self. Its musical idiom is integral to his project of locating and realising the interiority that forms the core of selfhood and the inviolate spirit of a community. D. R. Shashidhar argues that the figure of the poet in Tagore's novels brings out the dialectical relation between the poet and the nationalist as opposing figures: 'The poet's character is indicative of Tagore's engagement, fascination and disenchantment and disengagement with nationalist thought and action. The poets, with the doubtful exception of Amal, are all lovers whose "poetry" stops at some stage in their life' (Miri 2016, 111). The fractured selves of the most sensitive characters in Tagore's fiction point to a deeper schism in the historical context where they could save their sensitivity only by endangering themselves. By conforming to the demands of modernity, they lose their legitimacy and also undo themselves.

This is not to say that Tagore envisages an uncorrupted interior world in the world of imagination, or its allegorical representations of the pastoral in the local or the regional. The song by the Baul poet Madan (cited above) shows how Tagore was aware of the oppositional content of the local. Tagore's objection to the modern, as a discourse of the normative that homogenises experiences and erases differences, needs to be remembered here. What remains essentially local is also cosmopolitan and universal. Tagore saw no contradiction between the two. This is where we take into account his poetry where the idiom and the experience embody the very texture of the everyday as it is lived and felt. This texture cannot be abstracted or approximated into a cosmopolitan discourse. The recurring images of the road, the cloud, the boat, the distant river, the stranger, the traveller, the child, etc., invoke an intimate, interior space that is charged – the poems here perform a movement that transforms and transports the self. This act of fashioning a self out of a state of inertia and melancholy is the first act of decolonisation. This shows that long before the political decolonisation began in India, the poets had invented an idiom for its artistic articulation. The act of becoming aware is at the centre of this new poetic.

There is a moment in Asan's *Chinthavishtayaya Seetha*, where Sita compares her moment of self-awakening to being suddenly engulfed by flames of fire. Tagore also describes a similar moment in a similar metaphor that is suggestive of a violent encounter with oneself:

The agonizing edge of your sword
Flashes like awareness
At life's very end
Whatever in the mind is left
Will be burnt in a trice
By its piercing, fearsome fire. (Radice 2011, 142)

## References

Chakrabarty, Dipesh. 2008. *Provincializing Europe: Postcolonial thought and historical difference.* New Jersey: Princeton UP.

Chaudhuri, Amit. 2008. The flute of modernity: Tagore and the middle class. In *Clearing a space: Reflections on India, literature and culture*, 69–84. New Delhi: Black Kite and Rupa.

Horkheimer, Max. 1947. *Eclipse of reason.* New York: Oxford UP.

Majeed, Javed. 2010. Geography of subjectivity, pan-Islam and Muslim separatism: Muhammad Iqbal and selfhood. In *An intellectual history for India,* ed. Shruti Kapila, 133–49. New Delhi: Cambridge UP.

Miri, Mrinal. 2016. *The idea of surplus: Tagore and contemporary human sciences.* New Delhi: Routledge.

Nandy, Ashis. 1994. *The illegitimacy of nationalism: Rabindranath Tagore and the politics of the self.* New Delhi: Oxford UP.

Parekh, Bhikhu. 2015. *Debating India: Essays on Indian political discourse.* New Delhi: Oxford UP.

Radice, William, trans. 2011. *Gitanjali: Song offerings.* New Delhi: Penguin.

Sen, Amartya. 2005. *The argumentative Indian: Writings on Indian culture, history and identity.* New Delhi: Penguin.

Tagore, Rabindranath. 2002. *Four chapters.* Trans. Rimli Bhattacharya. New Delhi: Srishti.

——. 2005. *The home and the world.* Trans. Sreejata Guha. New Delhi: Penguin.

——. 2006. *Tagore on books.* New Delhi: Rupa.

——. 2007. *Gora.* Trans. Sujit Mukherjee. New Delhi: Sahitya Akademi.

——. 2008. *The English writings of Rabindranath Tagore.* 4 vols. Ed. Sisir Kumar Das. New Delhi: Sahitya Akademi.

Taylor, Charles. 2007. *Modern social imaginaries.* London: Duke UP.

## Chapter Seven

# Narrating a Community: The Secular Modern and the Discourse of Marginality in the Fictional Works of Vaikom Muhammad Basheer

The works of Vaikom Muhammad Basheer, the first major novelist to emerge from the Muslim community in Kerala, unravels the contradictions between the ideological thrust of the mainstream novel and the compulsions of the communitarian perspective of a novelist from the margins, enabling us to examine the problematic of representation in the modern novel. His *Balyakalasakhi* (Childhood friend, 1944) was a breakthrough in presenting an insider's view of the Muslim community with its own customs and rituals, from a perspective informed by compassion and tragic awareness. In *Shabdangal* (The voices, 1947) and a series of novellas written in the 1950s, Basheer indicts and satirises the absolutist and hegemonic traits of the nation state, providing a critique of the prevailing power relations. His best-known novel, *Ntuppuppakkoranendarnnu* (1951, translated into English as *Me Grandad 'ad an Elephant*), brings out the impossibility of narrating a community from the perspective of the subaltern and minority points of view. He endorses the secular modern but distances himself from the homogenising logic of modernity. Basheer is at his subversive best in *Pathummayude aadu* (Pathumma's goat, 1958) where he shifts towards a minimal mode of anecdotal, digressive narration, problematising the novelistic form and its inherent elitist proclivities. Basheer has fashioned a complex ironic mode rooted in the regional experience that critiques and contests received notions of the nationalist narrative on identity, community and modernity.

When a novelist emerges from the marginalised section of a society, he or she challenges the social hegemony that constitutes the 'common sense' of the society. But do novels constitute reality in particular ways, permitting only certain orders of reality to pass through its form? In other words, does the novelistic form 'plot' the narrative even before the novelist comes to use the form, and thus 'process' the material that enters into its formal domain? This question is urgent and relevant because novels were used in several societies including India to imagine collective identities such as 'region' and 'nation', thereby generating foundational fictions that constituted the imaginative space that later came to be inhabited by social structures. Categories such as 'nation', 'region', 'class' and 'caste' become visible only when they are narrated, and the act of narration presupposes a social location and perspective. It is presumptuous to suppose that every novelist has access to a privileged point of totality from where the society is revealed in all its complexity. A novelist deploys discourses in the act of narration, but these discourses inform his or her subjectivity, denying him or her an objective understanding of the way they work in language. The novel, as a form, is unique in its ability to embody the speech of the 'people'. But the novelistic form also regulates direct speech within a format of reported speech where the rational and the judgemental takes over. Thus, the direct speech is 'framed' and mediated through the legislative function of the form itself. An understanding of the ideological function of the form is essential to grasp the larger function of the novel in society. This chapter will examine some of the major fictional works of Vaikom Muhammad Basheer (1908–94) with reference to their engagement with the ideology of the novel and the consequent problematic of representation.

Basheer became increasingly aware of the mediatory role of form in the construction of fictional reality during the 1950s. He did not write a major novel after the publication of *Pathummayude aadu* (Pathumma's goat, 1958) which problematised the very form of the novel. Did he become aware of a deeper layer of resistance within the form? If yes, does it have anything to do with his minority identity? Does the novelistic discourse as constituted by mainstream Malayalam tradition inhibit the articulation of minority experience? Though clear answers may elude us, a close reading of Basheer's novels may provide some pointers to certain formulations. Here we should also add that among Basheer's novels, only *Ntuppuppakkoranendarnnu* (1951, translated into English as *Me Grandad 'ad an Elephant*) can be said to have the form close to what is considered the normative in a novel.

## I

Basheer's *Balyakalasakhi* (Childhood friend, 1944) is notable for its use of bildungsroman, a form that embodies the narrative of a character's formative years or spiritual education. The novel is largely autobiographical. R. E. Asher, Basheer's translator, notes, '*Childhood Friend* is, in a certain sense of the word, ninety or ninety five per cent "true" and is based on an episode in Basheer's own life' (Basheer 1980, ix). There is something idyllic about the childhood world of Majid and Suhra, the childhood friends of the novel, who gradually drift into a romantic relationship that turns out to be tragic. In one of the famous passages in the novel, which carries the imprint of Basheer's characteristic vision, the writer evokes the essential harmony of this childhood world:

> Once the schoolmaster had asked Majid, 'What do one and one make?' Now it is a fact known the world over that one and one makes two. But Majid produces a remarkable solution to the question that caused the teacher to burst out laughing. The whole class laughed. The solution he gave became his nickname. Before answering, Majid reflected: as two rivers join together and flow as a broader river, so two ones joined together to become a broader 'one'! Having calculated thus, he announced proudly, 'A rather big one'! (Basheer 1980, 11)

The narrative communicates a level of ironic self-awareness that may be traceable in the form of the bildungsroman itself. In this genre, the movement of time is central, and the socialisation of the self coincides with a progressive deepening of one's own initiation into self-knowledge. The novel has several moments of initiation, the description of Majid's circumcision ceremony being an early instance. It created a stir in Malayalam fiction, since it was the first time that a ritual only known to a minority community was described in mainstream Malayalam fiction. In his comments on the novel, M. P. Paul, a well-known critic of the first half of the twentieth century, described the novel as a major work and added that the Muslim community in Kerala had not found any representation in literature till this novel was written (1963, 278).

Basheer must have confronted the problems of embodying the minority experience in the novelistic discourse, since the genre had evolved in Malayalam through the depiction of the experiences of dominant communities. In this context, there is a gap between what the author knows and what the form admits. This becomes manifest in the disjunction between the characters described and the general reader addressed by the author. The novel does not 'dis-cover' the minority community, since its inbuilt discursive regime 'covers' what is culturally specific to the minority community. This happens through a process of individuation that is elaborated through Majid's conflict with his father. In the genre of bildungsroman, such a conflict is a defining theme and leads to the final assertion of the protagonist's identity. In Basheer's novel, Majeed leaves home, becomes an exile, and finally ends up a destitute. His individual assertion does not allow him to rise above the community and clear his own space in the larger world. During his absence, Suhra is forced to marry a man who already has a wife and two children. When he returns home after seven years, Majid's own family is in decline, the father having lost his business. His sisters cannot be married off, as the family has no money to pay the dowry. Suhra now looks a ghost of her former self. Majid now leaves home again, determined to come back with enough money to marry off his sisters. But he meets with an accident and his legs are amputated, and he is reduced to a cripple. When the news of Suhra's death reaches him, it is as if his world has finally collapsed and robbed him of his sense of purpose.

The sense of mourning and melancholy that pervades the latter part of the novel does point to a waking consciousness at a deeper subliminal layer in the narrative. But this resolution cannot admit the culture-specific aspects of the minority experience. The tragic remains personal and subjective, and cannot accommodate the destiny of the community as a whole. This has to do with the form of the novel itself. The novel has a scene where Majid meets a philanthropist, Khan Bahadur, who boasts that he has built four mosques while other millionaires in the community have only built one mosque each. However, all that he gives Majid is a rupee and some hollow words of sympathy. Basheer does not think there is a viable idea of the community that can transcend the individual's personal destiny in the context of modern society. The alienation suffered by Majid is set against the city and its predatory impulses. The narrative does not constitute a communitarian space as capable of imparting a new direction in Majid's life. Nor are there modern institutions which take care of the individual's welfare by investing him or her with a sense of purpose in life. If we examine the early part of the narrative, we find the culture-specific elements of Muslim community that shape Majid's self. In the childhood experiences of rituals and festivals one finds the presence of a collective social identity that can influence the destiny of individuals. But as Majid grows up, this larger space of affiliation withdraws into the background, but it nevertheless sets the limits for individuals' aspirations or worldly progress. Suhra's marriage, for instance, points to a collective failure of the community. In the foundational fictions of the nation, romantic love has always been a resource of the self and community formation. However, in *Balyakalasakhi,* love does not transcend these divisions or invest the main characters with a new life.

This may be explained with reference to Raymond Williams's idea of 'knowable community'. In social realist novels, narrative conventions make the community 'knowable' by scrupulously excluding details that do not conform to a particular view of the world. Williams comments, 'What is knowable is not only a function of objects—or what is there to be known. It is also a function of subjects, observers—of what is desired and what needs to be known' (Williams 1973, 168). The novel, as a narrative of modernity, cannot accommodate the culture-specific aspects of a minority community. In this sense, the novelistic desire, in the sense of an implicit narrative disposition, excludes the communitarian space. Majid's growing up in the Muslim community and his identity as a lover are accessible to the novelistic treatment, but his further movement in the world would involve a struggle against the desires of the community. But Majid is not Madhavan (of O. Chandu Menon's *Indulekha*) who has the educational and cultural resources to stand up against the community; and Suhra is not Indulekha who is endowed with the training to call into question the conventions of the community. Basheer's novel does not rewrite *Indulekha* from a Muslim point of view, because the novel's space of desire extends to an individual assertion and not to that of the community. In that sense, Basheer is true to his experience and grasps the dynamics of the tragic as formative for the individual whose move towards individuation is constrained by his or her location in society. This is why the novel ends on Suhra's unspoken sentence. Majid is forever imprisoned by her unspoken words which could have set him free. That the novel does not give such agency to a Muslim woman is a measure of its legacy from a particular trajectory of the 'progress of modernity'.

This can also be explained in terms of the obstinacy of the form as inherited by Basheer. The Muslim dialect used by Basheer is framed by a 'standard' Malayalam which has its own ideological orientation. Here the language carries the imprint of the 'literary', which is exclusivist in its approach to the minority community. The form legislates the experiential content of the novel and also interprets it. The novel ends with a question mentioned above:

> "Standing in the garden with her hand on the shoe-flower tree, and with tears in her eyes—Suhra.
>
> What she had started to say must have been still in her mind. What was it that Suhra started to say? (Basheer 1996, 50).

This makes the novel open-ended. The lack of closure allows us to read the experience that led to the unspoken sentence in a critical manner. Suhra is dead, and she remains beyond representation as her speech is not heard in the novel. This ending is a narrative gesture that enacts the silence of the minority as subject. It is not an accident that this subject is gendered. The novel, as created by Basheer, is haunted by the spectral presence of unspoken words. The shoe flower here signifies the idyll of the childhood where both Suhra and Majid were at home.

The motif of the garden recurs in Basheer as suggestive of a communitarian space. In *Mathilukal* (The walls, 1965), where Basheer speaks of his own days in prison as a convict, he is seen as nurturing a garden of roses with great care, right next to the row of cells housing convicts condemned to death. Here he falls in love with a woman prisoner housed in the women's prison on the other side of the wall, without ever meeting her. The day they were to meet the order releasing him from the jail is delivered, and Basheer is crest-fallen. He shouts in anger, 'Who wants freedom?' Such interrupted conversations and unspoken words are characteristic of Basheer's fictional world which problematises the distance between the ideological limits set by the mainstream Malayalam novel and the nuanced discourse of minority experience.

## 2

Basheer's *Shabdangal* (The voices, 1947) uses a different set of discourses to indict the nation state at the very moment of its formation. The narrative of this short novel is spoken by an ex-soldier who is afflicted by a venereal disease. He seeks out the writer because he has read his books. He talks to the writer of his life as a soldier and his struggle for survival after he was let off from the army. There is very little in his life that inspires trust in humanity. Born an orphan, he was raised by a priest. Once in the army, he was exposed to brutal scenes of death and suffering that kept haunting him. He recounts how once a whole battalion of soldiers drank water from a barrel, only to discover that the barrel contained blood, and not water. He keeps repeating that water is the blood of the earth. He has been living in the streets among the most marginalised of the society, such as petty thieves, prostitutes, pimps and tramps. They constitute the nation's Other – its outcastes. The soldier questions the legitimacy of the nation state which has centralised its power in a handful of people:

> "Do you think these riots and violence will ever end?"
> "So long as there continues to be more than one view about anything . . ."
> "Who is in the right?"
> "Think for yourself and decide. If you can't do that, accept the more convincing opinion." (Basheer 1994, 82)

Basheer was one of the earliest Malayalam novelists to recognise that the nation state, in actual practice, functioned as a massive, impersonal machine. War is a means of justifying its omnipotence. While the nation state invokes the people, and rules on their behalf, it does not represent their will. Basheer distances himself from the nationalist discourse. The apocalyptic tone of the novel informs the ex-soldier's view of his society – he sees every institution in ruins. The nascent nation is born out of blood and distrust. The dialogues between the nameless soldier and the author-narrator emphasise the present moment as one of a momentous moral crisis that cannot be resolved within the existing socio-political frameworks. Basheer raises radical questions about the nature of relationships among individuals, the community, the nation and the nation state. The function of the apocalyptic tone in the narrative is to trace the collapse of the moral order that cannot be restored. While talking of the function of the apocalyptic discourse,

Derrida comments, 'By its very tone, the mixing of voices, genres, and codes, and the breakdown of destinations, apocalyptic discourse can also dismantle the dominant contract or concordat' (1982, 89). The discourse of the apocalypse rejects the consensus that sustains the status quo. It allows the narrative to capture the voice of the disenfranchised and the marginalised. The breakdown of the moral order creates a fluid situation where multiple voices can be heard. Basheer points to this possibility; but in the bleak moral landscape of the novel, there is no suggestion of a fresh breakthrough. Here is a scene that graphically illustrates Basheer's anxiety on the eve of the birth of the nation state, when he tries to save an infant from ant bites:

> "I went to that lonely orphaned child.
>
> "A citizen of tomorrow. What did he know of things? He was just born just like everyone else. He would grow up with passions and desires like everyone else. Whiskers and beard would appear as he grew into manhood. . . .
>
> "Perhaps he would become a beggar. Or a thief. He could become a poet. Or a writer of stories. He could become a political worker. Or the future President. He could be a scientist. Or the prophet of a new religion." (Basheer 1994, 101)

In enumerating these possibilities, Basheer is both serious and ironical. The nation as a social contract is an inclusive concept that promises to strive for realising the potential in every individual. But the nation state finally becomes an impersonal war-machine using people as fodder and betraying the trust the people have reposed in the idea of the nation. The integrative logic of the nation state perpetuates violence as a means of realising its will. *Shabdangal* is a significant statement from a writer who understood that the voices of the disenfranchised will for ever haunt the idealistic narrative of the nation, turning it into a contested category.

## 3

Novels like *Shabdangal* deal with the failure of the grand narrative of the nation, imagined in idealistic terms during the nationalist struggle. It is in the everyday life of the speech community that one encounters questions of caste, class, gender, race and language. It is here – in this domain of the self, language and communication – that consent is manufactured, hegemony of the dominant class or caste is legitimised and organised coercion from any class is resisted. The relationship between culture and power is central to the civil society. The novel, in the act of narrating the community, intervenes in the civil society. It has a critical stake in clearing the society of its illusions and false consciousness. Basheer's ironical novellas set in *sthalam* (the 'Place') bring out the ideological in the self-fashioning of modern Kerala society.

Alexis de Tocqueville, in his classic *Democracy in America,* saw civil society as a sphere of intermediary associations between the individual and the state. He was deeply impressed by the vibrancy and autonomy of church groups, literary associations, public groups, town councils and similar organisations, which he found missing in Europe. For him it constituted a third sphere, apart from that of the state and the market. He is closer to Hegel in conceiving it as a mediatory space between the family and the state, where the individual can realise his or her potential without becoming an individualist. Hegel saw that individualism was the chief driving force of modern society that is constituted by the logic of capitalist economy. He recognised the predatory impulse in the economic organisation of such a society that needed to be regulated by community formation at various levels. Marx felt that civil society is the space where the state is contested and reformulated. As the setting of everyday life, it is here that civil society becomes an arena of struggles between competing ideological forces and formations. For Basheer, civil society is the space where the conflicts between hegemony and subjugation are rewritten, and the dialectical relation between culture and power is redefined. Antonio Gramsci made a distinction between civil society and political society, and argued that the function of civil society was to legitimate the coercive function of the political society. Civil society works through educational, cultural and religious institutions to discipline the mind and spirit of the people. Gramsci could see that the state included all those networks of affiliations and practices that enable it to maintain its dominance. The symbolic realm is crucial for the state, from this perspective.

In the discussion of Basheer's *Shabdangal*, we have seen his critique of the state as a domain of absolute power. Once the nation state becomes a reality, nationalism loses its relevance as an ideology of resistance. It is in this context that in *sthalam* narratives, Basheer recounts a series of tales around a set of rustic characters whose exploits make them heroes of local folktales. We will discuss three such novellas here: *Sthalathe pradhana divyan* (The chief holy man of the place), *Anavariyum ponkurisum* (The elephant-thief and the golden cross) and *Mucheettu kalikkarante makal* (The daughter of the card-sharper). These are anecdotal narratives that are set in an interior village in Kerala. It is believed that Basheer had lived in such a village when he had gone 'underground' while fleeing from the police during his days of political activism. In these stories, the two local policemen are universally hated for being 'agents of the foreign government'. The stories have the characteristic 'Basheerian' quality of orality, where he wears the mask of the storyteller. The unending feuds of this remote locality show that the people are for ever opposed to any governmental interference in their daily lives. The people of the 'Place' questions the 'common sense' created by the power structure through their actions and conversations. In the cast of characters are two brahmin feudal lords, their elephants, a mahout who attempts to steal an elephant, another veteran thief who steals a golden cross from a church, and a holy man whose predictions are coded in a mysterious language.

A sense of the carnival pervades these stories where the power structures and their codes are demystified through parodic and ironic commentary. The dominant point of view is always ridiculed and lampooned repeatedly through various means. Nothing is sacred and the 'Place' brims over with geniality and camaraderie. These tales do not admit an individualistic point of view. Everything happens in the public world. Even matters such as falling in love belong to this world of exchange and open debate. The world is turned upside down, as in all carnivalesque narratives. The normative is suspect here because it legitimates authority and hierarchy. In one of the episodes, we are told how 'Thoma the Gold-Cross' got his title. He was spending time in a police lockup when he took pity on a poor policeman who had several daughters to marry off. At his request, the constable let him off for a few hours and Thoma returned with a golden cross that had adorned a church. His logic is that Christ was not crucified on a golden cross and hence it has no sanctity. The people of the Place agree with his logic and do not consider his act as a crime.

Basheer consciously uses the discourse of historiography in these chronicles where he even uses footnotes and cross-references. The Place is sovereign in matters of political beliefs and social attitudes. This enables Basheer to show how false consciousness operates in society. He also demonstrates the dangers of absolute concepts of morality and essentialist categories, and their effects on society and politics.

In these stories, written in the 1950s, Basheer articulates a counter-discourse that brings out the moral evasions in the enactment of a nationalist discourse. The carnivalesque elements of the narratives, apart from interrogating the hierarchical structures of society, also provide a critique of elite nationalism. It is significant that this world of pickpockets, petty thieves and crooks, who inhabit the fringes of the society, constructs its world view based on myths, legends, face-to-face communication and local memories. There is a realm of the popular from which they cannot be separated. This, in turn, is also linked to the public sphere where the 'common sense' of the community is formed. In these stories, Basheer maps this deeper level of community formation. What is subversive in Basheer opens up ways of resisting dominant authoritarian viewpoints. One of the functions of civil society, as we have seen above, is to resist the monologic thrust of the nation state. In 1956, Kerala became a linguistic state, and since then, nationalisms of various kinds have gained momentum. That the state elected a communist party through a democratic process also makes Kerala a unique region with its own brand of popular politics. Basheer could see that the various castes and religious communities of the state were becoming part of electoral politics with their own sectarian interests.

## 4

*Ntuppuppakkoranendarnnu* (1951, translated into English as *Me Grandad 'ad an Elephant*) is one of the most significant novels in Malayalam to come out in the postcolonial period. It addresses the questions of reforms in the Muslim society of Kerala with seriousness and urgency. However, in the course of negotiating the question of modernity in the context of the community, Basheer also comes face to face with some of the paradoxes implied by modernity. At one level, the novel is a critique of a monolithic modernity embodied in the nationalist discourse. But at the same time, Basheer is aware of the undercurrents that make a simplistic position untenable in a multi-religious pluralistic society like that of Kerala. The central character is Kunjupathumma who moves out of her minority subculture, into the mainstream 'national' culture which is projected as a world of desire and aspirations. This trajectory of change has to be viewed against the losses such a shift involves. Kunjupathumma's naïve world view hides a complex mythopoetic attitude to the phenomenal world outside:

> In the world there are only two classes. Muslim and Kafir. Whether they are men or women, after death all kafirs will go to hell. They are all fallen ones. If Muslims imitate them they will become lost souls worthy of hell. The kafirs Kunjupathumma saw were schoolmistresses.
>
> Although they are kafirs, they smell nice. They all wear saris. They all have those small kuppayams known as blouses. Underneath their blouse they have a thin, tight bodice. What is more, they wear flowers in their hair. (Basheer 1980, 54–55)

Kerala Muslims had their own traditional dresscodes, just as they had their own dialect. Joining the mainstream, hence, meant moving out of these culture-specific markers of identity. Modernity demands greater standardisation and integration. Differences are seen as threats to the larger project of modernity. The formation of a unified Kerala on the basis of linguistic homogeneity also brought about greater standardisation and proved to be potentially disruptive for the Muslim community's cultural and social life.

Under the influence of Nisar Ahmad and his sister Ayesha, both from 'progressive' Muslim families, Kunjupathumma is initiated into a new set of habits of speech and behaviour. In the early part of the novel, we find that her world is made up of myths, fables, and religious sermons and customs. Her mythopoetic world is steeped in supernatural and exotic imagery. When Kunjupathumma sees Ayesha wearing a sari, she asks her, 'Are you like us?', to which the latter replies, 'No, we are genuine Muslims.' Obviously, Kunjupathumma cannot understand how a sari-wearing woman whose ears are not pierced can claim to be a Muslim. The distance between the mainstream progressive Muslim and the traditional Muslim is further underlined in those sections where Nisar Ahamad and Ayesha 'teach' Kunjupathumma to speak standard Malayalam;

> "You mustn't say 'noight'. Say 'night'."
> "Neight" said Kunjupathumma.

> "Not like that. "I" as in white. Say it. Night."
> Kunjupathumma said, "Night" and then asked, "Where's yer 'ouse?"
> "You must ask, 'Where is your home?'" (92).

The distance between the Muslim dialect that Kunjupathumma speaks and the standard Malayalam she is asked to learn can only be traversed through an act of cultural assimilation. In fact, formal education becomes a means of producing the normative national self where the will of the dominant community comes to be inscribed. Kunjupathumma asks Ayesha, her instructor, 'If you learn to read and write . . . and if you are well informed, it is not possible to live like a Muslim! Is this true?' This question is important in the context of the crisis that the community is going through. Kunjupathumma has been brought up on the myth of a feudal past that is now more of a delusion. Her mother, who perennially prides over her elephant-owning patriarchal father's ancestral world of pomp and wealth, has lost touch with reality after the family's decline. Her refrain, 'Me grandad 'ad an elephant', chains her to this remote past of imagined grandeur. Finally, when Kunjupathumma marries Nisar Ahamad, she comes out of this morbid world of delusion and decay, which has lost its power to sustain hope in the future. Kunjupathumma's 'backwardness' is inseparable from an identity grounded in the community. This is why she asks Ayesha if she can remain a Muslim despite being 'modern' and 'progressive'. Her assimilation into a standard national identity alienates her from the larger bonds of the community. But the question – whether you can relate to a national identity, which is an abstraction, without being part of a culture-specific local community – remains unanswered.

The local and the communal are specific ways of relating to 'higher' levels of collectivities. Basheer's tales discussed above, show how the local is constituted in terms of specific modes of knowing and experiencing the world. Subcultures have their collective wisdom, and their native ways of perception. Such modes of knowledge do not necessarily lead to 'ghettoisation', as is often feared. *Me Grandad 'ad an Elephant* apparently moves in the direction of Kunjupathumma's assimilation into secular modernity; but Basheer also seems to be uneasy about the violence inherent in the process.

The social realist mode that Basheer uses has an investment in the secular modern. Basheer must have become increasingly aware of the ideological dimensions of the novelistic form as he wrote this novel. He cannot possibly resist the integrative logic of the social realist novel which regulates the narrative's manner of representing reality. The mode of representation used in *Me Grandad 'ad an Elephant* privileges the point of view of Nisar Ahamad and Ayesha, and not that of Kunjupathumma. The social realist novel is complicit with the nationalist discourse, and this collusion renders it incapable of representing difference from within. It also turns the novelist a native informer for the nationalist elite. In Nisar Ahmad's idea of building toilets, creating a vegetable garden and emphasising sanitation and persoanl hygiene, we hear certain echoes of a Gandhian idea of communitarian identiy which had at one stage informed the nationalist discourse. Gandhi had strongly resisted the secular modern as interpreted by the West. As Dipesh Chakrabarty notes in his essay, 'Khadi and the Political Man', 'The Gandhian modern was thus, in a relation of both affinity and tension with the modernity of the citizen of the European political theory' (2002, 62). As we have seen in our reading of the novel, the development of Kunjupathumma is towards greater standardisation. The discourse of the community, embodied in her dialect, becomes the Other of the modern standard language. The novelistic discourse is closer to the normative language of the modern. The novel, as a spatial form, is unable to embody the consciousness inherent in the communitarian discourse as Basheer interprets it. The larger question he is concerned with is whether one can be grounded in the community without being part of the nationalist discourse.

## 4

After *Me Grandad 'ad an Elephant,* Basheer did not attempt another novel of the conventional kind. He must have come to realise that he cannot narrate a community without transforming the form itself. *Pathummayude aadu* is more of an anti-novel than a novel. It defies conventional ways of reading. Several of Basheer's family members – his mother, three brothers and their wives and children, and his sisters, Annumma and Pathumma – figure in the narrative. Nothing much 'happens' in this novella, except for the common squabbles and trivial banters and bargains among characters drawn from a lower-middle-class extended family. However, Basheer is able to raise several key issues regarding their subsistence and struggle for survival, while recounting what appears to be trivial on the surface.

Here it is necessary to take note of the extraordinary 'Introduction' that Basheer wrote for this novel. He recounts in great detail how he had undergone an elaborate course of Ayurvedic treatment for a bout of mental illness during the writing of this novel. In confessing to his mental instability, Basheer indirectly questions the normative standards of rationality that the society uses in evaluating people and events. In the digressive narrative, he also mentions the controversy surrounding the prescription of his novel as a non-detailed textbook by the government of Kerala. It was the communist party which was in power in Kerala at that point in time. Basheer recalls how the same party had attacked the book earlier when it first appeared. Obviously, the novel had come to acquire different meanings for different people and also for the same people at different times. The cult of the 'prescribed texts' is intimately connected with the question of the nationalist discourse. When a book is 'prescribed' for study it also becomes canonised in the mainstream. Basheer makes it clear that the book cannot be reduced to an essentialist viewpoint. Meanings/texts are constructed in the public sphere according to the prevailing power structures and dominant viewpoints, and they keep changing from time to time. Basheer is clear that the public sphere is where issues need to be debated and there should be no authoritarian control over the circulation of texts.

It is after describing this episode of a political nature that Basheer turns to his mental illness:

> Yes. . . . at that time my mind . . . like a tiny island that is starting to sink into bottomless ocean. . . . I don't know whether that makes any sense or not. Anyway, the mind gets drowned in darkness filled with frightful dreams. I myself am the mind. When I look up, there is only a small patch of light. In darkness and light. . .God!. . .Where am I? What is true? What is false? . . . Light . . . Light . . . I want only light. But darkness filled with terrible dreams . . . is approaching from all the eight directions, rearing and booming. Will I drown in this for ever? (Basheer 1980, 125)

This is the frame of mind in which the entire novel was written. Obviously, this sense of being on the brink sharpens one's sensitivity to the extreme where even a trivial event assumes grandiose dimensions. His encounter with the abyss has also taught him how vulnerable he is as a human being. Writing is the only source of regaining and sustaining a sense of normality.

In the later part of the introduction, Basheer gives a highly carnivalesque account of the treatment he underwent for his mental illness. Basheer fashions a language of the Other by defamiliarising himself through the narrative of his insanity. He gains a certain detachment about himself in this very act of narrating himself. This is what makes a novella like *Pathummayude aadu* possible. Basheer sees his own family as a microcosm of the world where the struggle for subsistence brings out the best and the worst in human beings. He writes, 'It was when I enquired that I came to know a pitiful fact. Umma, Anumma, Aishomma and Kunjanumma – none of them eat rice regularly. That is to say that they do not get any. There is the rice for the man and children only. The others live on tapioca' (Basheer 1980, 155).

The central image of the novel, the goat, has to be understood against this background of patriarchal organisation of the family. The goat roams through the novel blurring the boundaries between 'high' and 'low', inside and outside, victim and victimiser. The perennially hungry goat even eats up some of the books the author has written and he watches the goat nibble away with great amusement. He drives it away only when the goat begins to eat the blanket. The sublime and the gross are never separate in Basheer. Those who position art on a high pedestal indirectly endorse the other divisions in society in terms of class, gender, caste, religion, etc., creating exclusivist world views. The goat's omnivorous taste is a denial of the rigid classifications of reality into compartments. The goat delivers a kid and this proves to be the central event in the novel. The women of the house display none of the anxiety that the author feels at the delivery, as they view it as part of their everyday world. Birthing is an event that women understand, and Basheer the artist seems to suggest that men are unable to understand the secret of creativity.

In the novel, Basheer uses a minimalist language devoid of all literary embellishments. His use of everyday speech brings into the narrative the voice of women who are colloquial, garrulous, loud and assertive. *Pathummayude aadu* is essentially a woman's text. At its core is a concept of community formation that is grounded in the physical and the local. It is a self-sufficient world with its own internal rhythms. In this world, art cannot be separated from artefact. When Aboobacker, the writer's brother, who is given to using high-flung literary language, finds fault with his style of writing, Basheer shouts at him, 'Clear out from here! You and your predicate! I write the way I speak.' The oral speech, by its very nature, is fragmentary and tentative, ungrammatical and chaotic. It captures the lived reality of a community. The creative freedom of oral speech permits the author to effectively challenge the hegemonic power structure that legislates absolute views of identity. *Pathummayude aadu* also lacks closure as it ends in a question that the narrative cannot answer:

> Now, along with the goat, the kid also comes. Along with them, Khadija and half a bottle of milk.
>
> So we get two kinds of milk at home; one that they steal and the other that Pathumma gives. Poor Pathumma.
>
> One secret I have not been able to fathom as yet. Which of the women was the first to have this brainwave? (Basheer 1980, 195)

By turning away from the monumental to the minimal, Basheer forces us to see what is contingent and fragmentary in the construction of reality. The willed economy of Basheer's minimalist style pushes the language to its limits. This was Basheer's way of becoming an unrefined Kunjupathumma, an illiterate and a member of a community which can be represented in the mainstream narrative only through violating the prevailing aesthetic codes.

In a society of standardised identities, where all orality is domesticated by the tyranny of reported speech, the only way to defy reification is to challenge the political correctness of forms and norms. Basheer moves to the margins to listen to the gossip sessions of his women characters, the conversations in the kitchen, the stammering words of children, and even the speech of birds and plants. He enters into a conversation with a book-eating goat. What makes such things available to art is the author's perception of the normative as a construct that perpetuates its own authoritarian fictions. In *Pathummayude aadu,* he has found a discourse that will not 'contain' differences but articulate it. This is the furthest one can move away from the 'state' language, and its stable and solid discourses of modernity and identity.

## References

Basheer, Vaikom Muhammad. 1980. *Me grandad 'ad an elephant.* Trans. R. E. Asher and A. C. Chandrasekharan. New Delhi: Viking Penguin.

———. 1994. *Poovan banana and other stories.* Trans. V. Abdulla. Hyderabad: Orient BlackSwan/Sangam Books.

———. 1996. *Basheer: Sampoorna kritikal* [Basheer: Complete works]. 2 vols. Kottayam: D. C. Books.

Chakrabarty, Dipesh, 2002. *Habitations of modernity: Essays in the wake of subaltern studies.* Delhi: Permanent Black.

Derrida, Jacques. 1982. Of an apocalyptic tone recently adopted in philosophy. Trans. John P. Leavey, Jr. *Semeia* 23: 63–97.

Paul, M. P. 1963 *Novel sahityam* [The genre of the novel]. Kottayam: Sahitya Pravarthaka Sahakarana Samgham.

Tocqueville, Alexis de. 2003. *Democracy in America.* Trans. Gerald E. Bevan. London: Penguin.

Williams, Raymond. 1973. *The country and the city.* London: Chatto and Windus.

CHAPTER EIGHT

# Narratives of Memory: Representations of the Other in Postcolonial Indian Fiction

In postcolonial Indian fiction memory has become a privileged site to confront the travails of the present through exorcising the layered past of the community. This chapter examines how three fictional texts – Amitav Ghosh's *The Hungry Tide,* Mahasweta Devi's *Pterodactyl, Puran Sahay and Pirtha,* and Anand's *Vyasa and Vighneshwara* – problematise the cartographic, governmental and anthropological forms of representation legitimated by various forms of colonial epistemology. Set in the Sundarbans, *The Hungry Tide* invokes the multiple histories of the region through the interwoven stories of Piya Roy, a researcher on dolphins, Kanai Dutt, a businessman-cum-translator, Nirmal and Nilima, an activist couple, and Fokir, an illiterate fisherman. The novel exorcises the memories of the massacre at Marichjhapi, erased by official history, and demonstrates how Fokir's command over local knowledge turns him into a victim. In Mahasweta Devi's work, Puran Sahay, a journalist reporting a supernatural event in an interior tribal village, gradually wakes up to the community's sense of the sacred, rooted in a collective memory that goes back centuries, and is unable to resolve the ethical issues raised by their traumatised present. Anand, the well-known Malayalam novelist, brings out the complex relations between knowledge and freedom, against various narratives of the past, ranging from the myths of Ekalavya and Amrapali to the legend of the silk winders' self-mutilation aimed at defeating colonial oppression in nineteenth-century India.

In postcolonial fiction, memory is a site fraught with conflict and turbulence. This is particularly true of fictional works written in Indian languages and English. This chapter will examine fictional works from Bengali, Indian Writing in English and Malayalam to bring out the nature of memory as a complex mode of negotiation between different discursive formations that recover or suppress the past or the present, prevent events from coming to public view and create false notions of community or nation. Memory also takes forms which are mediated by the politics of collective resistance, activating myths and legends buried deep in the subconscious of communities into tangible contemporary forms. Memories can be organised around an event, a place, a person or even a projected future. The compulsive nature of memories (as revealed in the following analysis) points to a collective need to confront the travails of the present, within their own experiential space, and also to exorcise the past and come to terms with its traumatic content. Here, the term 'postcolonial' signifies a methodology that enables extracting and critiquing the complicity of cultural, historical, cartographic, governmental and anthropological forms of representation in the production of colonial epistemology, in the form of a thematic inventory. In this sense, it is a critical project that allows new modes of knowing and feeling to enter our social imaginaries. Since discourses or practices of representation are never neutral, new modes of knowing and feeling will contest dominant modes of representation. Truth claims of representations can be contested through such new modes of narrating events and places. There are many fault lines in the colonial epistemology that has stereotyped the content of the oral, the subaltern, the feminine or the orient, in various ways. They are revealed in a close reading of the exceptional fictional works under discussion in this chapter – Mahasweta Devi's *Pterodactyl, Puran Sahay and Pirtha* (1993), Anand's *Vyasa and Vigneshwara* (2000) and Amitav Ghosh's *The Hungry Tide* (2004).

## I

Ghosh's *The Hungry Tide* (2006) is a novel set in the Sundarbans, the vast archipelago near the Bay of Bengal. It is made up of the delta of the Ganges where swamps and mangroves have created a unique ecosystem that is not particularly hospitable to human habitation. The region is marked by perpetual human–wildlife conflicts – tigers and crocodiles often attack the villagers living in isolated pockets of these islands. Yet, waves of migrants have settled these islands, and their struggle to eke out a living in the hostile surroundings turn everyday living into a heroic struggle. The novel begins with the arrival of Piya Roy to carry out research on freshwater dolphins in the Sundarbans. She meets the Kolkata businessman and translator Kanai Dutt, who is on his way to Lusibari, one of the remote islands of the region where his aunt Nilima has set up a small hospital. She had come to this region along with her husband, Nirmal, a committed communist who believed in revolutionary change, with a sense of mission to serve the rural poor. Their lives got entangled with those of the locals in the next thirty years.

Ghosh invokes the multiple histories of the region in his narrative and weaves them into the collective memories that are retained in myths and folklores, to suggest the complex templates of time in which people live. Daniel Hamilton, a businessman who made his fortune in shipping during the nineteenth century, bought ten thousand acres of land in the Sundarbans to set up an ideal community. All that is left of his Utopian dreams of building a classless society is a collection of villages bearing strange names such as 'Shobnomoskar', 'Rajatjubilee' and 'Lusibari'. Since land was given away for free, people came in thousands; but the terrain was at the mercy of high tides which submerged it every day for hours. Nirmal says that Daniel's dream was to 'build a place where no one would exploit anyone and people would live together without petty social distinctions and differences. He dreamed of a place where men and women could be farmers in the morning, poets in the afternoon and carpenters in the evening' (Ghosh 2004, 53). Now, all that was left of the dream was a few 'rat-eaten islands' (53). By the time Nirmal arrived in Lusibari, Hamilton had already passed on into the collective memory of the villagers who worshipped him, 'if not quite a deity, then certainly a venerated ancestral spirit' (78).

Kanai first encounters the collective memory of the region when he watches a performance of 'The Glory of the Bon Bibi' by local folk artists. This was during his first visit, when he was a child visiting his uncle and aunt. Nirmal, the confirmed rationalist and Marxist, is dismissive of the popular realm of the sacred which, according to him, signifies 'just false consciousness' (101). But Kanai is deeply moved as he watches the performance of the myth. According to the myth, Bon Bibi and Shah Jongoli were twins born to a pious man, Ibrahim, who lived in Madina. When they came of age, they were sent on a divine mission, from Arabia all the way to 'the country of eighteen tides', to make it 'fit for human habitation'. There follows a long narrative of their fight against the demon king Dokkhin Rai who held sway over the entire forest land. When he was defeated, Bon Bibi decided to keep half of the tide country as wilderness, which was left to Dokkhin Rai and his hordes of spirits. The rest was reclaimed for human habitation. This was followed by the story of the orphan boy, Dukhey, who was handed over to Dokkhin Rai by Dhona, a greedy chieftain, in exchange of great forest wealth. Dukhey was saved by Bon Bibi at the nick of time, before he was killed by the demon. The child was nursed back to health and restored to his mother. Ghosh writes, 'Thus did Bon bibi show the world the law of the forest, which was that the rich and the greedy would be punished while the poor and the righteous were rewarded' (105). At a later stage in the novel, we come across an excerpt from the epic of the tide country as told by Abdur-Rahim: *Bon bibir karamoti orthat bon bibi johuranama* – 'The Miracles of Bon Bibi or the Narrative of Her Glory' – which shows the syncretic tradition of the region in its very Arabic–Bengali hybridity. The oral epic suggests a layer of the collective memory which is preserved in the subconscious of the people of the region. Fokir can recite the entire epic from memory, though he is illiterate. This shows how deeply the folk-memories have seeped into the subconscious of the community.

The collective memory of the local community that keeps the myth of Bon Bibi alive gives them hope and the will to strive for a better future, even as they are confronted with violence at various levels. The story of Kusum, whose mother is sold to a city brothel in Dhanbad, shows the extent of brutality faced by the poorest of the poor in the Sundarbans. Again, Ghosh is to the point when he says, 'the destitution of the tide country was such as to remind them of the terrible famine that had devastated Bengal in 1942 except that in Lusibari hunger and catastrophe were a way of life' (79). When Nirmal and Nilima first came to these islands, they discovered that 'a startlingly large proportion of the island's women were dressed as widows' (80). This was because these women had to live with the reality of the impending deaths of their husbands who could not be sure of their safety either in the forest or on the river. The act of draping their bodies in markers of widowhood amounts to inscribing their collective memory on their bodies, foreboding the inevitability of personal losses. In this sense, memory and mourning are inseparable. The inscribing of personal loss on the body turns it into a public spectacle of collective loss, turning everyday life into a ritual of loss. In this enactment of trauma, there is an attempt to recover a sense of dignity in suffering. This is what makes memory an ideological site for constituting identity and authority.

Piya comes into contact with Fokir, the illiterate fisherman who knows the topography of the rivers and the forest intimately but has no words to articulate his knowledge. His faith in Bon Bibi is revealed in an act of worship in a secluded place in the forest. Piya had noticed that his prayer contained a word that sounded like 'Allah', though he did not follow Islam. In fact, the people of the Sundarbans cannot be classified as either Hindus or Muslims. As we have seen, their folk beliefs speak of a certain crossing of the boundaries of institutionalised religions and nation states. This also makes them suspect in the eyes of postcolonial authorities. In fact, a fixed identity that could be explained in terms of the categories coined by the nation state would have saved them from destitution. However, they are 'refugees', the lost generation of the violent histories of the subcontinent. The partition of India brought a wave of refugees to the Sundarbans; and the 1971 war with Pakistan resulted in another influx of refugees. Terms such as 'refugees' and 'encroachers' suggest that the assigned identity of 'citizenship' is a guarded space in a modern nation state. This makes the private memories of those denied the right to belong a potential threat to the stability of the nation state.

The story of Marichjhapi is embedded in the layered memories of this novel, in the form of Nirmal's journals which he leaves for Kanai. The events of May 1979, which do not form the official narrative of modern India, are thus brought into the main narrative. It was by accident that Nirmal came into contact with the people of Marichjhapi. After retirement, he wanted to pursue some useful vocation and, hence, was on his way to Kumirmari, when an unexpected storm brought him to the island of Marichjhapi. There he met Kusum who had strangely disappeared from Lusibari many years before. The dislocations of the people of Marichjhapi come alive through her memories. Her search for her mother had taken her to Dhanbad where she found her mother in a brothel, wasted by the hard life she was subjected to. Later she, with her son, Fokir, joined the great march of displaced refugees who were fleeing from Dandakaranya towards the Sundarbans. When they were settled in the Sundarbans, the government wanted to evict them from the forest land. When Nirmal reached there, the people of the entire island had been living under the shadow of imminent eviction. He joined their fight, convinced that a government led by the Communist Party would definitely be responsive to the demands of the people. But what followed was traumatic. Even Nilima had warned Nirmal that there was no way to save the 'squatters' from eviction. The people, meanwhile, had already created their little worlds after settling down in the islands. All their lives they had been on the run. And now, the government, who had initially promised help, was threatening to uproot them. People who were trying to flee with their meagre belongings were set upon by police boats to rip apart their make-shift boats. Many women and children were drowned. Nirmal went to Marichjhapi along with Horen to bring Kusum and her son back to safety. When Kusum refused to leave, Nirmal also stayed back with the villagers. Horen took Fokir with him and went back. In fact, the journal kept by Nirmal ends here and all that we know about his last days comes from other sources: When he was discovered somewhere outside the Sundarbans, he was disoriented and not in a position to remember what had happened and how he had reached there. Kusum was never traced and it was presumed that along with many other settlers, she had also met with a tragic end. As the author writes in his note at the end of the book, the massacre of Marichjhapi has been largely forgotten. What the novel does is to retrieve it from oblivion for a new generation of readers, narrating the repressed history of the nation state through the memories of its victims.

## 2

In Ghosh's novel, Fokir is reticent and reclusive to the extreme, despite his unusual sensitivity to nature and his surroundings. It is his knowledge of the behaviour of the cyclone, gathered from his personal experiences and from the community memory spread over hundreds of years, that saves Piya from its brutal onslaught that kills Fokir. But at the end of the novel, we know that it is Piya's scientific knowledge that will triumph in the modern world. She has moved on, whereas for Fokir, it is the end of the road. Even if he had been alive, Fokir, at best, could only be the local informant in a project that would classify and enumerate nature. The myth of Bon Bibi embodies the spirit of the community which does not believe in boundaries and classifications. The community is caught between the past which is life-sustaining and a present that demands a certain collective amnesia. Moyna wants her son to be educated and not to become a crab-hunter like his father, Fokir. She herself is studying to become a nurse in the local hospital run by Nilima.

In Mahasweta Devi's novella, *Pterodactyl, Puran Sahay and Pirtha*, we come across a similar story of a community caught in hostile surroundings and fighting for its subsistence. The narrative is set in a tribal settlement in central India. Nagesia community is reduced to destitution, caught up as they are in barren surroundings that do not allow them to produce adequate food. They are unable to think of relocating themselves as their ancestors are buried there and for them the homeland is sacred. The state government replicates the colonial attitudes in following neo-liberal policies which have only benefitted moneylenders and middlemen: 'These roads have been built with the money sanctioned for tribal welfare so that the owners of bonded labour, the moneylender, the touts and the pimps, the abductors, and the bestial alcoholic young men lusting after tribal women can directly enter into the tribal habitations' (Devi 1995, 109).

The sudden appearance of a pterodactyl-like creature in this tribal region attracts attention of the outside world. The community considers this event as a visitation from their ancestors. They read it as a sign from the dead, warning them and reassuring them. They have gone into mourning, and Bikhia, the only tribal who has seen the bird-like creature, has withdrawn into silence. Puran Sahay is an urban journalist from Patna and has been assigned to report on this event. He gradually becomes aware of the enormity of the burden he is saddled with. He wakes up to the moral implications of violating the trust and privacy of a community which has been subjected to violence by successive authorities. It is not just the question of reporting an event objectively, but of understanding a community which does not share the language of modernity:

> Now Puran realizes that he's never been in such a situation before. Where an ancestral soul casts a roving shadow, Bikhia draws, the settlement remains unclean and in mourning, and Shankar says, from a millennial other space, "We were!" Upon the backdrop of the experience, there is the man-made famine. The same person, at the same time, banishes poverty in Constitution and Proclamation, creates poverty, protests in art-films. (141)

Mahasweta Devi draws our attention to the institutionalised violence of postcolonial society. The complicity of the nation state in keeping the tribal community in a state of backwardness, despite the presence of conscientious officers, comes through in the narrative. The postcolonial state has failed in its function of providing basic facilities to the tribal community living under hostile conditions. Droughts have recurred for years, reducing the people to penury. Women have been sold, showing the limits of despair the community has reached. The *sarpanch* (headman) of the village speaks the impersonal language of the state and his arguments finally put the blame on the tribal community for not doing enough on their own. Harisharan, the Block Development Officer (BDO), is eager to help but finds himself defeated by the insensitivity of the system. It is against this bleak landscape of destitution and ruin that the prehistoric creature reveals itself to Bikhia, who draws a picture of it on the wall of a cave. The tribal community, desperate to cling to hope, now believes that it is a sign from their collective past – the prehistoric creature is none other than their ancestor. Bikhia's silence complicates the situation. Perhaps he has grasped the implications of what he had seen, but he will never be able to convey to the outside world its significance. The media or the authorities will interpret it in their own ways, robbing it of its sense of the sacred that inspires awe among the members of the community. Shankar, the only literate person in the tribal community, tries hard to help the community. But he is caught between the authorities and his own people. Mahasweta Devi writes,

> Only Shankar is literate in the surrounding villages. He too cultivates the stony ground, lives on the hillside, eats mainly the root of the Khajra. How can he abandon the past? They don't know if that past is legend or history, and no researcher comes to separate the two. And who is going to tell us what is legend and what history from the perspective of these totally rejected tribals. (146)

The memories that are activated by the sight of the prehistoric creature are thousands of years old. Modernity is incapable of imagining anything on that scale. This is why Bikhia and his community feel alienated from Puran, the B.D.O and others who are sympathetic but unable to cross over to their world.

Puran has his encounter with the ancestor of the tribal community during the rainy night he spends in the village. After many months of drought, it rained the day Puran reached the village. That is enough to give him an aura of divinity in the eyes of the villagers. It is this trust that makes Puran even more responsible in handling the myth of the bird. He discovers that it is an 'embodied creature which can spread its wings and can fly' (104). Along with Bikhia, he watches the prehistoric creature and is deeply moved by the experience:

> From the other side of the millions of years the soul of the ancestors of Shankar's people looks at Puran, and the glance is so prehistoric that Puran's brain cells, spreading a hundred antennae, understands nothing of that glance. If tonight he had seen a stone flying with its wings spread, would he have been able to speak to it? (142)

Obviously, it would have been a big scoop for Puran to let the outside world know about the appearance of the creature in this tribal settlement. It would have brought him fame and professional success. But he decides not to let the world know about the incident. He had decided even earlier that he would not take pictures or record any conversations (135). He knows what would happen if this event is publicised:

> Newspapers and scientists from the world over are pouring into Pirtha, extinguishing the tribals altogether. Why Madhopura, Pirtha is on the map of the world. Internationally known Foundations determine the "why and how". If the world finally comes to the decision that "only tribal areas inhabited by starving, living human elements can discover the impossible, that these areas can help us determine the earth's real age and prove that, in some parts of India, a piece of the original earth still remains undiscovered"? (142)

Puran's moral crisis is connected to the nature of modernity that countries such as India have internalised. While Bikhia believes in the truth of the supernatural experience and has 'received his ancestral soul' (144), Puran is not sure how he can relate to this entire experience. He is awed by the experience but cannot understand its full significance. He addresses the ancestor-bird with these words:

> You are moveless with your wings folded, I do not wish to touch you, you are outside my wisdom, reason, and feelings, who can place his hand on the axial moment of the end of third phase of Mesozoic and the beginnings of the Kenozoic geological ages? That is the story of seventy five million years. . . . You were supposed to have become extinct then. Space separating, seasons and climate changing. Did your world have such dusks? What ocean, what weed, what fish, did you see?

> And were you extinct? Have you left the pages of some picture book, taken shape so that you can give some urgent news to today's humans, have you come here because Pirtha is also endangered, its existence is under attack for other kinds of reasons? (157)

Puran is not able to 'read' the symbol before him. Any attempt to attribute a 'meaning' to it will desecrate it. He knows that his education has given him no equipment to penetrate the veil that conceals the community's collective memory. In that sense, he is an illiterate, without memories, while Bikhia, whose sense of the sacred allows him to accept the bird as his ancestor, has access to another order of experience. Mahasweta Devi feels that for the tribals, nature is not a phenomenon located outside their being. A tribal does not feel homeless in the presence of nature – it is a part of his or her self. However, what makes Pirtha a site of prehistoric past also excludes it from the present. It is excluded from the narrative of development and progress that defines the march of the nation state.

Puran feels that 'the eye says nothing' (158). He feels that there is no point in communicating with the bird. Puran knows that this encounter with the supernatural will not be understood by the world outside. He rightly says,'There is no escape, we were torn apart so long ago, in fragments, in atoms, we are scattered everywhere' (161). Puran knows that Bikhia has become more vulnerable now, having encountered this prehistoric creature whom he recognises as his ancestor. The outside world will never understand his perspective, and will reduce him to a spectacle. When the SDO asks Puran if he will write about what he has seen, he replies in the negative, and adds, 'It is the soul of their ancestors, not mine' (171).

Puran and Bikhia go in search of a cave where they can bury the mortal remains of the bird, now dead, away from the invasion of the outside world. This cavern itself is a site of (geological) memory which modernity cannot fathom. In a lyrical passage, Mahasweta Devi invokes the template of time represented by this dimension of collective memory:

> Whatever is mine has been invaded. Where will the wild animal run when it is surrounded by a net fence? The present, encroaching from all sides, will eat the past whole. Yet there may be priceless truth worthy of being guarded in secret, that you cannot let anyone know, give it to me, I am that ageless timeless darkness of time, when the earth was under water, there was no light anywhere, darkness was everywhere,

> and the creator was in thought, how to create the earth and the living world. I am waiting since then, I keep everything in my lap, nothing is lost. (177)

In the last section of the story, Puran grapples with the ethical implications of his experience. He feels that the pterodactyl had a message for them, but they were unable to understand it. As he says, 'we belong to two worlds and *there is no communication point*' (196, italics in the original). Indirectly it suggests that we have no means of communicating with the tribals and their world. The modern Indian state has never tried to understand the tribals or their world. The community is haunted by a deep sense of loss. He feels that to communicate with the tribals, we should learn to love them. He sums up what is the essence of the story in these words:

> To build it you must love beyond reason for a long time. For a few thousand years we haven't loved them, respected them. Where is the time now, at the last gasp of the century? Parallel ways, their world and our world are different, we have never had a real exchange with them, it could have enriched us. (197)

Mahasweta Devi believes that our civilisation is aggressive and incapable of loving and nurturing anything. Bikhia is able to understand what the pterodactyl has come to say because he has access to a collective memory which excludes Puran. In a sense, this collective memory is unrepresentable. It can be experienced only as loss, as in a ritual of mourning. In that sense, mourning and memory become inseparable in the narrative. It is through mourning that the community partakes of the memory of their ancestors. One may recall here the women of the Sundarbans who are clad in white. These sites of collective experiences are beyond the grasp of the postcolonial state which presides over their fate. There is no way we can represent Pirtha without silencing it, erasing its essence. This is why Fokir's death is preordained in the narrative of *The Hungry Tide.* Fokir can only speak through his death.

The postcolonial state can only represent the tribal in facts and figures – their sense of themselves can never be deciphered by the officers of the state. For the postcolonial state, the tribals are like children to be adopted and tutored and brought into the 'mainstream'. Their memories are not seen as inherently worthwhile, and the templates of their time scale are not grasped by bureaucrats who think in terms of five-year plans.

In a dialogue between Judith Butler and Gayatri Chakravorty Spivak, the latter observes that 'we now have the managerial state on the free-market model', and continues, 'When these managerial states with these globally regulated priorities work, some kinds of demands do not come up. The market is never going to throw up demands for clean drinking water for the poor. Other kinds of institutions have to take up these behests away from something like the state' (Butler and Spivak 2007, 79–80). Pirtha's inability to forge a new institution results from its exclusion from all networks of power. In the prevailing political climate, where the nation state is itself in retreat, tribal populations will have to innovate and rely on their own resources for survival and subsistence. Their cultural capital may be outdated, but it allows them to mobilise people on a common platform of shared memories.

## 3

Anand's *Vyasa and Vigneshwara,* a novella which is postmodern in its approach to the question of time, raises larger questions about memory and history. Its metafictional features make it a text about texts. In fact, the author himself says in the course of the narrative that he intends to present yet another problem for the critics to crack – 'how about developing it [a text] through someone else's texts' (Anand 2000, 59). The two sections of the novella are called 'Kriti' (text) and 'Kaalam' (time). Anand observes that 'when smriti, what is remembered, and shruti, what is heard, get subsumed by vismriti, amnesia, and further by mriti, death, kriti alone remains' (126).

The central figure that runs through Kriti is that of Ekalavya, the forest-dweller (a tribal, to use the current terminology) who was punished by Drona, the brahmin guru, for excelling in the art of archery. Drona asked him to sacrifice his thumb as *gurudakshina* (offering for one's teacher or guru) and Ekalavya obeyed him without protest. This helped Arjuna, the great warrior of the *Mahabharata,* to remain invincible in the art of archery. However, in the story narrated by Anand, we come across a text called *Nishadapurana* which recounts a long conversation between Ekalavya and Abhimanyu, Arjuna's son. After many years of search, the narrator chances upon the text in a library in Delhi, but finds the crucial dialogue between Ekalavya and Abhimanyu, regarding whether Lord Krishna was responsible for Abhimanyu's death, missing from the text.

One of the recurring themes of Indian history has been the conflict between the 'Aryan' race and the 'non-Aryans'. *Nishadapurana* makes it very clear that the 'forest-dwellers' had their own highly developed culture. One of the issues discussed threadbare between Abhimanyu and Ekalavya is the nature of the relation between knowledge and freedom. Ekalavya does not believe that knowledge will ever set us free. He explains,

> Vidya is infinite. We are born with little missions which last but for a short span. Therefore everyone's vidya is only half complete. Man knows only to shoot the arrow, he cannot call it back. That is why I say that vidya is a mesh. It arouses a person, makes him fly on the wings of the desires and aspirations, and then abandons him in the midst of hunters. Vidya renounces him who does not renounce vidya; he who renounces it wins. One who attempts to embrace it becomes a slave. I spent my entire youth trying to understand this. (36)

This debate on knowledge and freedom has particular relevance to the question of colonial construction of epistemologies. Anand's novel begins with a reference to Romesh Chunder Dutt's famous book, *The Economic History of India* (1901). The book refers to the pauperisation of silk weavers in Bengal who were forced to sell their products at a very low rate to the East India Company:

> The price was so low that no manufacturer could possibly agree to it. Even then, the locals had no alternative but to sign these ex-parte contracts. If they refused to sign the bond, not only were they flogged, but their goods forcibly seized and auctioned. Bolts further testifies as to how several silk winders, who refused to sign such agreements, chopped off their thumbs, thus bidding permanent goodbye to their occupation. (12)

Here we have a repetition of the Ekalavya legend – knowledge brings these silk winders disaster. The act of chopping the thumb amounts to an act of castration. It is through this act of self-mutilation that the body is transformed into a site of history. The excised thumb is a permanent reminder of the injustice inscribed on the body. The bonded slave, or the Hindu widow on the funeral pyre (*sati*), is a reminder of such acts of injustice that have shaped Indian history. The past is a site of dismemberment for the colonised people. Since the Indian subcontinent has gone through several cycles of colonisation, the metaphor of the chopped thumb stands for its multiple levels of historical oppression. Anand, in the act of recovering a fragment called *Nishadapurana,* 're-members' the 'dis-membered' body, reconstituting the fragmented history from which tribals have been completely excluded. The very fact that Ekalavya has become one of the haunting metaphors – for the cumulative injustice heaped on the marginalised sections of the society – of postcolonial Indian literature is testimony to the ability of memory to resist hegemonic discourses of history. Images of Fokir, Bikhia and Ekalavya haunt the rational constructs of modernity erected by the nation state. In this sense, all the three fictional works discussed here present spectral figures from the past which can enter contemporary society only through memory, mourning and melancholy.

In the second section of Anand's narrative, we come across an activist who is inspired by the Utopian ideas of revolution and liberation – Vardhamana. He has been on the run from the authorities for plotting against the state. On his way to Delhi, the narrator meets Vardhamana on a train. They discuss the fate that befell ancient kingdoms like Vaishali, Kosala and Vajji. Vardhamana knows that democracy is no defence against injustice. He gives the narrator a part of a play he has written, titled '*Nagaravadhu*', which is about Amrapali (referred to as 'Ambapali' in Buddhist Pali texts) who is forced to become the *Nagaravadhu* through a democratic process by the wise people of Vaishali. In the words of Amarasena, we have the central argument of the whole story:

> "Today, you have dragged this state to the portals of prostitution." Amarasena's voice is firm. "You have dragged prostitution from its dark and sinister chambers to the street and enthroned it there in the name of social justice. You celebrate as democracy, the illegal conjugality between politics and adultery. Listen, you selfish and greedy people, society is the soil, from which germinate fine, dignified people. But you, you fear such people. You mow them to the ground, then you make them the pillars that bear the weight of the edifice of a decadent civilization which you yourself have constructed." (103–04)

Here we have – in all its essence – one of the recurring motifs of postcolonial Indian novels. Colonialism brought new knowledge, but it also alienated people from their own roots. Knowledge can liberate only if it is inclusive and just. Knowledge is not an unmediated and objective description of outer reality. Institutions and discourses mediate the production and distribution of knowledge. This is why Fokir or Bhikhia lack legitimacy, though they are intimately related to local discourses of knowledge. India has a long tradition of internal colonisation, as evidenced by the story of Ekalavya. It is not important to determine if *Nishadapurana* existed in reality. It is a fact that indigenous knowledge systems gradually went out of circulation whenever hegemonic power structures established their authority. Modernity has legislated normative subjects through education and training; and colonial modernity was a way of controlling the mind and body of the native. New knowledge subjects create new orders of power – and the power structure guards its boundaries closely. Towards the end of the narrative, Anand refers to a book, *The History of Torture.* He says, 'Torture is not a sectarian concept. It is ubiquitous. At times, it is inflicted on the faithful, at other times, on those who question faith, and yet other times, who are neither' (122). Like Ekalavya, Bikhia and Fokir knew, from their experiences, that they will for ever remain victims to the system of surveillance that micro-manages the production of knowledge in the regime of modernity. In such a penal colony, memories offer a site of resistance, since they hold out the hope of retaining alternative sources of knowledge production.

## References

Anand. 2000. *Vyasa and Vigneshwara.* Trans. Saji Mathew. Intr. Udaya Kumar. New Delhi: Katha.

Butler, Judith, and Gayatri Chakravorty Spivak. 2007. *Who sings the nation-state: Language, politics, belonging.* Calcutta (Kolkata): Seagull.

Devi, Mahasweta. 1995. *Pterodactyl, Puran Sahay and Pirtha.* In *Imaginary maps,* trans. Gayatri Chakravorty Spivak. Calcutta (Kolkata): Thema.

Ghosh, Amitav. 2004. *The hungry tide.* New Delhi: HarperCollins.

**CHAPTER NINE**

# Writing the Region, Imagining the Nation: A Reading of Bhalchandra Nemade's *Kosla*

Bhalchandra Nemade's *Kosla* (1963; translated into English as *Cocoon,* 1997) has attained a cult status in Marathi literature for its imaginative rendering of a young man's quest for identity against the moribund culture of Indian society in the 1960s. Nemade's nativist critique is directed against the philistinism of cultural and educational institutions. Pandurang Sangvikar's journey towards self-awareness, through an adolescent crisis that involves confrontations with his father and patriarchal authorities, reveals the deepening rural-urban divide in India, the growing gulf between ideals and practice, and a disoriented new generation adrift without a vision or commitment. His sister's untimely death throws Sangvikar into the vortex of an emotional turbulence that shatters him, and precipitates his open rebellion against his family and its values. Nemade subjects the complex relation between an individual and society to a close scrutiny through the lens of an ethical perspective derived from the tradition of the Marathi novel going back to *Yamunaparyatan* (1857). The chapter also shows how Nemade redefines the relation between form and content in the nuanced ironical structure of the novel, enabling the narrative to reflect on the unresolved ethical dilemmas of Indian modernity.

## I

Bhalchandra Nemade (b.1938) is one of the pioneers among the modern Indian novelists of the post–1960 period, who marked a departure in the way fiction was used to represent reality. His *Kosla* (1963, translated as *Cocoon* [1997]) appeared in the same decade as two other significant novels of Indian literature – U. R. Ananthamurthy's *Samskara* (1965) in Kannada and O. V. Vijayan's *Khasakkinte itihasam* (1969) in Malayalam. While A. K. Ramanujan's translation of *Samskara* (1976) soon made the novel an iconic work of modern Indian fiction,

*Kosla* and *Khasakkinte itihasam* did not receive the attention they deserved. Vijayan's self-translation of *Khasakkinte itihasam* was not able to capture the resonance of the dense idiom of the original, which had become a cult book for the generation of the late 60s. Vijayan was a well-known political cartoonist at the national level and had made a name for himself as a political commentator. Besides, his translation of *Khasakkinte itihasam* was one of the first translations to be issued by Penguin India. All this ensured a certain visibility for Vijayan's work, though it did not receive the attention that *Samskara* garnered. On the other hand, Nemade's novel had established itself as a classic in Marathi by the late 60s, but the English translation appeared thirty-three years after the publication of the Marathi original. Perhaps, among these three novels, *Kosla* was the most difficult to translate into English. Sudhakar Marathe's translation (1997) has done justice to the original, but the linguistic and stylistic complexity of *Kosla* is as much an attribute of its architectural design as its innovative narrative mode and tone. *Kosla* has to be studied as an Indian novel of seminal significance to understand the directions taken by Indian society in the postcolonial period. While we tend to celebrate even minor works of Indian Writing in English as 'international literature', works of crucial importance to the study of Indian society are routinely ignored, even when translations of such texts exist. Of late, social scientists have made use of Indian fiction in Indian languages to some extent, but no course in social sciences in India contains fictional works written in Indian languages.

The three novels mentioned above merit attention not because they appeared in the same decade, but they take a hard look at Indian modernity and provide us with insights into its fraudulent nature. They do it with involvement and compassion that does not carry the burden of ideological baggage. By the 1950s, the social realist tradition had become moribund and had lost its capacity to develop the narrative apparatus necessary to represent a society caught in moral dilemmas that could not be resolved in terms of simplistic idealistic solutions. The innovative nature of the experimental idiom used in these novels attests to the fact that a critique of society necessarily involves developing a new perspective on society. It is possible to argue that each of these texts has altered the relation between form and content and redefined the very direction of the novel in their respective languages. The new narrative idiom discovers and recovers social and personal spaces that were invisible and intractable to conventions of social realism. This discussion of *Kosla* will focus on its treatment of the moral crisis in the Indian society of the 1960s, and the search for a new and emergent social imaginary that is articulated in the novel.

Nemade has been identified with the group of Marathi writers advocating a 'nativist' approach to literature. Nemade's essay 'The Marathi Novel 1950–1975' outlines a history of the novel in Marathi, tracing its history from the colonial times (in the nineteenth century) to the present. He talks of three trends in the history of the novel – the *Yamunaparyatan* trend, the *Mochangad* trend and the *Muktamala* trend. The *Muktamala* trend gives primacy to convention rather than life and may be termed 'formalistic' in approach. This type of novels avoids action and has an affected way of narration. Nemade includes well-known Marathi novelists like V. S. Khandekar, N. S. Phadke, P. B. Bhave, P. S. Rege, C. T. Khanolkar, Madhav Kanitkar, Kusum Abhyamkar, Baba Kadam, etc., in this category. The *Mochangad* trend revels in fancy and may be counted as 'popular literature'. The dominant tendency here is to produce a 'non-existent reality'. Eminent writers such as V. S. Khandekar, Ranjit Desai, C. V. Vaidya, Nathmadhav, N. S. Inamdar, Shivaji Savant and Haribhau Apte are cited as examples of this category of writers. Obviously, Nemade considers the *Yamunaparyatan* trend as central to the history of the novel in Marathi. He defines this trend: 'A novelist selects the theme as a verbal action with specific moral angle in the context of the multi-faceted relation between the individual and the community. And in keeping with the theme, the style organizes the form through the medium of language using various techniques' (2010, 194).

According to Nemade, the works of novelists such as H. N. Apte, V. M. Joshi, Sane Guruji, Vaibhavari Shiurkar, Dinanath Manohar, Anant Kadam, Bhau Padhye, etc., come under the *Yamunaparyatan* trend. Nemade believes that this central trend in Marathi novels reflects a response to colonisation and modernisation. The creation of prose literature was an effective way of countering the oppression created by imperialist and colonial forces. The novel of the reformist kind should be seen as part of the organised movements and activities based on reason. It was the expression of a dynamic society which was responding to new challenges in the wake of the encounter with the superior technology of a dominant culture. The formalist novel of the *Muktamala* kind enters a 'mystified world of fantasy', affording escape routes from the crucial problems of the day. The realist tradition enunciated by *Yamunaparyatan* is notable for its activist role in addressing the larger moral issues. Baba Padamji's *Yamunaparyatan* (1857), considered to be the first Marathi novel, had talked of a young widow's plight in a convention-bound society. Nemade notes that this tradition subsequently became dormant in Marathi literature, as the society lost its larger moral direction. In the post–1960 period in Marathi literature, he finds a return to this tradition, and feels that it has the vitality to address urgent socio-political and moral issues. Nemade's own novel has to be studied in this context of the Marathi novel.

It will be a misnomer to term Nemade as a 'nativist' in the sense of being a 'revivalist' of the obscurantist variety. He has attempted to trace a critical tradition in the history of the novel in Marathi and emphasised its contemporary relevance. He states, 'Culture is not a hot-house, but a soil-bound process; literature is not a theoretical construct but a living phenomenon' (2010, 193). A novelist should have 'a nativist awareness' of the roots of his or her society and its history. Uncritical acceptance of alien traditions, without reference to native histories, will result in fraudulent discourses. An uprooted internationalism that parades itself as cosmopolitanism has the effect of disorienting the creative engagement of the artist in pursuit of false goals. The fantasy worlds created by the formalists did not address the living problems of contemporary society and hence, Nemade argues for a critical realism that engages social and political issues from the perspective of historical awareness. Nativism, in this sense, is not a celebration of a 'grand tradition' but an awareness of the socio-political issues that animate the larger moral issues a work of art is derived from. It is an attempt to retrieve and retain a strong sense of community that sustains an ethnic culture.

## 2

*Kosla,* seen from this point of view, is the harbinger of a critical realism that renovates the mainstream of the Marathi novel by interrogating its foundational principles. Though Baba Padamji's social realist tradition could revitalise Marathi society, it had lost its moorings in the twentieth century.

Pandurang Sangvikar is the main character in *Kosla.* The novel traces his journey from childhood to youth. It is divided into six sections, each focusing on a particular phase of his life. Sangvi is a village in the Khandesh region of Maharashtra. Pandurang's father is a rich farmer of the village, and his childhood is spent in the shadow of his disciplinarian ways. The first section deals with his unpleasant childhood and his relationships with his family members. He moves out of the village to study in a college in Pune. The second and third sections describe his life in the college for the next four years. He drifts away from his family during this time, with the father's menacing figure lurking in the background. Pandurang fails in the final examination and is haunted by a sense of failure. He stays on in Pune to retake the examination and feels lonely and lost in the big city. Finally he is back in the village, without anything to show for his years spent in Pune. The last two sections deal with his life in the village, alienated from his family and community, and haunted by questions he is not equipped to answer.

The novel is more of a digressive narrative with several loosely connected episodes, with its focus on the inner development of the protagonist's subjectivity. The tone is set in the opening sentence: 'Me, Pandurang Sangvikar. Today, for instance, I am twenty five years old. Honestly, there is only this thing worth telling you" (1997, 1). The tone is one of irreverence and rejection from the very beginning. Pandurang feels hemmed in by his family and the world around him. The towering image of his father leaves him no space for asserting his own identity. Once Pandurang, along with his friend Eknath, sets out to see the hills and comes back late in the evening. He gets punished by his father: 'My legs were throbbing. On top of that, of course, Father plied the switch. I may not mind anything else, but I cannot take being struck with a switch. I shouted at him that this was hardly in keeping with our Hindu religion. Damn your daily prayers in the temple' (3). What vexes Pandurang further is the father's miserliness and greed for money. He makes Pandurang apply for a 'freeship' at high school by claiming that they belong to a low-income category, though they were quite well off. The son faces humiliation in the class for this. Pandurang adds, 'Father was most terrifically after money' (3). Pandurang practises playing the flute, but his father hates the idea. This also can be seen as one of the earliest scenes in the novel where his family does not approve of Pandurang's artistic inclinations. He also has his problems with some bullies in school, engages in night-long battles with rats that damage his books, resolves to put his life in order according to a set time-table, and wants to 'do something great' in life. Most of all, he wants to escape from the village, primarily from his father who, he is afraid, will put him on some short agricultural course and force him into the family profession. He is greatly relieved when he is sent to a college in Pune to study.

*Kosla* is a bildungsroman which portrays the struggles of a young man in search of his own identity. The retrospective gaze of the twenty-five-year-old Pandurang Sangvikar documents those incidents and events that have a bearing on what he is now. His fancies, friendships, failures, all become coloured by the larger theme of the quest for an authentic self and a meaningful relationship with the society around him. In his father, Pandurang confronts patriarchy for the first time, in all its ruthlessness. Later, he would realise that all social institutions are built on hierarchies and they are all equally oppressive. The college and its environment have very little to inspire a creatively restless mind like that of Sangvikar's. He has to cross the gulf between the rural and urban worlds which seem to be miles apart. He disapproves of his Maushi dressing up and going out, and even suspects her morality: 'Everybody in Pune dresses up, it is true. But it is not nice for one's own Maushi to dress up and strut about. . . . But even after behaviour like Maushi's if a woman's husband calls her his wife, why anyone else say anything about him' (28). Later, he discovers how his friend Madhumilind Ichalkaranjikar seduces girls and feels no guilt about abandoning them. The rebel in him cannot approve of the indulgences of his friends. Sangvikar is a victim of the contradictions within himself.

In every letter from home, Pandurang's father mentions the money he has been spending on his son and urges him to study well. Pandurang is profligate with money and this lands him in quite a few troubles. The boys from Pune, with their superior ways, extract money from him and exploit him. They are full of self-importance and correct his English pronunciation. Pandurang says, 'Heck! These three were crooks. You'd have to call them crooks. Mind you, once I conveyed my intention to go to dine with them at home—saying, I would do one Sunday with each of you in turn—they even stopped passing by my door' (31). Pandurang is quick to notice, behind the urban sophistication, the same greed and duplicity he had noticed in the village, in his father and others. He notices the same shallowness even in matters of art. He finds the comic plays that are performed in college, which incited virtual laugh riots, extremely disturbing. Pandurang's own sensibility is at a formative stage and his confrontation with the duplicity and philistinism that characterise the elite institution in Pune alerts him to the complexity of his surroundings. Since self-development takes place in relation to the environment of one's own being, Sangvikar's self-creation becomes psychologically harrowing. His disillusionment with the 'learned teachers' adds to this state of confusion. He says, 'Truth to tell, the notions I used to have before about the erudition of my teachers proved correct in only one or two cases' (55). Most of the teachers have nothing new to say. The teachers of Sanskrit and Marathi leave him cold. He is the secretary of the College Debating Society, but his attempts at public speaking are disasters. Even serious occasions, such as a speech by a Gandhian or a debate on 'War and World Peace', arouse laughter when handled by Sangvikar. He rarely attends classes; and when he does, he and his friends distribute parodies of famous lines from Marathi poems.

Sangvikar is unable to handle money and this lands him in a series of problems. He is incharge of the hostel mess, and at the end of the year, he discovers a deficit of six hundred rupees in the mess fund. He has been sympathetic to Ramappa, the cook who has spent a lifetime in the hostel's kitchen, and is unable to accept that the cook is telling lies. He had entrusted the job of collecting money to Vaidya and now Vaidya blames Ramappa. Finally, Sangvikar has to send a letter to his father requesting for money, keeping aside the humiliation it involved. The theme of money is central to narratives of growing up. In Sangvikar's case, it is his sensitivity and lack of ruthlessness that turn him into a victim. While those who can exploit the system flourish, students like him end up as failures. When he decides to leave the course in history and opts for Marathi and English, the father is again furious. He writes, 'You are an ass. If you must read the *Dnyaneshwari,* why go to college for that? Don't we read it at home too?' (122)

After his initial unpleasant experiences as office bearer in the college mess and the debating society, Sangvikar withdraws completely into a cocoon. The novel's title suggests the formative phase of an insect before it emerges, fully grown, into light. Sangvikar's struggles with his environment bring out the contradictions in himself as well as the system. The middle class of Maharashtra had become self-seeking and consumerist in the post–1947 period. The individual was the measure of all things. This meant that community values, or anything that would benefit the society at large, had very little relevance for the young generation. After withdrawing from all his public activities, Sangvikar reads recklessly and is plagued by thoughts of all kinds. He even observes silence for eight days in a row. There are times when he walks entire nights through the hills or the streets – once he is even arrested for wandering at night.

Sangvikar had a Marathi teacher, Gune, who had the reputation of being a good scholar and writer. He kept a house in Mumbai and another in Pune. However, Sangvikar finds his teacher's obsession with security in life at odds with the lofty ideas of modernism he often elaborated on. Gune would buy all the latest books and comment on ideas that were in vougue in his critical works. Sangvikar meets many Marathi writers at Gune's place and finds most of them pompous and insincere. He has a long argument with an eminent Marathi writer who states that poets writing in English have made much more progress than poets writing in other languages. Finally, he parts ways with Gune, whose annoyance at Sangvikar's critical tone is reflected in his words: 'Your reading is inadequate and your chattering excessive' (189). One of the final arguments they have is over Gune's statement, 'literary writers are superior to ordinary human folk' (189). Sangvikar's line of thought shows that he is against setting the literary as an insular domain of sanctity cut off from ordinary life: 'Now I have myself seen many people who are great and yet haven't written a single line. Only fifteen per cent can read and write, so does that mean there is no greatness in the remainder of humanity?' (189). The larger moral question that *Kosla* raises can be located here – literature need to be anchored in the ordinary life of the community. The flow of common life that brings out the contradictions in the ideological positions of intellectuals who live a double life – one at the personal level and the other at the intellectual level – bothers Sangvikar. The opinions of critics like Gune have something spurious about them. Sangvikar would rather align with the ordinary and observe life critically, than profess any theory that may sound lofty but contradict the life he himself led. In this sense, one of the central themes of *Kosla* hinges on the question, how to bring life and art/literature in consonance with each other?

Sangvikar finds the fascination with the new or 'modern' inauthentic, since it does not enable Indians comprehend the life around them. The intellectual fascination with the West should not become a narcissistic pursuit of self-importance. Nemade's own nativist position may be read into the text here but, as argued earlier, it is not a celebration of the obscurantist and regressive.

## 3

Sangvikar suffers a traumatic loss in the death of his sister, Mani. He was very close to his younger sister. When he gets the news of her death, he cannot believe it: 'I was so shaken I thought, How can anyone just die like that?' When Mani was ill, his father was busy demolishing their house and rebuilding it. He feels that his father had not paid enough attention to her. Only occasionally he would bring a doctor to check on her. Sangvikar blazes with rage after hearing the news: 'I said, I will murder Father. I'll kill Grandma. Then I will set fire to that whole house. I'll burn all their cadavers in that house. Spare only Mother. O to die thus' (150). For many days, Sangvikar cannot contain the fury and rage at the death of his sister. He buys a yellow sari – the kind that little girls wear – cuts it into pieces and burns them, and burns his own fingers in the blaze. He wanders through the streets of Pune during nights. The anguish he feels at her death is his initiation into the mystery of death. Perhaps Sangvikar had never felt such intense pain all his life. His anger against the insensitive father now becomes an awareness about the vulnerability of life itself. He travels to Ajanta around this time. The huge sculptures of the Buddha there, and the paintings on his life and philosophy, move Sangvikar deeply. His own pain appears small and trivial in comparison with the burden of pain that the Buddha had internalised in his gestures and visage:

> This suffering at once expansive and infinitesimal cannot be grasped between one's fingertips. It is a sorrow that whirls round and round. Even to drink of sorrow one needs to cup palms of sorrow. It is impossible to measure this desert-vast sorrow by my cowrie-sized sorrow. Mine are circumscribed little woes. How can I perceive this face through the narrow chink of my pain? I crash down into the abysmal sorrow on that stone face. Now the circumference of my pain too becomes immeasurable. (153)

The tone of this passage is markedly different. The awe inspired by the artworks of the Ajanta caves is reflected in the dense writing in this section. This becomes an 'intertext' that captures the grief at the death of Mani. Sangvikar's passage through this traumatic experience amounts to a rite of passage – from the innocence of a carefree adolescence to a stage of greater maturity. Now he distances himself from the new house built by his father, since it signifies the latter's patriarchal arrogance and insensitivity. He sees it as a tomb built on the dead body of his sister. He feels that the old house was better. His lost childhood, spent in open spaces in the company of people, comes back to him. The new house is like a fortress, shutting off people from gaining easy access. When he goes to his new room, he finds it isolated and closed to the outside world. He looks for an opportunity to have a showdown with his father. Finally, he talks back to his father for an hour without pause, addressing him irreverently. His mother has to drag him away from there. The break with his father is now complete.

Pandurang's emergence as a young man is accompanied by a deepening sense of alienation from his family, village and community. It is here that Nemade's ironic comments on the historical discourse become relevant. We have noted earlier that one of the pastimes of Sangvikar and his friends was to parody famous lines from Marathi poetry. Sureh, one of Sangvikar's friends, writes a parody of history textbooks which gradually becomes a way of lampooning nationalist historiography. Once, both Sureh and Sangvikar were locked up in a police station for a night, for wandering in the streets of Pune. Here they tested the policemen's patience by resorting to the discourse of history textbooks:

> *Every government used to have a Police Department.*
>
> *Now you might ask who is this Government? What does Police mean?*

> *Now, that gentlemen, who in the public street went about openly in a pair of shorts, with a stave in his hand, and caught thieves for you—that was a Policeman.*
>
> *It appears that Policemen must have been born out of an inherent desire for law and order in the Nation. Because, why else would anyone do the work of catching thieves, in shorts at that, and on a measly income of eighty or ninety rupees a month.*
>
> *Now what does Government mean? Every nation used to have a Government.*
>
> *Some eight or ten ancient persons would come together, and for a salary they would look after the balance sheet of the Nation.*
>
> *Once in a way, two or three governments would come into conflict.*
>
> *This does not mean the Oldies themselves came to blows. First having created some quarrel out of nothing, the Oldies would send altogether different younger men to their National borders to fight, while they themselves watched the fun from the rooftops.* (178; italics in the original)

There are many such passages in the novel that are hilarious interludes in the narrative. The idea of history as a grand narrative documenting the momentous events in the life of the nation is lampooned from the perspective of youth who do not see themselves as part of the nation. Sangvikar's alienation from the family and society assumes a larger political dimension here. In his introduction to the English version of the novel, Chandrasekhar Jahagirdar has noted that the Maharashtrian middle class's shift towards the values of material success, careerism, social status and prestige, has created a crisis of values and this results in Sangvikar's alienation from the larger society. He also adds that Sangvikar is put off by the pervasive 'phoniness' of the system:

> What hurts is to find that in the adult world that surrounds him, values are systematically distorted behind facades of social decency and institutional security. The hypocrisy blankets both the rural and urban so that in *Kosla* there is no nostalgia for some kind of rural stability destroyed in the process of social change. The hypocrisy pervades every area of life—from agriculture in the villages to the literary circles in the cities. (xi)

The nation as a moral idea has to be anchored in the life of the community. Modernity, as it was defined in the colonial context, had questioned the unbridled individualism of the Western culture and emphasised the moral values that would enable us to define an inclusive nation. The 'phoniness' that Sangvikar experiences at every stage of his journey, from the village to the city, indicates the failure of the moral imagination that underlies the idea of an Indian nation. In writing the region of Maharashtra, Nemade is pointing to the illegitimacy at the core of the nation and the need to reimagine it.

In the last two sections of the novel, Nemade points to the resources that may hold out the possibility of such a reimagining. Sangvikar is now back in his village, having failed in his BA examination. His days are given to aimless wanderings and reflections. He reads the Mahanubhav literature of the eleventh century and finds a kindred soul in the figure of Chakradhar Swami who had preached renunciation as a way of discovering oneself. He quotes the following lines from Chakradhar with approval:

> One's own country needs to be forsaken:
> One's own village needs to be forsaken:
> The relation of relations particularly needs to be forsaken. (222)

Sangvikar is unable to follow the path of renunciation, caught as he is in moral doubts for which there are no clear answers. However, his friend Giridhar, who shares his alienation and sense of futility, is capable of taking the right action, and chooses to put into practice what he felt was right. Sangvikar, on the other hand, feels a sense of void, unable to believe in anything. He knows that it takes courage to say 'no', and that is what is needed to reconstitute oneself. It is this realisation that makes this novel a comment on Indian modernity.

A discussion of Nemade's use of linguistic and stylistic experiments in the novel deserves a separate chapter altogether. His use of colloquial speech, particularly the slang used by the college youth, gives the novel an expansive rhythm and flow which can absorb a variety of experiences that are comic, gross, profound and, sometimes, even sublime. He moves to the densely lyrical passages on Ajanta and the meditative passages of the last two sections, without disrupting the energetic tempo of the narrative. Words such as 'for instance' and 'etc.' suddenly crop up and lighten the narrative even as it allows us to see the mind of the narrator in a flash. The subtle humour of the parodic passages mimicking the nationalist historiography must be the first example of postmodernist pastiche in modern Indian fiction. The range of his stylistic variations –

from rustic humour and folktale to Baudlairean wanderings in the city – communicates a variety of moods and attitudes that gradually build up the anguish and agony of a generation caught in a moral crisis without easy solutions. *Kosla* is a novel that needs to be studied deeply for what it offers in terms of style and substance.

## References

Nemade, Bhalchandra. 1997. *Cocoon* [*Kosla*]. Tr. Sudhakar Marathe. New Delhi: Macmillan. (Republished in 2014 by Popular Prakashan, Bombay)

———. 1997. *Teekasvayamvara* [Literary criticism in Marathi]. Aurangabad: Saket Prakashan.

———. 2010. The Marathi novel 1950–1975. In *Indian literary criticism. Theory and Interpretation*, ed. Ganesh Devy. Hyderabad: Orient BlackSwan.

## CHAPTER TEN

# Modernity, Memory and Magic Realism: Gabriel García Márquez and Malayalam Fiction

The reception of translated Latin American fiction in Malayalam, especially the works of Gabriel García Márquez, is an interesting instance of cultural translation and intertextual affiliation between languages and cultures. In countries such as India and Colombia, colonialism had made it impossible for writers to access their pre-colonial oral traditions. With his stunningly inventive idiom, Márquez broke the narrative mould modelled on European realism, and reinvented the novelistic form to embody the polyphonic plurality of a society where multiple time zones, with their shifting centres and expanding peripheries, co-existed. This chapter discusses the role of the storyteller as an institution with reference to the works of Márquez and Mario Vargas Llosa. Kerala's confrontation with colonial modernity had similarly created a crisis of authenticity, necessitating the search for an introspective idiom that could bring out the contradictions within. In this context, the chapter discusses Malayalam writers such as Sarah Joseph, M. Mukundan, N. S. Madhavan and Benyamin, to show the moral crisis of a society caught between materialist compulsions and mindless violence. For writers in Kerala, Márquez has become an enabling presence in the quest for an imaginative idiom that would recover alternative visions of indigenous modernity and life-giving community.

Apart from its passion for football and its history of communist and other radical Left movements, Kerala has these things in common with Latin American countries: a tropical climate; the history of colonialism; a rich store of folklore and mythology replete with magical and supernatural events and beings; a multicultural heritage with Christianity, Islam and Hinduism and 'pagan' beliefs coexisting in harmony; a long history of struggle against feudalism and colonialism which makes the state one of the most politically conscious (and volatile) regions of the subcontinent; and an openness to new experiences that reflects itself in constant experimentation in creative expression in literature, theatre, painting, cinema, and classical and popular art forms, ranging from the traditional to the modern. The Malayali diaspora is one of the largest and most visible among Indian diaspora communities – spread out as it is across the Gulf region, Europe and North America, not to mention Australia and other regions. Kerala is highly urbanised; and though it does not have a major metropolis, its culture is in constant contact with the global and the transnational through its citizens who are cosmopolitan in their outlook, even when their tastes in matters of culture can be extremely local. The large number of Malayalis who flock to the international film and theatre festivals held in the state every year and the large number of translations that appear in Malayalam, from languages beyond Europe and North America, further attest to the cosmopolitan character of the Malayali community. Of course, there is a dark underbelly to Kerala's modernity which complicates any discussion of contemporary Kerala. This will be dealt with in detail later in the chapter in the context of Malayalam fiction. The popularity of Márquez in Malayalam has to be understood against this complex web of political, social and cultural phenomena that sets the highly literate state of Kerala apart from the rest of India.

One may argue that the incomplete nature of Kerala's project of modernity is the most significant factor responsible for its readers' fascination with Márquez, who captures the contradictions of a society which lives in several time zones, from the primordial to the postmodern, in a language that transcends the binary of tradition–modernity or local–cosmopolitan. As we probe deeper, we find concerns and issues – which agitate Márquez – that have a bearing on the immediate context of the Malayali community. Before we explore Márquez's reception in Kerala, in terms of his influence on Malayalam fiction, let us discuss the breakthrough achieved by the narrative mode he popularised – magical realism. This narrative technique cannot be understood merely in terms of craftsmanship but has to be related to issues of the political in all its complexity. The peculiar combination of colonialism and modernity that had informed the writing traditions of Kerala since the nineteenth century, alienated writers from their own past, denying them access to their oral roots which now became remote and exotic. To get a clearer picture of the undercurrents of these writing traditions, we may examine the moral economy of social realism that attained a hegemonic status in the production of narratives in Kerala in the first half of the twentieth century, with reference to Raymond Williams's idea of 'knowable community'. This will help us delineate how Márquez made a fundamental difference to the knowledge subject and the knowing subject by shifting the optics of narration from the print-directed page to the oral context of storytelling. The crisis of narration that Márquez had to confront can be further illustrated with reference to Mario Vargas Llosa's *The Storyteller* (1987). This will help us map the epistemological leap achieved by magic realism and comprehend its telos in terms of a new conceptual grid. The nature of this shift will be outlined with examples from *One Hundred Years of Solitude* (1967) and subsequently, the implications of this shift for Malayalam writers will be elaborated with reference to some of the major representative fictional works of Malayalam during the last three decades.

## I

Raymond Williams, in his *The Country and the City* (1973), demonstrates how the country came to be invested with values and traits that suggested idyllic innocence and natural grace, even as the forces of industrial capitalism were pauperising the country to inhuman levels. The tendency to locate a golden age in one's childhood or back in the remote past was evidenced by successive generations of English authors, particularly poets, as the present became increasingly uninhabitable. Against this context, Williams observes that the pace of sweeping changes during the eighteenth century rendered the idea of a 'knowable community' unsustainable (1985, 165) – what is 'knowable' is not only 'a function of objects, of what is there to be known' but also 'a function of subjects, of observers—of what is desired and what needs to be known' (165). As the pace of urbanisation quickened, all those values that could not be sustained by the cultural environment of the city came to be associated with the country, creating a binary where the country becomes the Other of the city. As Williams observes, 'knowable community' is still a 'matter of consciousness, and of continuing as well as day-to-day experience' (166). The critique provided by Williams allows us to understand the way the social realist novelists of the nineteenth century shaped 'reality' from their limited perspectives. The moral economy of social realism operates from within a regulated social space where entire sections from lower classes are rendered invisible. For instance, in Jane Austen, the propertied class become neighbours even though removed by distance, while, those below that class never figure in the narrative. If and when poorer sections became visible in English fiction, 'it was not a certain disintegration of a traditional rural order but a change in literary bearings which bring into focus, a persistent rural disturbance that had previously been excluded or blurred' (166). This brings out the nature of the underlying transaction between the moral economy of social realism and the world view of the emergent bourgeoisie class. The central consciousness of a work of art has to recognise the social contradictions of a particular period, as part of an everyday world informed by prevailing ideological limits, to shape a narrative mode adequate to represent them. In the Latin American fiction of the first half of the twentieth century, the prevailing modes and models fail to recognise the ideological limits of the narrative structures in use. Does the emergence of magical realism mark a rupture in the tradition of narrative, or is it only a further stage of an earlier evolution in progress?

Gerald Martin, in his *Journeys through the Labyrinth: Latin American Fiction in the Twentieth Century* (1989), has argued that at the centre of Latin American experience, there is a sense of the violation of Mother America, 'aboriginal, virgin, fertile, creative and productive', by the 'superior' European outsider, 'cold, rationalist and covetous', creating 'the illegitimate Mestizo' who is afflicted by a dualism born of 'an unending dialectic of violation and vengeance' (1989, 10–11, 16). As the Latin American countries evolved into separate nations, the creolised Mestizo culture came to the forefront, and the political assertions symbolised by the long history of revolutions, from Mexico to Cuba, turned this figure into a native hero. The theme of 'solitude' that runs through Latin American literature is a reflection of the isolation of this figure of the Mestizo from the larger narrative of history. The writers in the nineteenth and early twentieth centuries were divided between the European and North American models, each claiming its own relative advantages for a people who did not find the choice between a collaborative Ariel and a rebellious Caliban easy in providing a viable alternative in their search for a stable identity.

During the first half of the twentieth century, the accent on regionalism produced a group of novels across Spanish America that were characterised by descriptions of landscapes, customs, local traditions, linguistic peculiarities, etc. 'The novel of the land' was a sub-category of the same group of novels which turned towards rural settings and physical environment as the shaping agents of the lives of characters. As can be seen in retrospect, the regionalist novel dealt with the external realities of the living environment, with little awareness about the subliminal layers of collective identity that shaped the consciousness of the people. Between the 1920s and 40s, social realism emerged as the dominant mode and its use privileged a certain 'knowable community' which shared the ideological world view of the novels. However, there is a paradigm shift in the manner in which the 'boom novels' of the 1960s evaluated the moral foundations of society. Martin's argument that magical realism is a climax and consummation of the earlier 'social realist' mode, is misplaced for several reasons. He argues that the 'boom novels' owed their creative breakthrough to the insights that James Joyce provided in *Ulysses* (1922). This seems to be farfetched. The 'Ulyssean moment' is significant for its critique of several hegemonic Euro-centric narratives, but it is still framed and contained by the tenets of Anglo-American modernism. Martin fails to note that the metaphor of the labyrinth has something organic about it in the context of South America, and was not borrowed from Joyce as a strategy. It emerged out of the specific cultural and historical conditions of Latin American authors who had no means of transcending them. The exploration of the resources of a spoken, local language as different from the standard imposed by a central authority; the fascination with the mythical; the obsessive immersion in popular culture; the condition of exile providing a critical point of view on European hegemony – all these are factors that cannot be traced to the sole authority of Joyce. Miguel Ángel Asturias's *Hombres de maiz* (*Men of Maize*, 1949), Juan Rulfo's *Pedro páramo* (1955) and Márquez's *Cien anos de soledad* (*One Hundred Years of Solitude*, 1967) are novels that break the narrative mould of Europe and North America to locate a specifically South American mode of knowing and representation. For the first time, in these novels, Latin American society becomes a knowledge subject as seen by the knowing subject which is, again, Latin American, and they are not constituted on European terms.

To see the crisis which Asturias, Rulfo and Márquez confronted, it is instructive to turn to Mario Vargas Llosa's *El hablador* (*The Storyteller*, 1987). This novel is as much about the act of writing the novel about Latin America as about the process of recovering the resources of oral tradition in a time and place where they are getting irretrievably lost. The novel begins when the narrator reaches Florence to spend some time away from Peru, his homeland. But he comes across some photographs in a gallery depicting the life of the 'natives of Amazon forest'. This brings back his memories of time spent with the Machiguenga community living on the banks of the Amazon, way back in his youth in 1958, when he was attending a 'Summer Institute in Linguistics' organised by an American Protestant organisation. One of his classmates in the University was Saul Zuratas who was indignant at the way the indigenous tribes of Peru were being treated by 'civilised' people. He mysteriously disappears after his graduation, rejecting an opportunity to carry out advanced research among the indigenous communities, which would have made him an authority in anthropology. He felt the discipline had only helped the colonisation of the indigenous people. They have been on the run during the last four centuries – from the Incas, from colonisers, from missionaries – and now they are scattered with all their cultural resources in shambles. In one of the early conversations between the narrator and Saul, the latter says, 'The extraordinary thing is that, despite so many disasters, they haven't disappeared. They are still there, surviving' (Llosa 2001, 20). In the course of the novel, we come to know how Saul has now abandoned the modern world altogether and become a member of the indigenous community. He raises the ethical problem in dealing with the pre-modern culture which disciplines like anthropology had refused to acknowledge:

> Do our cars, guns, planes, and Coca-Colas give us the right to exterminate them because they don't have such a thing? Or do you believe in civilizing the savages, pal? How? By making soldiers of them? By putting them to work on the farm as slaves to Creoles like Fidel Pereira? By forcing them to change their language, their religion, and their customs, the way missionaries are trying to do? (26)

The story is told from multiple perspectives, alternate chapters embodying the voice of the modern sceptical narrator, who thinks there is no escape from the compulsions of modernity, with that of the age-old storyteller, which is an institution among the indigenous tribes, keeping the scattered people together with their counterparts and also with their own past. The chapters spoken by the storyteller form a flowing narrative that defies the gravity of linear narrative modes, moving between creation myths, trickster stories and tales of death and redemption, often reminding us of Greek tragedies, Shakespeare and Kafka, but transcending the demands of social realist or modernist narrative modes. There are many references to Kafka's *Metamorphosis* (1915) in the narrative. We are told that Saul almost knew it by heart. In one of the chapters, we hear the storyteller, who is none other than Saul transformed into a member of the indigenous community, speak of his own transformation in terms of Kafka's story:

> I had people. I had a family. I was asleep. Then I woke up. I had barely opened my eyes when I understood. Alas, poor Tasurinchi! I had changed into an insect, that's what. A buzz-buzz bug, perhaps. A Gregor-Tasurinchi. I was lying on my back. The world had grown bigger, it seemed to me. I was aware of everything. Those hairy, ringed legs were my legs. Those transparent mud-colored wings, which creaked when I moved and hurt me so much, had once been my arms. The stench that surrounded me: was that my odour? I saw the world differently: I could see the underside and the top, the back and the front, at the same time. Because now, being an insect, I had several eyes. What's happened to you, Gregor-Tasurinchi? Did a bad witch eat a lock of your hair and change you? Did a little kamagarini devil get into you through your ass-eye and turn you into this. I was covered with shame at seeing myself the way I was. (203)

This moment of self-loathing captures the plight of the Latin American mestizo who is trapped in an alien body with no reprieve for his tortured consciousness. We can also remember the defining moment when Márquez discovered Kafka through *Metamorphosis* and remarked that he never knew he had permission to write in this manner.

The storyteller's voice is at the centre of the magic realist narrative, problematising the project of modernity that countries like Colombia had known as predatory plunders of their natural resources and ruthless exploitation of the community, disrupting their own native ways of living, feeling and relating to the world of humans and animals. Cultures such as that of the Machiguenga have no defence against the 'superior' artefacts of modern civilisation. They are condemned to live in the periphery with no sight of a viable alternative to build a new life. It is this impasse that Márquez sensed and articulated from the other side of the divide, siding with the indigenous community and its everyday world of constructing a fictional habitat for the living community. Here, we may also see the underlying reason why fictional works from Latin America fascinate the Malayali reader. For a society where radical movements have failed and consumerism has triumphed with its unbridled predatory impulse, fragmented selves are unable to piece together a communitarian narrative on the foundation of shared values. The project of modernity has brought them to an impasse, from where they can neither turn back nor go forward. Márquez's, or Llosa's, writings are about neither magic nor realism – they talk of the limited ethical choices that confront those who had invested in modernity and have now come to recognise that they have been betrayed. The question of form in Márquez points to a deeper moral crisis to which we will turn in the following section, in a brief analysis of *One Hundred Years of Solitude.* This is why attempts to position magical realism as 'a modern and contemporary global narrative genre', as done by Wendy Faris in her *Ordinary Enchantments: Magical Realism and the Mystification of Narrative*, are not convincing (Walker 2007, 511), even when Faris recognises it as a genre with its own textual poetics and cultural politics.

## 2

Márquez was deeply constrained by prevailing narrative conventions, because those conventions were complicit in the act of reproducing the dominant ideology. One of the first things that *One Hundred Years of Solitude* (hereinafter referred to as *One Hundred*) does is to erase the idea of a referential frame of reality, problematising the limited perspective of knowability cultivated by the social realist mode. A sentence such as the following, 'The world was so recent that many things lacked names, and in order to indicate them it was necessary to point' (1996, 1), simultaneously stages an erasure and an inscription. The optics of the narrative are altered and the limits of knowability, as regulated by prevailing perspectives, are dislocated from the page. We enter an enchanted world which has been restored to its primeval freshness through immersion in the language of the storyteller who is inseparable from the community. The celebrated first sentence of *One Hundred* is not spoken by an individual but performed by a 'community voice' as an act of ritual which weaves us into its sacred space as participants. The novel breathtakingly moves along the axis of the community space of collective memories, invoking the historical through a matrix of metaphors that register every event as a deep sensation.

In the story of the Buendía family, running into generations, we have the saga of a small town as well as the history of Latin America in the last century. Lost in the wilderness of the swamp, much like Aracataca, the author's own village, it is shaken out of its isolation by the colonising American banana companies which finally abandon it to oblivion, thoroughly ravaged. Before the invasion of the banana companies, the only visitors Macondo had from the outside world were the gypsies who every year brought the marvels of science such as the magnet, the magnifying glass or the ice. The colonial onslaught on the primordial rhythm of Macondo upsets the inhabitants to such an extent that no one knew for certain where the limits of reality lay. The first time a railway train makes its appearance in Macondo, a woman who was washing clothes in the river ran screaming down the main street in an alarming state of panic: 'It is coming', she finally explained, 'something like a kitchen dragging a village behind it'. The people of Macondo could not accept the new age of wonders as they had welcomed the gypsies' marvels. When an actor who was playing a character who died and was buried in one film reappeared in another film as another character, the audience would not accept that outlandish fraud and vandalised the seats in the theatre. The banana plague turns Macondo into a tormented society without dignity. The old policemen came to be replaced by hired assassins with machetes. When a seven-year-old boy accidentally bumped into a corporal and spilled the soft drink he was drinking on the policeman's uniform, the boy was cut into pieces. The corporal also beheaded the old grandfather accompanying the boy. Márquez writes, 'The whole town saw the decapitated man pass by as a group of men carried him to his house, with a woman dragging the head along by its hair, and the bloody sack with the pieces of the child' (196).

The sixteen children of Colonel Aureliano Buendía are murdered in different parts of the country on the same night, under the colonial dispensation. The braiding of the mnemonic and the historical is constant throughout the narrative, as the author invokes a world which was never documented in official versions of history. The wretched passivity that the people of Macondo sink into is juxtaposed against their heroic exploits in the Civil War which lasted twenty years. Colonel Buendía's efforts to start another war against the colonial invaders evoke no response from the veterans of the earlier war. They were waiting for old-age pensions, 'dying of hunger, living through rage, rotting of old age amid the exquisite shit of glory' (200). In his youth, Colonel Buendía had fought on the side of the Liberals, who were reputed to be free thinkers. It was the sight of soldiers killing a woman with rifle butts which prompted Colonel Buendía to become a rebel and a legendary warrior. He had organised thirty-two armed uprisings, all of which he lost, survived fourteen attempts on his life, seventy-three ambushes and a firing squad. In his twilight years, he finds his society reduced to impotence and lethargy. He observes in disgust, 'The only difference today between Liberals and Conservatives is that the Liberals go to mass at five o'clock and the conservatives at eight' (200). Marquez rightly comments that races condemned to one hundred years of solitude do not get a second chance on earth.

Obviously, the Third World reality is a comedy of terrors that demands a constant redefinition of the past. This is where Kerala and Macondo become indistinguishable. Márquez was reclaiming the past in all its polyphony so that official versions of history can be resisted. In Latin America, or India, one comes across sanitised versions of the past which deny the present generation access to the complex stages through which the society has passed through. This has to be seen in the context of the 'plotting' of history by imperial powers. As Dipesh Chakrabarty points out, 'Europe remains the sovereign, theoretical subject of all histories, including the ones we call Indian, Kenyan, Chinese and so on' (2008, 147). History, with a capital 'H', is always already plotted into a European code that erases non-European experiences. To create a non-European code means recovering a location that provides effective resistance to its ideological moorings.

Márquez worked on the material for this novel for more than twenty years, till the narrative emerged as a whole from a tone that was elegiac and comical at the same time, because he was condemned to remember what his tribe wanted to forget. As Márquez once observed, 'Latin American history is made up of immense useless enterprises and great dramas which are condemned to oblivion in advance. We also suffer from the plague of memory. With the passage of time, nobody remembers that the massacre of the banana company workers actually took place. All they remember is Colonel Aureliano Buendía' (Mendoza 1982, 73). The act of narration thus becomes an act of resistance against accepted notions of truth, because the novelist has the power to challenge the 'common sense' which is promoted through authenticated voices of authority. That Márquez is aware of this fact comes through in his words:

> Description is itself a political act . . . . Redescribing a world is the necessary first step towards changing it. And particularly at times when the state takes reality into its own hands, and sets about distorting it, altering the past to fit the present needs, then the making of the alternative realities of art, including the novel of memory becomes politicised. "The struggle of man against power," Milan Kundera has written, "is the struggle of memory against forgetting." (Butcher 1983, 78)

Culture is memory, and the dynamics of memory sets in motion acts of imagination that opens up the world. Faced with the strong compulsions to orient themselves towards the colonial world and its rationality, countries like Colombia and India are forced to forget their past. One of the striking metaphors in the opening chapters of *One Hundred* is the plague of insomnia and amnesia that strikes Macondo. José Arcadio Buendía decides to build a 'memory machine' which will bring back the essentials of the life they have been living: 'He conceived of it as a spinning dictionary that a person placed on the axis could operate by means of a lever, so that in very few hours there would pass before his eyes the notions most necessary for life' (49). It is at that point that the old gypsy, who had been a constant presence in their lives through his annual visits, arrives and he is able to cure the entire village of its plague in a matter of hours.

The figure of the gypsy merges into that of the storyteller because he holds together a pre-modern world where life is not classified or categorised into hierarchies. The 'marvellous' is another term for the blurring of boundaries. The liminal figure of the gypsy allows a blurring of the boundaries between the everyday and the infinite, the mundane and the mythical, a guarded interior of customs and rituals with a wandering periphery of ever expanding knowledge. We must remember that the figure of the gypsy is a literary construct, European in origin, with the mark of otherness deeply imprinted through several literary echoes. Issues of migrancy, social marginality and exclusion from hierarchies of power are written into this figure who cannot be assimilated into the given frames of 'knowable community' without disrupting it. The effect of his presence in the opening page is not unlike the unhinging effect of the magnet that is dragged along the street, by Melquiades:

> He went from house to house dragging two metal ingots and everybody was amazed to see pots, pans, tongs, and braziers tumble down from their places and beams creak from the desperation of nails and screws trying to emerge, and even objects that had been lost for a long time, appeared from where they had been searched for most and went dragging along in turbulent infusion behind Melquiades' magical irons. (2)

Melquiades unsettles the set rhythms of the provincial town withdrawn into its privacy, allowing it access to a wide world of imagination.

When Melquiades returns as a decrepit old man, he finds shelter in the Buendía family home. He spends all his days furiously writing the past of the tribe on parchments. Soon it appears that he is decoding not the past but the future, and the parchments run parallel to the novel as it records in minute details the fate of the Buendía family: 'At that prodigious instant Melquiades' final keys were revealed to him and he saw the epigraph of the parchments perfectly placed in the order of man's time and space: the first of the line is tied to a tree and the last is being eaten by the ants' (420). Aureliano now reads the parchments loudly, standing in the dim light of the room where he has shut himself up – the history of the family, written by Melquiades, down to the most trivial details, one hundred years ahead of time. Revealing the master key to read the present novel, Márquez writes, 'Melquiades had not put events in the order of man's conventional time, but had concentrated a century of daily episodes, in such a way that they co-existed in one instant' (421). The contingency of everyday life as lived from day to day, and the fragmented narrative of collective memory in all its sensuous intensity, collapse into each other, where nothing exists outside the instant of its apprehension and physical possession. What the novel reveals is what is unspoken but preordained as a prophetic course of collective destiny:

> Aureliano skipped eleven pages so as not to lose time with facts he knew only too well, and he began to decipher the instant that he was living, deciphering it as he lived it, prophesying himself, in the act of deciphering the last page of the parchments, as if he were looking into a speaking mirror. Then he skipped again to anticipate the predictions and ascertain the date and circumstance of his death. Before reaching the final line, however, he had already understood that he would never leave that room, for it was foreseen that the city of mirrors (or mirages) would be wiped out by the wind and exiled from the memory of men at the precise moment when Aureliano Babilonia would finish deciphering the parchments, and that everything written on them was unrepeatable since time immemorial and forever more, because races condemned to one hundred years of solitude did not have a second opportunity on earth. (422)

Finally, the voice that we hear in the novel is that of the wandering Jew, the marginal man who is excluded from all written histories, and who is condemned to tell the stories that will return the people to their homelands. He is the healer who knows that there is nothing outside the story – the community will survive as long as they have the will to tell and listen to stories. It is difficult to find another text that leaves such a deep sense of loss and bleakness along with an equally strong sense of exhilaration and freedom in the mind of the reader.

## 3

In this section, we will briefly discuss some representative fictional works with certain Márquezian traits from Malayalam literature. This is not to suggest that the writers have borrowed narrative strategies or thematic concerns from Márquez, but to point to a subliminal stratum of shared socio-political experiences and patterns of thought, shaped by ideological conditions and implicated in history. Sarah Joseph's *Aalahayude penmakkal* (Alaha's daughters, 1999) and M. Mukundan's *Kesavante vilapangal* (Kesavan's lamentations, 1999) are both accomplished works in Malayalam. I use them here to suggest how concerns and issues treated in these novels remind us of similar questions dealt with in Latin American fiction.

Sarah Joseph's vision is informed by ideologies that have liberatory potentials, but it eschews the reductive tendencies one associates with such categories. She uses the potential of the form of the novel to communicate the transformation of Kerala in the post-Independence period with a retrospective look towards the community formation in Kerala. Many novelists in Malayalam tend to use the novel without knowing that the form has its own ideology, and this often results in the form contradicting what they are trying to say through the content of the novel. But in *Aalahayude penmakkal*, the visionary element is built into the structure and woven into the silence that envelopes the central characters – Annie and Ammama (Annie's grandmother).

It is the power of the language to map a locality and invoke a community that makes *Aalahayude penmakkal* refreshingly different. The local dialect is implicated in community history and to bring it into a dialogic relation with the world of imagination, it is necessary to see that a living society is more than just the sum of its parts. It is not a mere inventory which social realist novelists make it out to be. One has to locate its organic bonds in its clusters of tales that encapsulate the very habitat of its language. It is here that the central character Ammama reminds us of Ursula in *One Hundred*. In both Márquez and Sarah Joseph, the figure of the grandmother is the unifying factor. All through the chaos of the civil war and the mindless violence of the banana companies, Ursula had ensured the survival of the family as a unit. When she finally becomes senile, the familial authority is eroded to such an extent that the world of Macondo falls apart. In Sarah Joseph's novel, through the tragedies and travails of the family, Ammama carries the burden of the entire family with a will power that makes her a memorable character.

*Aalahayude penmakkal* is set in Kokkanchira, which had once marked the outer limit of the town of Thrissur in central Kerala, and was used as a dumping ground. This *poromboke* (wasteland) becomes home to the homeless and the abandoned, and starts bustling with life. The original inhabitants of this land were the scavengers, butchers, rickshaw pullers, bootleggers and other such marginals of the town. We learn these facts from what Ammama tells the young Annie. Annie is close to her grandmother who is perennially busy tending to the unending daily chores of the family. Of her five daughters, only Cherichi has found a happy home after marriage. The eldest daughter's husband died on the eighth day of her marriage. Another daughter is married to the brother of Annie's mother, Lasser. He tortures his wife because his sister has been abandoned by her husband. The other two daughters are unmarried. Of the two sons, the younger one, afflicted by tuberculosis, is bedridden. The elder one, Annie's father, left home about eight years ago and has been untraceable. Annie's mother often blames her mother-in-law for all these tragedies. This is because Ammama, the grandmother, has her own rituals which many consider un-Christian and profane. For instance, she has a special prayer, which she calls *Aalaha's namaskaram* (homage to Aalaha). She recites it with her eyes closed and the body in a trance. Women from the neighbourhood often bring their children to her when they refuse to stop crying. Once on her lap, and under the magic of the recitation, the children will sleep calmly. Annie's mother, a God-fearing Catholic, disapproves of such practices. She bares her bitterness in vicious outbursts. She blames all the misfortunes of the family on Ammama's sacrilegious ways. At the outset of the novel, we see Ammama reciting her magical prayer because they have come across a bone while digging in the courtyard. The fact is, anywhere you dig in Kokkanchira you will come up with a skull or a broken bone.

The world in the novel is seen through Annie's consciousness which registers every small movement in her environment. The bean plant with its white and violet flowers in the courtyard casts a spell around her and transforms the everyday world of grief and despair into one of light and grace, dispelling the larger evils of the everyday world. This represents an ecological vision which the novel gradually weaves into the material and the metaphorical world of women. This novel is essentially about women's struggle to sustain their world against heavy odds. The men are either missing or wasted characters who have no 'presence' even when they are around. Annie finds the adult world mysterious and unintelligible. Her bedridden uncle uses words which remind her of the language of her textbooks. He was once a political activist and still retains his secular beliefs. (The only time he gets up from his bed and comes up to the door is when Annie's mother splits his charka [spinning wheel] into pieces for use as fire wood in the kitchen.) Annie constantly thinks of the words she does not understand. Ammama calls the woman next door '*machi*' (a barren woman) but Annie does not know what the term means. She also does not understand why she is forbidden to use the word '*mula*' (breast). Aunt Cherichi's visit, along with her husband, a Protestant priest, is an occasion Annie still remembers. It was on that day that Annie understood that her mother was poor and shabby, and that she herself was dirty compared to her cousins. The days are hard and there is famine constantly round the corner. Rice is a scarce commodity. Her mother, a committed Catholic, spends all her time in the church because the entire Kerala is on the boil as the Catholic Church and the Congress Party are on a warpath against the first elected communist government of Kerala. Annie knows that her father, whom she has never seen, was not a believer. And so she cannot shout slogans against the '*commus*' (the communists) whom her mother finds embodiments of evil. The manner in which Sarah Joseph interweaves the political turmoil and religious conflicts into the everyday of the family's struggle provides the narrative a rare resonance, as in Márquez's fiction.

There is no way one can keep the relentless march of time at bay. Kokkanchira is changing and 'big money' and 'market' invade it. In Márquez, we have seen that societies which are brought up in the privacy and solitude of their conventional wisdom become powerless in resisting the predatory violence of capitalist forces. One area of Kokkanchira known as 'ettummuri' is purchased by a business man, Emandon Varu. The local church is hand in gloves with him. The women try to convince their men to protest but they lose their courage before the priest. Annie's activist uncle tries to mobilise the locals against the eviction, but he is ill and helpless. Varu takes over the locality and pulls down the houses. Annie walks through the broken bricks of the houses which now house memories of many generations. The people who have lost their homes are scattered and leave, without any idea about how they are going to survive. The lumpen elements of the locality, who always used to be seen around the market, also disintegrate as they have no place to hang out. Swanky offices of financial enterprises dot the street now. One can mortgage land or gold here to borrow money at exorbitant interest rates. The open land that belonged to Konni Mestry is purchased by the church and a new convent school comes up there, for rich children who can eat with forks and knives. The bean plants in the courtyard were crushed by the steamroller which came to widen the road. The old Kokkanchira is dead and gone and in its place, gated communities with warnings such as 'Keep Silence' and watchdogs come up everywhere.

The novel ends on an apocalyptic note, reminiscent of the dust storm that erases Macondo at the end of *One Hundred.* When Ammama sees the steamroller she is reminded of the British army she had seen long ago in the town of Thrissur. Torrential rains which continue for weeks flood Kokkanchira. Their house is tottering on its foundations. Annie sees her father coming towards her with an apple, rowing on the floodwaters. The activist uncle's last words are: 'All movements are finally betrayed'. The bleakness one finds in the apocalyptic vision at the end is negated by the energy of the language that redeems and rebuilds. In both Márquez and Sarah Joseph, the language approaches the incantatory force of a collective chant towards the end of the narratives. Ammama clasps Annie to her body and stands against the floodwaters in a final gesture of defiance against the impending doom. She recites *Aalaha's namaskaram*, this time instructing Annie in its contents, binding her in its message of survival through struggle. This oral performance in Malayalam invokes Kerala's rich history of oral folklore and complex poetic of ritual performances that confront the violence of contemporary dislocations in a desperate struggle to hold on to an idea of collective society. This is a message that only a woman who has survived through the force of her will and the power of her hope can give. Its power to create and sustain a community is what makes it the poetic of a communitarian discourse. That the novel integrates it into the economy of its narration makes it a metaphor for an order of experience that is yet to find full articulation in the Malayalam novel.

Ammama reminds us of the 'Earth Mother'. She is the storyteller and the deity of birthing, preservation and survival, who lives in the present. She stands against the forces of ruin that envelope an entire society. Annie's character holds out a lot of promise which the novelist has not fully utilised. She remains in the shadow of her grandmother. But their bonding lightens up the pages of this novel. At the end, she spits blood, even as her uncle collapses and dies, and floodwaters enter their rickety house. Ammama has passed on to her the ability to invest space with charm and meaning. The chanting of *Aalaha's namaskaram* is one of the finest moments in the narrative, where language becomes pure energy, kinetic and consoling. Sarah Joseph reminds the reader of writers such as Toni Morrison and Márquez, who use the power of orality and myth-making to reinvent a community. This is also true of Sarah Joseph's novel. Her ability to invent the prayer is a tribute to the imaginative power of an entire society. Myth and memory are, finally, repositories of survival for a community. The activist uncle dies a broken man, but Annie sees her grandmother standing against the storm waters, assertive and emphatic. When we look back, we remember how Ammama never lost her sense of human dignity, all through her dehumanising misery. Annie has always been possessed by words. Words are haunted because they always carry traces from the past. The novel does not talk of the 'Word' but words, as enactments of our everyday world of hope and misery. When ideologies fail, the magical power of storytelling can reclaim a lost community from the ruins of life.

Another novel which compels our attention here is M. Mukundan's *Kesavan's Lamentations* (*Kesavante vilapangal* in Malayalam) published in 1999. Márquez repeatedly wrote about the political reality of Latin American countries where the line between politics and mythification is narrow. In novels such as *The Autumn of the Patriarch* (1975) and *The General in His Labyrinth* (1989), Márquez maps the decay and decadence that set in after revolutionary movements lose their capacity to inspire people. The unnamed general of the former lives for more than two hundred years, only to see his empire crumbling, but clings to the illusion of his omnipotence by recasting his memories in the present. He had exercised power with such brutality and ruthlessness that no one would believe that he has been reduced to a shadow of his past, drifting in his own nightmares and imprisoned in his jumbled memories. What Márquez unveils is the mystique of power and the pathos of human life against the myth of invincibility perpetuated by popular perceptions. This is done with greater authority and precision in *The General in His Labyrinth*, which portrays the last days of Simón Bolívar, the liberator of Colombia. He flees his own land to become an exile in Europe, but during his last journey from Bogota to the coast, his health deteriorates, and he dies a broken man, aware of his country descending into anarchy and violence.

Mukundan raises an important question in his novel: what happens to the dreams that inspire people's movements? Here it has to be mentioned that M. Mukundan is a major Malayalam novelist with more than twenty-five novels to his credit, all of them well-known to Malayalam readers. Mukundan is not indebted to Márquez in any manner as he is a writer with a clear vision of life and politics. However, what I find relevant in the discussion is Mukundan's exploration of the process through which a man becomes a myth and passes into popular imagination. Written in 1999, after the breakup of the Soviet Union and the emergence of a globalised India, *Kesavan's Lamentations* is also a critique of the decline of values that is sucking Kerala into the quagmire of violence and communal hatred.

The novel is about E. M. S. Namboodiripad, the legendary communist leader from Kerala, the deified hero of revolutionary Marxism whose sharp intellect shaped the official party line for close to five decades. The novel does a tightrope walk between the myth that is EMS and the reality of everyday living in Kerala, creating a double-voiced discourse which scoffs at all manners of grandiloquence, whether it is the radical variety of extreme Left or the theoretical variety of scholarly writing. The novel presents two characters who speak the truth bluntly and fearlessly – the two drunkards of the village who have no allegiance to any ideology.

In the novel, the protagonist Kesavan is a novelist with four novels to his credit. He works in an office. The dull rhythm of his eventless life is disrupted by the occasional visits of his literary friends like Ravunni and Pavithran. When Ravunni comes to know that Kesavan's latest novel is about EMS, he asks him, 'What do you know about Eeyyemmess? One should not write about what one does not know' (2006, 11). He goes on to quote Vaclav Havel to the effect that one should always write about what one knows. The novel within the novel traces the story of Ananthakrishnan and his son, Appukkuttan. Ananthakrishnan is a former Naxalite, the radical Left outfit which believed in violent means to overthrow the state, and has now become a convert to orthodox Hinduism. After his wife's death, he brings up his son all alone. Appukkuttan, right from his days in the cradle, is devoted to EMS who is the sole subject of his devotion. Ananthakrishnan wants to bring him up as an apolitical being but in the company of Aaman sir, a teacher in the local school and a card-carrying communist, Appukkuttan becomes even more drawn towards the myth of EMS. Under Aaman's tutelage, he does well in studies, but also becomes a regular member of the Communist Party, to the great distress of Ananthakrishnan. His worst fears are finally proved right when the young Appukkuttan is arrested in a murder case. He had murdered one of the drunkards in the village who was about to dishonour a photograph of EMS.

The 'lamentations' of the title suggests the travails of Kesavan, the novelist who feels constrained in contemporary Kerala by its polarisations of various kinds. As a creative artist, he feels suffocated in his society. The thirty-seventh chapter of the novel contains a speech given by Kesavan to some college students. The speech makes it apparent that he is under pressure to align himself with public and political positions. He finds such compulsions detrimental to an artist whose real struggle is with the material at hand, which involves the lives of his imaginary characters drawn from life around him. At the beginning of the novel, we see Kesavan's intense loneliness as he tries to transform his mental images into the verbal form. He drifts through the routine acts of attending to work at his office and living his domestic life with a sense of unreality. For the people at large, he is a celebrity, but he considers himself a failure. Kesavan is pestered by neighbours for recommendations and his friends blame him for not pursuing positions of power in literary academies. He is forever discontented as a writer as he is not happy with what he has produced as a writer. When he is happy with the title of the novel he is writing, he feels the kind of relief one feels 'upon coming back home from walking in the scorching sun' (73). He feels the pressure of the thousands of yet-to-be-written words of the novel as he pushes forward with its storyline. What isolates him from the world around him is the invisible struggle of a creative artist whose final test is not his ideology but his self-expression through a medium which poses constant challenges. He is amazed when EMS, the great leader of whom he is engaged in writing a novel, pays a visit to his house, to bless his project. Kesavan is obviously confused because his quest has very little to do with the real EMS.

This is also the moment when the two narratives in the text – the novel and the novel within the novel – meet and the fictional and the metafictional confront each other. In a poignant moment in the novel, Aaman sir and Appukkuttan travel all the way to Kannur to participate in a political rally. The huge maidan explodes into excited slogans as EMS appears on the stage: 'Far away, on the stage, decorated by red flags and streamers, EMS rose like a red sun. As if the sun, which had already sunk in the western horizon, had come back, the entire stage was imbued with a red light'(143). Here Mukundan captures the mystique of EMS as a mass leader, from the outside. But this is more of a spectacle than substance. One should note that mass movements are produced by such single-minded devotion to leaders and their ideologies. Those who know the history of modern Kerala cannot deny that the communist movement was emancipatory in the real sense, bringing dignity to peasants and workers from the lower castes, oppressed for ages. But it is equally true that those achievements appear remote as the Communist Party, now splintered into several groups, haggle after political power with little idealism of any kind. This is why Appukkuttan's obsession with EMS looks more like a morbid affliction than a pursuit of an ideal. Kesavan ironically writes that Appukkuttan had impaired vision, and when he is prescribed a pair of glasses, he is glad to find that he resembles the young EMS with his glasses. He is not inspired by the dream of emancipation, which is personified by EMS, but is fascinated by the myth of EMS which makes him a larger-than-life figure. The communist movement in present-day Kerala has become moribund, unable to reinvent itself in the globalised environment. In this sense, Mukundan is lamenting a certain erosion of imagination, a loss of creativity within Kerala society. Aaman sir, the mechanical Marxist, we are told, 'doesn't know how to dream' (173).

Kesavan writes that the two alcoholics in the village are the only two people who have no illusions of any kind. Saravanan, the failed Naxalite, also joins their ranks and gives a stirring speech about the failure of our political movements: 'The Congressmen who brought about the first Independence and the Communists who brought about the second Independence are two sides of the same coin. What they wanted was only power' (196). Adressing the other two drunks, he says, 'We three drunks are the creation of the two Independences earned by spilling blood, and sacrificing lives' (196). The grand narrative of political revolution is reduced to a farcical footnote with a cynicism that is characteristic of the present Kerala society. After completing his novel, Kesavan himself takes to drinking. And one night, while on his way home from the local toddy shop, he is brutally killed by unknown assassins.

The original novel in Malayalam ends with a footnote that says, 'Kesavan had bequeathed his copyright to the novel to Aravindan. After Kesavan's death, Aravindan became rich.' However, in the English translation, the endnote goes like this: 'The axe (used to kill Kesavan) symbolises the RSS–Marxist conflicts in Kannur region that have claimed many innocent lives' (228). It is true that the novel hints at the gradual drift of the society into a communal frenzy. Mukundan seems to be pointing at a larger collective failure to preserve the state's achievements gained through reformist and resistance movements over a period of time, creating a secular-modern Kerala with its own regional brand of social liberation. Its achievements in literature and films testify to this regional modernity that has deep roots in the popular consciousness. The rise of mindless consumerism and the death of ideological debates have led Kerala to the brink of a moral precipice. Mukundan feels that fiction has the ability to raise moral issues that rigid ideological positions cannot address. He reminds us that questions of creativity, love, hate, the desire to dominate and control others, and moral questions of failure and success and countless similar existential issues will continue to haunt us, despite the solutions provided by ideological positions.

## 4

Mukundan's novel points to a failure of moral imagination in contemporary Kerala. He also hints at the demons that are incubating in the social space, which can further break up the society. While writers of preceding generations played an active role in setting the socio-cultural agenda of Kerala, shaping its future priorities and directions, the same degree of involvement and concern for larger social issues is not found among the young generation of Malayalam writers. With the unprecedented spread of media, the space for literature seems to have further shrunken. Literature demands a longtime perspective and a concern for humanity at large, beyond the narrow limits of the society one lives in. One of the challenges that the young writers in Kerala face today is to develop the capacity for reflection and self-criticism that enables them to go against the grain, wake up from the stupor of the shallow conformism that characterises the consumerist middle class and take a principled stand which may involve challenging the 'establishment'. Writers have to battle the demons that are both within and without. The larger moral crisis faced by the society has to be creatively confronted by writers, within the space of their art and through the rigour of their medium.

We will now discuss a few well-known contemporary short stories in Malayalam, to discuss how present-day Malayalam literature captures the demonic and contingent within the frame of everyday experience. They will also remind us of the parallels between the Latin American and Kerala situations. This discussion may indicate an artistic way of confronting a deeper moral crisis which cannot be resolved in terms of earlier modes of expression or articulation. The literary texts cited here as examples deal with the everyday life of contemporary Kerala. However, they also cross the limits of the state's boundaries, in search of a transcendental moment of transgression. That both the stories discussed here allude to Latin American situations, through figures or texts, adds to their significance. These are stories that have, during the last decade, delineated the moral crisis that Kerala is passing through. The stories that need to be highlighted in this context include C. Ayyappan's *Bhrantu* (Madness, 2008), K. R. Meera's *Aave Maria* (2006), Chandramathi's *Ratnakarante bharya* (Ratnakaran's wife, 2011), S. Sitara's *Agni* (The fire, 2001), Santhosh Echikkanam's *Comala* (2005), Benyamin's *Eeyemmassum penkuttiyum* (EMS and the girl, 2012) and Subhash Chandran's *Parudeesa nashtam* (Loss of paradise, 2000). These stories are able to internalise into their very verbal texture the tension of having to live a double life in a society where conformity has become a way of life and creativity is suspect. In the following section, we will briefly discuss N. S. Madhavan's *Higuita* and Santhosh Echikkanam's *Comala*.

*Higuita*, which has been voted as one of the ten best Malayalam short stories of the last century, uses metaphors of visual media to examine questions of power and marginality. This story is notable for its use of visual imagery which charges the narrative with a heightened sense of perception. The story is about how a tribal from Bihar, Lucy, now a housemaid in Delhi and threatened by a tout called Jabbar, is saved by Father Geevarghese, a priest from Kerala. Father Geevarghese has been a football enthusiast and is inspired by the Colombian goalkeeper, René Higuita, to transcend his traditional priestly role to take on Jabbar. In the final scene, Madhavan uses the language of the game of football to describe Geevarghese's act of transgression:

> The Colombian goalkeeper, Higuita, appeared on TV as a footnote to Father Geevarghese's study of goalkeepers. Higuita, with his long black hair – emulating Lord Shiva in his cosmic dance – dark, granite face and thin moustache, was an exception among goalkeepers.
>
> A goal keeper's regular function is that of a mute witness. He forgoes it only when he faces a penalty kick and acquires, instead, a short spell of stage-fright. But Higuita marched nonchalantly into the thick of events. Like a sailor discovering new latitudes, he would dribble left and right and advance right into the centre of the field, a territory no goalkeeper has ever seen.
>
> . . . . . . . . . . . . . .
>
> At last it happened. The opposing team's forward took possession of the ball from the advancing Higuita's legs, scored into the open goal and sent Colombia crashing out of the World Cup. But only Father Geevarghese noticed the ghost of a smile which played on Higuita's lips as he ruminated over his role in the incident. (1992, 62)

The rest of the story describes how Father Geevarghese goes in search of Jabbar and confronts him with a resolve inspired by Higuita's act of transgression. He beats up Jabbar till 'blood oozed from Jabbar's nose as he hit the floor with a thud' (64). He warns Jabbar that he should not be seen again in Delhi. What makes the visual metaphor of the game of football acquire the mystique of a moment of terror and beauty – that is often at the core of magic realism – is its combination of controlled violence and transgression. In breaking the rules of the game, Higuita becomes a hero and an outcast, a winner and a victim at the same time. Madhavan's story revolves around this ambivalence that constitutes the Higuita moment of self-discovery, which needs the act of transgression as an essential condition. There is a moment of self-reflexivity here which Madhavan shares with Márquez in several of his fictional works. In locating a parallel from the everyday, where the same moment of moral ambivalence is enacted on a different plane, the story enacts the everyday moral crisis of inertia and passivity that has afflicted Kerala society, and opens up a possibility to represent something that had hitherto lacked a metaphorical articulation.

Santhosh Echikkanam's story, *Comala*, is another narrative that was received in Malayalam with great enthusiasm and approval. The title establishes an intertextual relation with Juan Rulfo's *Pedro páramo* (1955), a novel located in a town of the dead, Comala, where all inhabitants have been dead for a long time. As Gerard Martin observes, 'Do they exist in myth, in memory, in the historically constructed consciousness of every Mexican peasant, or indeed, every modern Mexican? We do not know. We do not need to' (1989, 180).

Echikkanam's story is about a villager, Viswam, who is tricked into standing surety for a loan by a close friend who then vanishes without a trace. The bank now threatens to attach or auction off a small plot of land that Viswam owns, to recover the loan. Out of despair, he puts up a note in front of his house – that he, along with his family, will commit suicide on the coming Independence Day. The narrative begins in the form of a live discussion being conducted on a television channel, which alternates between the naïve laments of Viswam in his heartrending rustic words, the bureaucratic arrogance of the bank manager who quotes the relevant clauses from law books, and the impersonal comments of a psychologist who provides a 'scientific' discourse on the act of committing suicide. The writer deftly caricatures the insensitivity of the media which turns the tragic plight of a poor villager into a public spectacle, to exploit its commercial possibility. However, the story moves out of this frame when Viswam goes for a long journey to look for his missing friend. He fails to trace the friend; and while returning, he witnesses an accident where a young man who has fallen from a motorcycle lies unattended on the road, bleeding to death. When no one comes forward to help, Viswam takes him to the hospital. But the young man dies, even as Viswam gives him water. At that moment, Viswam recovers his will to live and struggle.

In Rulfo's novel, Comala has no signs of life left when the protagonist reaches the town in search of his father. Echikkanam seems to suggest that present-day Kerala presents a similar state of bleak lifelessness and insensitivity. What is remarkable about the story is the protagonist's turning away from death and despair through a traumatic encounter with death. The rawness of this encounter is a descent into hell that lifts the veil from the character's defeatist stance.

In the stories of Madhavan and Echikkanam one comes across images of visual media. In Echikkanam's story, during the televised debate, the psychologist refers to Comala, while drawing attention to the high suicide rate in Kerala: 'If we go on like this, in a span of about eight years, Kerala will become a state of the dead, like the town of Comala described in the famous novel *Pedro páramo* by Juan Rulfo. All of us become dead people. Kerala becomes Comala and Comala becomes Kerala' (2012, 147; translated from the Malayalam original). Subsequently, Viswam goes to a library to borrow a copy of the book and reads it. Though he is not highly educated, Viswam is able to understand that Comala is a village of spectral figures who have been dead for years. Viswam underlines the following lines in the novel: 'There is nothing here. Except a stale stink, wherever you look. This village is a misfortune. Only misfortune' (148; translated from the Malayalam original). Viswam understands that his life has become unbearable, like life in Comala. He still has a week left for the Independence Day on which he has decided to publicly commit suicide. He wanders far and wide, looking for Sudhakaran. On the fifth day, he is standing at a crossing on a national highway waiting for a lift. None of the vehicles passing by cares to stop for him. There is only a wayside eatery in that area, but he has no money to buy his lunch. He orders a cup of black coffee, and is about to take a sip when a motorcycle, coming at a high speed, skids on the wet road. The rider, after being thrown into the sky, lands on the road, hitting his head on its hard surface. Nobody comes forward to help the bleeding man. Vehicles continue to move on the road, splashing blood. Viswam feels he is in the land of ghosts, in Comala:

> From those having their supper there, there was not even a consoling gaze towards the victim of the accident. They continued to eat, like dead people. Is this place really Comala?
>
> Am I watching a short film on death? Viswam thought, are all these eating their supper people who have resolved to commit suicide in the coming days? Have the worms of death already eaten all the green leaves within them? Is each of them a tree of worms? A truck sped past the body and something warm touched his feet.
>
> Blood!
>
> Tyres are speeding up and down through his blood. He could not stand the scraping sound of sand and blood on the road. Viswam went running to the young man and pulled his heavy body out of blood. (150; translated from the Malayalam original)

The turning point in the story is provided by the awe-inspiring vision of a spectral city. Viswam, who had decided to give up life, now undergoes a change. He manages to stop a jeep, puts the bleeding young man into it and rushes to the medical college. Midway, Viswam understands that the injured man is dying. He asks the driver to stop the jeep, goes to a nearby stream and gets some water. Before dying, the young man gulps down two drops of it. Now Viswam thinks to himself – these two drops of water, this was the debt he owed the world. He has paid that debt. The threat to commit suicide, which he had proclaimed, now appeared absurd. He decides to move on, and live and struggle, as he walks home.

The story raises issues of subsistence and survival against today's media-driven, consumerist lifestyle. During the commercial break that punctuates the live discussion, the television channel airs advertisements for dream houses which promise 'better locations, better lifestyle; creations for generations'. But the demonic element in predatory capitalism finds an adequate metaphor through the metaphor of Comala. Though it enters the story through the televised debate, it gradually assumes a presence with the pervasive images of lifelessness, inertia and stupor that Viswam confronts all around him. The vision of Comala has all the attributes of the myth and magic where the mind confronts its limits and is threatened by dissolution. One's power of expression is unable to cope with the demands of the demonic that cannot be transformed into an aesthetic whole. With the invocation of the Latin American novel within the space of the text, the story is able to transgress into the domain of compassion and love.

The fascination with Latin American literature, particularly fiction, among contemporary Malayalam readers may also be traced to this desire to 'defamiliarise' the environment of the self caught in a web of inarticulate powerlessness. Latin American fiction opens up a liminal world where the self is able to transgress without the fear of being engulfed by its vortex of turmoil. In Benyamin's *Eeyemmassum penkuttiyum*, the setting is America where a person of Mongolian origin brings out the traumatic history of displacements his family has gone through (Benyamin 2012, 229). In the heart of the story we have the figure of a Mongol–Vietnamese man, a veteran of the Vietnam War, now irretrievably lost to depression and condemned to silence. Through this figure, the writer is able to confront the worst fears of the contemporary Malayali society, which feels threatened and insecure in the extreme in their unreal palatial homes, where the sense of the real is lost in endless virtual images. Their everyday can only be enacted through the unfamiliar and the nightmarish; and the moments of terror and beauty that these fictional works present strive to make the trauma of this everyday existence bearable, by giving it a local habitation and a name, in terms of metaphors and images.

## References


Benyamin. 2012. *Eeyemmassum penkuttiyum. Mathrubumi Weekly Onam Special* 26 August–1 September: 229–42.

Butcher, Maggie, ed. 1983. *The eye of the beholder: Indian writing in English.* London: Commonwealth Institute.

Chakrabarty, Dipesh. 2008. The public life of history: An argument out of India. *Public Culture* 20: 143-68.

Dragas, Areti. 2014. *The return of the storyteller in contemporary fiction.* London: Bloomsbury.

Echikkanam, Santhosh. 2012. *Comala. Mathrubhumi Onam Special:* 144–52.

Joseph, Sarah. 1999. *Aalahayude penmakkal* [Aalaha's daughters]. Thrissur: Current Books.

Llosa, Mario Vargas. 2001. *The storyteller.* Trans. Helen Lane. New York: Picador.

Madhavan, N. S. 1992. *Higuita.* Trans. K. M. Sherrif. *Indian Literature* 151: 62–72.

Marquez, Gabriel Garcia. 1996. *One hundred years of solitude.* Trans. Gregory Rabassa. New Delhi: Penguin.

Martin, Gerald. 1989. *Journeys through the labyrinth: Latin American fiction in the twentieth century.* London: Verso.

Mendoza, Pilinio Apuleyo. 1982. *The fragrance of guava: Pilinio Apuleyo Mendoza in conversation with Gabriel Garcia Marquez.* London: Verso.

Mukundan, M. 2006. *Kesavan's lamentations.* Trans. A. J. Thomas. New Delhi: Rupa.

Walker, Janet A. 2007. Review of *Ordinary enchantments: Magical realism and the remystification of the narrative. Comparative Literature Studies* 44.4: 510–14.

Williams, Raymond. 1985. *The country and the city.* London: The Hogarth Press.

**CHAPTER ELEVEN**

# The Poet as Witness: Ethnicity and the Discourse of the Nation in the Poetry of Jean Arasanayagam and Agha Shahid Ali

This chapter discusses the poetry of Jean Arasanayagam and Agha Shahid Ali, both of whom gave voice to the tragic divisions and traumatic violence that followed in the wake of ethnic conflicts in their countries. Both Sri Lankan Tamils and Kashmiri Muslims have confronted monolithic, unitary nation states that were insensitive to the collective affirmation of religious and cultural differences from the margins. In her poems on the events of 1983, Arasanayagam extensively documents the decimation of an ethnic community which had separate traditions of rituals, customs, worship and everyday living. She turns self-critical when she finds her own Burgher legacy dubious as it had internalised the violence of the colonial gaze. The poetry of Agha Shahid Ali mourns the irretrievable loss of the Kashmir of his childhood which is now reduced to the size of a postage stamp. His poems are replete with images of the outsider, such as the snowman, the gypsy and the stranger. In the embittered elegiac poetic discourse he perfected with precision, Ali documents the gradual deepening of ethnic tensions into a point of no return, rendering him a permanent exile in search of a lost paradise. Both Arasanayagam and Ali are haunted by divisive pasts but sustain a humanist vision deeply rooted in the communitarian traditions of their ethnic communities. These poets stand witness to the oppression of minorities and their displacement in South Asia in the postcolonial period.

South Asian countries have gone through similar phases of historical experience – such as those of colonialism, national movements, formation of the nation state and efforts at decolonisation. The politics of South Asia still bears marks of a colonial legacy. The state boundaries, which were politically drawn, often contradicted the cultural boundaries that had taken shape over centuries. The process of nation building in these countries had been influenced by collective memories, but the same logic did not inform the process of state formation. The 'minorities' came into being, through political processes of exclusion which were often the result of policies prescribed by the state, and electoral policies made them increasingly self-conscious about their distance from centres of power. They were forced to defend their cultural identity against the aggressive assimilationist policies of the state. As a result, their cultural identity took on aspects of a political identity. They were caught in a conflict between atavistic sentiments and compulsions of civil politics. This process of othering can be seen as relevant to both Kashmiri Muslims and Sri Lankan Tamils.

The cultural 'givens' that constitute ethnic identities can often mobilise people in times of crisis. Both Kashmiri Muslims and Sri Lankan Tamils can be described as ethnic communities, since they are objectively different from other communities in customs, rituals and beliefs, and they subjectively accept these differences as the basis of their distinctive identity. From this perspective, one may argue that the prolonged civil conflicts in Sri Lanka and Kashmir have their roots in a conflict between ethnicity and the nation state. This chapter will study the poetry of Jean Arasanayagam, a Sri Lankan poet, and that of Agha Shahid Ali, an Indian poet – both writing in English – to see how they respond to the crisis in their respective communities.

Let us examine the case of Sri Lanka. When Sri Lanka secured independence in 1948, it was the Sinhalese Buddhist elite which constituted the ruling class. Minority communities constitute around 26 per cent of the Sri Lankan population – 18.5 per cent Tamils, and 7.4 per cent Muslims. The divisive politics followed by the Sri Lankan state in the 1950s progressively alienated the Tamil minorities, largely concentrated in the northern and northeastern parts of the country. The dialetic of the monolithic, unitary state and its deliberate suppression of differences, linguistic and religious, led to the demand for a separate nation by the Tamils. It should be remembered that the Buddhists have no special claim to Sri Lankan territory. There are strong cultural and racial similarities between the Sinhalese and the Tamils, the linguistic and religious differences notwithstanding. It is impossible to differentiate the Sinhalese and the Tamils from their physical appearance. The Tamils have lived in Sri Lanka for centuries and have contributed substantially towards the country's economic and cultural wealth.

After the formation of the independent Sri Lankan state, the Tamils were systematically marginalised by the state apparatus. The Sri Lankan national flag shows a Sinhalese lion. The secular national discourse of the state became increasingly irrelevant as Buddhist culture and the Sinhalese language became markers of the Sri Lankan nation state. In 1956, Sinhalese was made the official state language. The rhetoric of cultural nationalism ('Sinhala Only' was their slogan) was used by Bandaranaike's Sri Lanka Freedom Party to mobilise the majoritarian forces into a formidable political formation. The Tamils, who were a highly educated minority, gradually lost their access to opportunities in higher education and representation in government jobs, and this oppression united them across religions. As Juergensmeyer observed, 'The original link between Tamil ethnicity and the Hindu religion has come to be severed. Instead, Tamil ethnicity replaces Hinduism as the focal point of nationalist pride among Tamils. As a result, some of the most active participants in the Tamil separatist movement have been Christians, even Christian clergy (1993, 120). It is to be noted that the Tamil resistance movement has primarily targeted the Sri Lankan state.

The poetry of Jean Arasanayagam gives us an insider's view of the Sri Lankan ethnic strife. By birth, she is a Dutch Burgher. The Dutch came to Sri Lanka in the seventeenth century and the Burghers constitute a microscopic minority in Sri Lanka. During the colonial period, they were a privileged group, and this had alienated them from the mainstream. Arasanayagam's marriage to a Sri Lankan Tamil, despite the disapproval of her family, meant embracing another minority identity. The year 1983 marked a turning point in the history of Sri Lankan Tamils. In response to the killing of thirteen Sri Lankan soldiers on 23 July of that year, riots erupted all over the country. More than 2000 Tamils were killed in the violence. President J. R. Jayewardene did not condemn the rioters. This was the beginning of a long-drawn-out civil war which claimed thousands of lives on both sides. Arasanayagam's poems in *Apocalypse 83* record her trauma as a refugee and a victim of political violence. In the poem titled '1958 . . . '71 . . . '77 . . . '81 . . . '83', she traces the recurring history of ethnic strife in the country and concludes,

It's all happened before and will happen again
And we the onlookers
But now I'm in it
It's happened to me,
At last history has meaning
When you're the victim
When you're the defeated
The bridges bombed
And you can't cross over. (1984, 26)

Some of her major poems from this period deal with the trauma of dislocation and displacement of the Tamil community in the context of the ethnic strife. Several poems such as 'Innocent Victim – Trincomalee' and 'Eye Witness – Nawalapitiya' give first-person accounts of the inhuman violence perpetrated on innocent people who had no inkling of the magnitude of the tragedy that was to befall them. For instance, 'In the Month of July' describes the scene of a man being chased by a mob and brutally killed. 'It's Got to End' speaks of the need to speak out against violence. Several of the poems in the volume deal with the plight of refugees who are unable to come to terms with the sudden collapse of the familiar world they lived in. In 'I Watch My Own Death – Refugee Camp 1983', Arasanayagam writes,

It is easier now to die than live,
One waits for the burning to be over
One waits for the final conflagration
To end, seeing death and murder face to face
In the eyes of enemies, strangers, predators,
The degradation of the fugitive, the hunted
Fleeing from the burning mazes, threats and death. (1984, 67)

In 'The Dalada Bombing', she shows how violence is routinised in the civil-war-torn Sri Lanka. A family of worshippers is caught in a crossfire when they visit a temple. A woman set ablaze, 'runs demented along the street, the flames surging out of a singed glass of body-globe' (2003, 46).

The Nallur poems, in the same volume, are a poignant record of the temple town's slide into violence and chaos. Nallur houses a famous Murugan temple around which a minority culture of devotion and worship has grown. In 'Nallur', Arasanayagam laments that the '*thirtham*' which had tasted like nectar is now bitter and at the entrance of the town, 'the silent guns are trained upon a faceless terror' (1984, 3). Smoking ruins, blackened stones, empty roads and trails of blood mark the landscape outside. The pilgrim town has turned into a ghost town. The images of the 'burial urns filled with the ash of bodies cremated by the fire of bullets' and 'the waves of rust that swell and billow, beating into the hollow caves' convey the barrenness of the empty land and the traumatised sense of isolation that afflict the people who have become refugees in their own country (2003, 107).

In 'Remembering Nallur – 1984', she recalls the annual festival of Nallur temple. The festival used to attract lakhs of people, but now no one comes when the conch blast 'summons the penitents to sacrifice' (2003, 109). She also remembers the wandering singers who once travelled through the villages and bound the people together in their enchanting devotional music:

> Where have they vanished,
> The Bhakti singers in their trance,
> Bodies bent backwards leaning against
> Wind, borne by its surge
> Across the empty plain singing thevarams,
> Clashing cymbals. . . . (109)

The memories of devotion and communion, which form a counter-narrative to the dominant one of arson, murder and dispossession, constitute a site which assumes significance in her subsequent poetry. 'Remembering Nallur – 1984' ends with these lines:

> This time the poojas are not made
> With laden trays of flowers, tulsi, camphor,
> Fruit, kumkum and thirtham,
> The poojas are made with their bodies,
> As they come thousands and thousands
> Traveling from distant villages. (115)

As people march with weapons, instead of offerings to gods, Nallur turns into a battlefield.

The context of ethnic violence forces Arasanayagam to review the content of her minority identities. She offers a critique of the nationalist discourse by producing self-critical narratives of her Burgher and Tamil identities. In *A Colonial Inheritance and Other Poems*, she recovers her past, and in the process, takes stock of the colonial past. This is, by no means, an easy task because now she has to recognise that her ancestors have left her a dubious legacy of violence and shame. The rusted cannons and the ancient swords stained with blood speak of a history of violence and oppression. She feels implicated in that history: 'and in my face – a semblance' (1985, 5). The present violence echoes the colonial onslaught on Sri Lanka and the brutal subjugation of its people. To own up to this dubious legacy is to be self-critical about her community:

> We were once invaders
> On our brows eating into skull
> We bear branded the marks Cain. (1991, 85)

In a long poem titled 'Exiled Childhood', in the volume *Shooting the Floricans,* Arasanayagam confesses to her privileged status as a Burgher (1993, 9–10). To situate her own legacy is to accept that her relation with the mainstream is historically determined. The critical distancing she achieves in her narration of the past is a pointer to her awareness of the complications of history informing the present. In the middle of the poem, she compares herself to a migrant bird which has overstayed its summer and has chosen to stay behind, to cohabit with the native kind and has now grown 'into a rare genus' (13). Here she achieves a stasis of sorts without any final resolution of her problem of belonging. The nationalist discourse, by its very nature, demands assimilation, and the critical distance she acquires, through her examination of her own location within Sri Lankan history, enables her to realise the inherent vulnerability of minority identities. Elaine Ho and Harshana Rambukwella have argued that Arasanayagam's writing is heavily invested in the idea of 'national belonging'. They suggest,

> It is from within the Sri Lankan nation and as an individual who desires to belong that Arasanayagam writes, but she is also acutely aware that in this national space, she is persistently marked as alien. The desire to belong co-exists with an equally urgent process of rewriting her own alien-ness, and to reinvent alienation as critical irony and poetic agency. (2006, 66–67)

She will remain a vulnerable member of a minority community, ever marked and singled out for differences. This burden of self-consciousness will also prevent her from being part of a dominant imagined community.

Arasanayagam tries to find an alternative to the colonising model of nation-building which characterises both colonial and postcolonial nation states. This becomes apparent in the manner in which she negotiates her Tamil identity. The insular nature of her mother-in-law's Tamil Hindu (vellala) culture denies her an entry into that culture. The culture and customs that constitute Tamil identity can also make it hegemonic in its own way when it excludes other identities from its day-to-day life. In the long narrative poem, 'The Women Goddesses and their Mythologies', the narrator describes how she is allowed to enter the 'pooja room' of the matriarch only to be aware of an intractable symbolic logic of Tamil cosmology that excludes her and constructs her differently. Here we are made to feel the matriarch's centrality in Tamil culture. As a daughter-in-law from another minority culture, the narrator feels both unwanted and threatened. She has to subscribe to the codes of this new culture, to gain entry. As she says,

> Yet I entered, treading uncertain and wavering with
> Naked sole, my feet, now unpolluted, washed and bathed
> In turmeric, first having shaken off the dust of many Journeys on roads and streets I trod . . . (1991, 30)

The dialectic of purity and pollution, which is at the root of this narrative of the sacred, clearly speaks of the essentialising tendency at work in the Sri Lankan Tamil culture. The writer feels the need to resist this hegemonic element, because it is the same factor that is at work in the construction of the majoritarian discourse of the nation state. In 'Mother-in-law', she points to the hollowness of all claims to purity:

> "Aachi you have Sinhala blood.
> You drank milk of a Sinhala woman"
> "Who told you that? A Sinhala nona
> gave me milk. They all were
> respectable Sinhala nonas." (Wijesinha 1998, 71)

The term 'nona' means 'an honourable woman'. The narrator wants to preserve the purity of her 'blood', but realises that we are all 'polluted' in one way or the other. The ironic comment in the above lines points to an inclusive vision of the idea of identity and the need to resist the fictions of purity. In a plural society, one has to be wary of essentialist claims to insular spaces of identities.

## 2

The poetry of Arasanayagam compels us to reconsider the 'modernity' of modern nations. In his *The Ethnic Origins of Modern Nations,* Anthony D. Smith argues that the core of ethnicity resides in 'myths, memories, values and symbols' and in 'the characteristic forms or styles or genres of certain historical configurations of populations' (1986, 15). Ethnic communities carry the potential to emerge into nations, as shown by the struggles of several such communities during the twentieth century. Citing the example of Eastern European nations, Smith observes that such transformations meant a triple movement: 'from isolation to activism, from quietism to mobilization and from culture to politics' (154). We have discussed how the Sri Lankan situation forced the Tamil community there to stake claim for a separate nationhood. The Kashmir context is equally complex. During its long history, Kashmir has gone through Hindu, Buddhist and Islamic phases and has remained a confluence of cultures. The political crisis of modern Kashmir is, however, traceable to the partition of the subcontinent and the emergence of two nation states – Pakistan and India. It is also linked to a strong sense of *Kashmiriyat,* the term for Kashmiri identity deeply implicated in the history and culture of the region. This cultural ethos was politicised during the 1980s due to the interference of the central government in New Delhi, which was deeply suspicious of the Kashmiri's loyalty, and this created the mutual antagonism which persists to this day (Bhattacharjea 1994, Srivastava 2001).

Agha Shahid Ali spent his childhood in Srinagar, before he moved to Delhi and then to the United States where he settled permanently. He became acutely aware of his ethnic roots during his life in exile. His poetry is not concerned as much with the routinised violence in Kashmir as its politico-cultural identity which he invokes through myths, metaphors and memories. While Arasanayagam documents the trauma of ethnic violence, Ali embodies the trauma of Kashmir in the embittered elegiac poetic discourse he went on to perfect with chiseled precision.

Both Arasanayagam and Ali know that there are larger ethical questions behind the ethnic conflicts they have witnessed. Their poetry is an attempt to negotiate the homelessness inherent in their contexts. While Arasanayagam distances the tragedy with an ironic examination of the very processes of exclusion in the construction of all identities, Ali is more concerned with memories as a source of cultural identity. T. K. Oommen's formulation of ethnicity may be applied to both these writers and their work. Oommen observes,

> In order to get rid of the prevailing confusion, we need to conceptualize ethnicity as an interactional, as against an attributional notion. We must view ethnicity as a product of conquest, colonization and immigration and the consequent disengagement between culture and territory. It is the transformation of the "outs" into "ins" that leads to the process of ethnies becoming nations. (May et al. 2004, 131)

One may argue that this question of internal colonisation is relevant to both Sri Lankan Tamils and Kashmiris. Both Arasanayagam and Ali have experienced the disjunction between 'culture and territory', which Oommen speaks of. As an exile, Ali's alienation from his 'land' is more acute; and this is reflected in his works that are full of anguish.

In his *The Half-Inch Himalayas* (1987), Ali shows how the Kashmir of his childhood is now untraceable. As a homeless exile, he is condemned to his memories which unspool from the hallucinatory images of violence in the valley: 'This is home. And this is the closest / I will ever come to home' (1987, 1). The Kashmir of his childhood has shrunken to the size of a postage-stamp. The over-exposed memory turns his memory into a 'giant negative, black / and white, still undeveloped' (1). He turns to the mythical images of the snowman to capture that elusive identity which is a haunting absence. In 'Snowmen', Ali says that his ancestors came from Samarkand, with 'a bag of whale bones'. He still travels with generations of snowmen on his back: 'They tap every year on my window / Their voices hushed to ice' (1987, 8). In this surreal vision, Ali recognises his own otherness and homelessness. To recover his voice, he has to speak from within the marginal space of an exile. It is by going back to the cadences of Urdu that he retraces the collective memories of his community. 'In Memory of Begum Akhtar' uses memory as a source and recourse to map a layered view of Kashmir:

> Ghazal, that death-sustaining widow,
> sobs in dingy archives, hooked to you.
> She wears her grief, a moon-soaked white,
> corners the sky into disbelief.
> You've finally polished catastrophe,
> the note you seasoned with decades

Of Ghalib, Mir, Faiz:
I innovate on a noteless raga. (1987, 28)

It is significant that his memory is mediated by the aesthetic form of the ghazal and its classical heritage. In 'Homage to Faiz Ahmed Faiz', Ali again invokes the ghazal as the form that speaks the language of exile:

. . . Your lines were measured
so carefully to become in our veins
the blood of prisoners. In the free verse
of another language I imprisoned
each line – but I touched my own exile. (1987, 32)

In many of Ali's poems, the figure of the stranger appears in various forms: the previous occupant of the apartment, the riverside jogger, the 'someone' who lives in the house. The interiors of these poems become haunted as the poet feels unable to relate to a living community.

The crisis in Kashmir was precipitated by the failure of the state to ensure people's right to dignity and identity. When the nation state delegitimated the demand for identity, the collective identity took on an aggressive political role. As T. K. Oommen observes, 'But in the case of the new multicultural polities of Africa and Asia, there is a shift of emphasis from sequentiality to simultaneity. That is, the nations, ethnies, and minorities in the federal polities of these continents are increasingly insisting on equality and identity simultaneously' (May et al. 2004, 131). For 'ethnies', region and nation are contiguous. The 'disengagement between culture and territory', which Oommen talks about, renders both Arasanayagam and Ali as 'public poets' speaking as members of ethnic communities who voice concerns of a larger collectivity. It will not make sense to read their poetry in a strictly personal, individual context. The displacements they have suffered cannot be accounted for in individual terms. Ali reclaims a fragment of the inward-looking Kashmiri society through his scattered memories, which range from those of Begum Akhtar to those of saffron farmers.

The poems in *The Country without a Post Office* (1997) employ metaphors of mourning to come to terms with the trauma of displacement and loss in the wake of the violence in Kashmir. The postcolonial state in India had become highly unitary, and in the process, the marginal had become increasingly invisible. Ali documents Kashmir, its geography, myths and rituals, from the fragments of his memories. This 'region' he constructs is a site of resistance to the monolithic, unitary nation state. The nation state, as a centre of power, operates through codes that strictly define the boundaries of allegiance politically. Terms such as 'domicile', 'citizen', 'immigrant', or 'foreigner', are creations of these codes. Our liberal nationalist discourse fails to recognise ethnic, linguistic and regional identities as legitimate categories in themselves, as it has become highly exclusivist and essentialist.

Ali constitutes his ethnic identity as a site of loss, hurt, injury and denial. It feeds on embittered exile and apocalyptic epiphanies. The discourse of mourning becomes the dominant way of dealing with life and its experiences. We have seen how Ali's poems about the snowman and the gypsy invoke the Other. Here we may also recall one of his early poems, 'Eurydice' from *A Nostalgist's Map of America* (1991), which retells the myth of Orpheus from the perspective of Eurydice. It is set in a concentration camp in Nazi Germany where a crippled Eurydice limps past 'howl-chocked dogs' to disappear in 'a sudden tunnel of mustard twilight' (1991, 17–19). There is a suggestion of homelessness in these portraits. In his epigraph to the poem 'A Footnote to History', Ali writes of 'Gypsies . . . coming originally from India to Europe a thousand years ago . . .' (2001, 43). In his references to Begum Akhtar and the classical tradition she stood for, we have another clue to the separate cultural identity of Kashmir. In the concluding lines of the poem 'I Dream I am the Only Passenger on Flight 493 to Srinagar', we can read a deep sense of hurt that is at the core of the Kashmir crisis:

> He holds my hand speechless to tell me if
>
> those smashed golds flying past those petrified
> reds are autumn's last crimsoned spillage
>
> rushing with wings down the mountainside
> or flames clinging to a torched village. (1987, 16–17)

*Rooms are Never Finished* (2002) uses Hussain's sacrifice at Karbala and its commemoration in Muharram as the central metaphor. Memorialising is the poetic mode which Ali perfects in his final collections. Memory and mourning become inseparable here. In working the martyrdom and its memory into the musical structure of the English ghazal, Ali, an exile who cannot return to his homeland, explores the possibility of a community. Karbala becomes Kashmir and Palestine; the mother becomes both Zainab and Kashmir; and the pain becomes physical and its overwhelming burden can be captured only in gestures. He uses translation as a verbal gesture of containing and communicating pain. One of the poems here is a translation from Ghalib who says, 'Grief crushed me so / again and again it became the pain that pain erases' (46). Translation is a mode that Ali's poetry internalises right from the beginning. We have seen references to Begum Akhtar, Ghalib and Faiz Ahmed Faiz, in his earlier poems. His use of the ghazal also involves translation. Rajeev Patke has argued that there is a homology between translation and migration in Ali's poetry: 'The unavailability of communion (with God) or connection (with parent, community, friend, home or country) is like the impossibility of full translation. Reversed, it becomes a denial of univocity, and thus a sanction for plurality of speech as dialects, of poetry as translation, of exile as migration, and guilt as a restitution' (Patke 2006, 234). The need to translate and the impossibility to arrive at a proper translation go together. While translating Faiz Ahmed Faiz, Ali touches 'his own exile' as the English free verse turns his hand 'to stone' (1987, 32). His efforts to transplant the ghazal into English have to be seen in this context. The English free verse was not free enough to embody the larger pain of his private context. Ali says that 'suffering is seldom, perhaps, never, private' (1987, 32). It is this aspect of suffering, which is public and private at the same time, that he is able to articulate through his English ghazals.

Ali moved closer to the metropolitan poetic discourse in the later part of his career. But this is also the time he experiments with the ghazal form in English. This use of the ghazal creates a dialogic space in Ali's quest for identity as a displaced exile. Traditionally, the ghazal has spoken about love and desire. In their essay on the English ghazal, Chandrani Chatterjee and Milind Malshe have shown how the traditional male gaze inherent in the traditional ghazal is redefined in the ghazals of the American poetess Phyllis Webb (Ramakrishnan and Dasgupta 2006, 197). In his English ghazals, Ali subverts the form from within by investing the tone with a collective voice. His use of the ghazal in the context of the metropolitan tradition of American poetry is both an act of resistance and affirmation. It involves a border-crossing that questions the assumptions behind such boundaries. In this, he opts out of the normative strategies adopted by hegemonic discourses and majoritarian languages. The ghazal, as Ali reinvents it in English, comes closer to the idea of 'minor literature' as defined by Deleuze and Guattari in *Kafka: Towards a Minor Literature* (1986). A 'minor literature' contests the norms that constitute the normative codes of the literary. It renders the world and the word provisional.

For Ali, what mattered in the ghazal was its paradoxical nature – as reflected in its restraint and freedom, rigour and release, and reticence and eloquence. It could talk of the divine and the earthly love simultaneously. As he says in a small note on the ghazal form, the second line of each couplet 'delivers on the suspense by amplifying, dramatizing, imploding, exploding' (2004, 19). The ghazal gets deterritorialised as it moves out of its context. In its English version, it embodies the voice of an exile who cannot identify with any of the given identities constructed by hegemonic structures of power. Writings of Kafka's use of Prague German, Deleuze and Guattari comment,

> He will tear out of Prague German all the qualities of underdevelopment that it has tried to hide. . . . He will turn syntax into a cry that will embrace the rigid syntax of this dried up German. He will push it toward a deterritorialization that will no longer be saved by culture or myth, that will be an absolute deterritorialization, even if it is slow, sticky, coagulated. To bring language slowly and progressively to the desert. To use syntax in order to cry, to give a syntax to the cry. (Deleuze and Guattari 1986, 26)

This corresponds to what Ali does in his English ghazals. He is able to find the syntax of a cry. His ghazals are 'in-formed' by his lamentations for the loss of his mother, his home, community and Kashmir. The ghazals allow him to find a midway home, an in-between space, between the shadow lines created by nation states and his own present location. It renders the borders porous, making it easy for the exile to be 'in' and 'out', to be 'at home' in his homelessness. He creates a 'minor' language within the majoritarian language of English by eschewing its affiliations and normative cosmologies. This also enables him to release the bodies that are mapped into objects by the nation state. We may remember here that the English language is the associate national language of India. It is the nation state's privilege to interpellate an individual as 'citizen', 'refugee' or 'outsider'. The 'minor' language neutralises this power by transforming itself through the deterritorialised collective voice, which is detached from a unified subject or body. Thus, the English ghazal becomes the speech of a person who has lost his or her speech. In 'Arabic', Ali says, 'The only language of loss left in the world is Arabic' (2004, 24). In another couplet in the same poem, he addresses Amichai and says, 'I too Amichai saw the dresses of beautiful women. And everything else, just like you, in Death, Hebrew and Arabic'. The poem ends with the line: '"The Beloved" in Persian, "witness" in Arabic' (2004, 25). This is the paradox of which the ghazal becomes emblematic: of belonging and not belonging, of defying prescribed affiliations and loyalties. Ali says this with clarity in the ghazal titled 'Land': 'If home is found on both sides of the globe / home is of course here – and of course a missed land' (2004, 50). It is the geography of this 'missed land' that his ghazals map with great verbal precision.

To conclude, both Arasanayagam and Ali refuse to endorse the terms and conditions set out by the nation state to secure a sense of belonging. Arasanayagam has lived in Sri Lanka, but as a witness to the tragic divisions that have extracted a heavy human cost, she documents the violence inherent in all discourses of identity. Both the writers remain exiles, acutely aware of the traumatic consequences of essentialising one's sense of identity. They take their ethnicity as a matter of fact and refuse to celebrate it. As they stand witness to the tragic conflicts in their societies, in their separate ways, their poetry questions and affirms, even as it contests and consoles.

## References

Ali, Agha Shahid. 1987. *The half-inch Himalayas.* Connecticut: Wesleyan UP.

———. 1991. *A Nostalgist's map of America: Poems.* New York: W. W. Norton.

———. 2001. *The country without a post office.* New Delhi: Ravi Dayal.

———. 2002. *Rooms are never finished.* New Delhi: Ravi Dayal.

———. 2004. *The final selections: Call me Ishmael tonight; Rooms are never finished.* New Delhi: Permanent Black.

Arasanayagam, Jean. 1984. *Apocalypse 1983.* Colombo: International Centre for Ethnic Studies.

———. 1985. *A colonial inheritance and other poems.* Kandy, Sri Lanka: Privately Published.

———. 1987. *Trial by terror.* Hamilton: Rimu Books.

———. 1991. *Red water flows clear.* London and Boston: Forest Books.

———.1993. *Shooting the floricans.* Kandy, Sri Lanka: Samjna.

———. 2003. *Fusillade.* New Delhi: Indialog Publications.

Bhattacharjea, Ajit. 1994. *Kashmir: The wounded valley.* New Delhi: UBS.

Bose, Sumantra. 1994. *States, nations, sovereignty: Sri Lanka, India and the Tamil Eelam movement.* New Delhi: Sage.

Colebrook, Claire. 2007. *Gilles Deleuze.* London: Routledge.

Deleuze, Gilles, and Felix Guattari. 1986. *Kafka: Toward a minor literature.* Minneapolis: Univ. of Minnesota P.

Ho, Y. L. Elaine, and Harshana Rambukwella. 2006. A question of belonging: Reading Jean Arasanayagam through nationalist discourse. *The Journal of Commonwealth Literature* 1.2: 61–81.

Juergensmeyer, Mark. 1993. *Religious nationalism confronts the secular state.* New Delhi: Oxford UP.

May, Stephen, Tariq Modood, and Judith Squires, eds. 2004. *Ethnicity, nationalism and minority rights.* Cambridge: Cambridge UP.

Patke, Rajeev S. 2006. *Postcolonial poetry in English.* Oxford: Oxford UP.

Ramakrishnan, E. V., and Subha Chakravarty Dasgupta, guest ed. 2006. *Translation Today* (Special issue on Indian translation traditions) 3.1–2.

Rothschild, Joseph. 1981. *Ethnopolitics: A conceptual framework.* New York: Columbia UP.

Smith, Anthony D. 1986. *The ethnic origin of nations.* Oxford: Basil Blackwell.

Srivastava, Madhumita. 2001. *International dimensions of ethnic conflict: A case study of Kashmir and Northern Island.* New Delhi: Bhavana Books and Prints.

Wijesinha, Rajiva. 1998. *An anthology of Sri Lankan poetry in English.* English Association of Sri Lanka.

# Section 3

# Colonialism to Comparatism: Translating/Historicising the Other

CHAPTER TWELVE

# Hegemony, Ideology and the Idea of the Literary: The Emergence of Comparatism in Colonial India

In the present chapter, the term 'comparatism' points to a new language of comparison that emerged in the wake of the pluralisation of the literary field in colonial India in the nineteenth century. In the writings of a new class of educated elite who were complicit with Western world views, the 'literary' became a site of contestation and containment. The existing norms of cultural production were altered as the 'vernacular' discourse used the symbolic capital of English to critique the dominant aesthetic of neo-classical Sanskrit. The project of modernisation is examined here through close readings of its manifestations in the translation of Shakespeare, the practice of the new novel and the discourse of literary criticism. Translation became a mode of self-fashioning as it mediated between multiple conventions of the literary, reinforcing the critique of the hegemonic structures of the feudal world view. A literary novel such as *Indulekha* stages this confrontation in its narrative. Malayalam novels dealing with Dalit experience, besides documenting the practice of slavery in Kerala, problematise the elitist nationalist discourse from the perspective of the disenfranchised. Comparatism, as a mode of deciphering the emergent critical consciousness reflected in the new literary genres, is a defining feature of the dominant episteme produced by colonial modernity.

## I

Comparative literature as a discipline has had its origins in the West, but has found acceptance in India from the late nineteenth century onwards – both as an academic discipline and as a critical method that helps the 'native' languages of India to negotiate issues of power and ideology. This chapter attempts to trace the context in which comparatism emerged in nineteenth-century Indian society against massive shifts in the cultural domain. These shifts need to be studied in relation to the transition from the pre-modern period when Sanskrit had occupied a position of prestige and hegemony, to the modern period when English came to replace Sanskrit as the principal language of intellectual discourse. Behind this shift was the rise of a new class of English-educated elite who were exposed to colonial modernity. The educational and cultural policies of the colonial administration enabled this transition that marked a moment of rupture. The nature of this rupture occasioned a need for new discourses of evaluation and analysis from a comparatist perspective. This rupture was most obvious in the rise of a new idea of the 'literary' as manifested in the rise of new genres of literature and their ability to embody Indian society and reality, from a perspective that was validated by colonial modernity. The new language of comparison was an effect as well as a response to the colonial encounter.

Many theorists have drawn parallels between Europe and South Asia while analysing the process of 'vernacularisation' which took place in the period between 1000 AD and 1500 AD. Sheldon Pollock has argued that the 'vernacularisation' of Europe was accompanied by 'a pronounced ambivalence toward a cosmopolitan order that simultaneously enabled the vernacular to speak literarily yet constrained it' (2006, 470). In South Asia, the Sanskrit cosmopolis continued to hold its sway over the vernacular literary production (469). Elsewhere in this volume, I have contested Pollock's argument that literary culture in modern Indian languages continued to subscribe to the aesthetic norms and ideas of the literary based on the Sanskrit cosmopolis in their long periods of evolution. There were exchanges between Sanskrit and modern Indian languages throughout their histories, particularly in the fields of philosophy, theology and science. Languages such as Persian and Tamil had their separate histories in the subcontinent, which need to be taken into account when we discuss the relationships between Sanskrit and Indian languages. In Europe, multilinguality was suspect, and had negative associations of chaos and guilt as the myth of the Tower of Babel indicates. In India, 'diversity was not a sign of divine wrath, nor was multilinguality a crime that demanded punishment' (477). Early writers of modern Indian languages did not use their literary writing as a means of mapping a political territory, while in the West, the underlying links between language, polity and identity continue to this day. In India, where the society was marked by religious pluralism, the literary was not regulated by the agency of an authoritarian Church which legislated what was worthy of publication or circulation. Hence, the pre-modern Indian idea of the literary was more secular than that in the West, though the idea of the secular itself is associated with Enlightenment modernity.

The Sanskrit cosmopolis was elitist in its world view, and this resulted in a hierarchical social structure that did not allow any dialogic relation between the pan-Indian Sanskrit scholars and the writers of modern Indian languages. In the West, vernaculars became strong enough to appropriate intellectual functions with the result that discourses of modernity emerged in these languages. This was not the case in India. Modern Indian languages had their moment of confrontation with rational discourses only after the advent of colonialism, when the status of Sanskrit as the source of intellectual resources came to be challenged by English. By the end of the eighteenth century, most of the Indian territory was under the direct rule of the British. The language policy of British colonial administration was aimed at 'reforming' modern Indian languages so that they are altered from within. As Bernard Cohn has shown, the British used English to displace Sanskrit from its pedestal and align modern Indian languages with the normative structure of English (1985, 282–83). The study of Indian languages became a matter of official concern with several grammars and dictionaries appearing in Indian languages. The languages had to be 'refashioned' to conform to the modern standards of English. Persian, which was the language of revenue and judicial administration, was replaced by modern Indian languages by 1840. As the publication of *A Glossary of Judicial and Revenue Terms and of Useful Words Occurring in Official Documents Relating to the Administration of the Government of British India*, in 1855, indicates, India was now a 'rich field of philological enterprise' (Lelyveld 1993, 672). By the end of the nineteenth century, the monumental *Linguistic Survey of India* (1894–1928), undertaken by G. A. Grierson (1851–1941), was commissioned by the British colonial administration.

'Comparatism', in a different sense, was also a defining feature of the colonial project to objectify, enumerate, document and classify Indian languages in an attempt to regulate and deploy them in the service of an imperial order. Disciplines such as philology, geography and ethnology came in handy in converting the facts of language into a comparative framework. The observations of Reverend John Stevenson, a Scottish missionary who undertook a study of Marathi, is typical of the attitude of many such colonial scholars of Indian philology: 'The assertion that no language can be thoroughly understood till it has been compared with others, belonging to the same family, is nowhere more true than in relation to the vernacular languages of India' (qtd. in Naregal 2001, 45). These scholars were led by assumptions regarding 'pure' and 'impure' languages, the theory of 'original' languages, the superiority of some languages, and the evolutionary nature of linguistic development. The director of the Indian census for 1901, Herbert Risley (1851–1911), was 'a true believer in the relevance of biological evolution to language' (Lelyveld 1993, 674). Some languages were now seen as 'primitive' and some as closer to 'European' languages. Naregal rightly comments, 'The course of colonial policy, especially in the field of education, showed how the mapping and regulation of "native dialects" was a necessary prelude to their "rebirth" as the languages of a colonial modernity under the normative authority of English' (2001, 48).

Colonial modernity altered the existing norms of cultural production. This chapter, as mentioned at the outset, is concerned with the idea of the 'literary' as a site of contestation and containment. We have noted that the Sanskrit cosmopolis had no space to accommodate the cosmology of the 'vernacular'. On the other hand, the colonial educational policy became a means for transforming the natives. The liberal ideology of the new education policy was aimed at a minority of elites who belonged to the upper castes of India. Though it invoked universalist positions, the policy did not attempt to empower the masses through literacy and incorporate them into the ruling class. By effectively confining access to modern ideas to a select class, the colonial power could create a 'collaborative' class who had internalised Western rationality and could articulate those positions in the 'native language'. At the same time, the Orientalists were responsible for assembling a massive archive of classical 'Indian' literature which selectively retrieved the Indian 'Aryan' past that further reinforced the idea of intellectual decline in the subcontinent and justified the 'civilising' mission of the colonial administration. Modern Indian languages now came to be restructured to suit the codes of colonial modernity which operated as a conceptual grid underlying various structures of power, from the political to the social and cultural.

The introduction of history as a subject of academic study, for instance, illustrates the massive penetration of Western ideas into the native consciousness. Let us take the situation in western India as an example. By the turn of the nineteenth century, the British rule was formally established in this part of the country. After dislodging the Peshwas from their positions of power, the colonial administration reinstated a descendant of Shivaji in the Satara court, thus reversing the caste equations within the province. James Grant Duff's *History of the Mahrattas* (1826) was a historical project which reclaimed the history of Shivaji, the Maratha king, and this narrative became a model for nationalist historiography in subsequent decades. With the spread of colonial education, Grant's book, originally published in 1826, became a definitive work and was reprinted in 1863, 1873, 1878 and 1912. It was also adopted into a shorter Marathi version in 1830 (Deshpande 2007, 80). Soon after the appearance of this book, Marathi adaptations from well-known English histories of England, Europe and India were also published. History became a powerful means of endorsing Western supremacy and helped colonial administrators reimagine collective identities from a position that benefitted them. As Deshpande observes, 'The first generation of Western-educated Marathi intellectuals eagerly approached history as an important pedagogical tool for becoming modern, progressive individuals; their writings betray an acute sense of the "lack" of a historical tradition in India' (95). Hence, in the case of Marathi, the choice of a new script and a new highly Sanskritised idiom was dictated by the demands of colonial modernity.

Dipesh Chakrabarty has argued that the two concepts of 'historicism' and 'the political', as engendered by Europe in the nineteenth century, are integral to the idea of modernity (2000, 7–8). Historicism enabled Europe to trace the origin of modernity to Europe on an evolutionary scale that relegated 'non-Europe' to the status of 'pre-modern'. This meant that Africans and Asians have to necessarily traverse a considerable distance from their state of 'backwardness' to reach the European pinnacle of 'civilisation'. As Chakrabarty puts it, Indians and Africans are consigned to 'an imaginary waiting room' (8) where they will have to wait till they acquire a historical consciousness that qualifies them to enter modernity, the domain which is already chartered by Europe. This colonial historiography became the model for the study of Indian history. For instance, R. G. Bhandarkar (1837–1925), the well-known Marathi scholar of Sanskrit, advised Indian scholars to follow the Europeans' 'critical, comparative and historical method' (Chakrabarty 2008, 146–47).

The context of colonial modernity also contained a deep-rooted ambivalence towards the European claims of superiority which now came into conflict with nationalist thought. The educated elite was haunted by a division they had no means to heal, caught as they were between a deep sense of inadequacy in comparison to Europe and its rational apparatus of thought, and a strong desire to assert their identity against such deprivation and sense of inferiority. Culture, thus, became a site of struggle against the constraints of a tradition on the one hand, and the hegemonic tendencies inherent in the process of colonialism on the other. Traditions had to be retrieved and reinvented as part of modernity, to establish their continuity. At the same time, the legitimacy of modernity depended on how it conformed to tradition. To understand the cultural production of the nineteenth century, it is important to recognise the deep-rooted anxieties ingrained in the social imaginary of the time.

## 2

This section will discuss two related issues: the manner in which the 'literary' becomes a site of struggle, and how the larger epistemological constructs derived from the West were put into circulation in nineteenth-century Indian society in various allied fields such as literary criticism, social and political thought, and pedagogy. I use Malayalam for a focused investigation into these related issues.

As argued in the previous section, due to the colonial intervention, the Sanskrit cosmopolis gradually came to be replaced by English. This is reflected in the manner in which translations from English into Malayalam became significant in numbers through the nineteenth century. Translation was used as a mode of setting up an authority that legislated and legitimated the literary. Sanskrit, as the Orientalists testified, was complicit with the colonial imaginary, reinforcing the image of India's decadent present; while English penetrated deeper into the domains of education, culture and polity, and finally, into the normative world of the 'aesthetic', breaching the self-validating claims of Sanskrit. Translations from English became the habitus of a new epistemology. To illustrate this point further, I will briefly discuss Kandathil Varughese Mappilai's (1857–1904) translation of Shakespeare's *The Taming of the Shrew* into Malayalam, *Kalahinidamanakam* (1893).

*Kalahinidamanakam* uses the everyday language used by the Christian community in Kerala, with a remarkable dramatic effect. This has to be understood against the stamp of authority enjoyed by Sanskrit with the active support of the feudal elite in Kerala consisting of brahmins and nairs. It was this authority that came to be challenged in the deployment of an 'everyday' variety of Malayalam that is backed by English. The prestige and power associated with Shakespeare was deployed in the service of a cultural battle against the supremacy of Sanskrit in matters of cultural production. It is significant that the newly emergent class of lower and middle castes and Christians formed the driving force behind the translation practices of nineteenth-century Malayalam. In dislodging Sanskrit from its pedestal, they deployed the symbolic capital of Western canon to question the legitimacy of a pre-modern aesthetic. Hence, translation became a mode of self-fashioning in the epistemological context of colonial modernity where the grand narratives of the East and the West confronted each other, often mutually reinforcing an essentialist view of India. This view of India was in conflict with the contingent, fragmentary and fluid perspectives of contemporary India that were being shaped in the emergent literary genres of the lyric, the modern proscenium play, the novel, the short story, the autobiography, the travelogue and the discursive essay. These new genres emerged from encounters with colonial modernity, and they shared a 'translational' orientation in the sense that they carried sub-texts which had a dialogic relation with the West. The role played by the print medium in securing this transition from Sanskrit to English also has to be underlined. The first English medium school came up in the southern city of Thiruvananthapuram in 1834; but by 1824, the first printed Malayalam book had already appeared. By the end of the nineteenth century, there were forty-seven printing and publishing houses in Kerala, and of the 1177 books published in Malayalam in the nineteenth century, 500 were related to literature.

Mappilai's translation of *The Taming of the Shrew* has to be seen as part of a larger sociocultural project of questioning the prevailing literary culture and social values. In his introduction to the second impression of *Kalahinidamanakam,* Mappilai claims that his translation is aimed at introducing the dramatic mode of English plays to those who are not familiar with English (1972, 22). He had 'Indianised' the original settings by making the characters '*par-desi*' (non-Keralite) Hindus. Lord in the original becomes Tharakan, a title used among Syrian Christians, Christopher Sly becomes Chirattakkakathu Varkey and the hostess is Chekkothi; and Baptista, Padua, Vincentio and Verona are Pavanasayan, Pataliputra, Vighneswaran and Varanadesh, respectively. One of the contemporary critics, C. P. Achutha Menon, who praised this translation for its use of colloquial Malayalam and effective dramatic quality, wanted more songs and also suggested that, like the original Shakespearean play, *Kalahinidamanakam* should have been in verse. Mappilai strongly argued that the play 'lacked' profound themes which would have justified the use of verse. He had used 'natural' prose, close to the everyday speech of the reader, which conveys the experiential content of the book. He also dismissed the suggestion that the play should have had songs in it.

In fact, in the translation, Mappilai used the induction scene to satirise the prevailing zeal in Kerala for 'Sangita Natakam' (musical drama), a form of theatre. In the second half of the nineteenth century, most of the languages in India had a tradition of musical plays which dealt with mythological and historical themes in a melodramatic and spectacular manner, with a large number of songs with no relevance to the main theme punctuating the development of the plot. Mappilai used his translation of Shakespeare to satirise the norms of such plays, to highlight their artificiality. Translation functions here as a self-reflexive mode mediating between the conventions that satisfy the leisure class of the feudal elite and the critical realism that characterises a new set of norms that are embedded in the cosmopolitan, secular and rational world of colonial modernity. The ability of this translation to engage with the real and the contingent, as opposed to the closed world of the Sangita Natakam, points to the collapse of the brahminic tradition which had stagnated over the years. Translation here mediates between two ideas of the 'literary' – one which is unable to embody the real and the other capable of confronting the contingent and the contemporary. The new language of comparatism emerged in Indian languages in the second part of the nineteenth century, in the context of this confrontation between two irreconcilable world views and aesthetic norms. This language of comparatism is realised in the self-reflexive structure of the novel, the play and other literary forms that developed in the second half of the nineteenth century.

The opening scene of Mappilai's translation uses the Christian dialect of Malayalam which was yet to be consecrated as a literary language. The graphic muscularity of this dialect enables the translator to stage the confrontation between the feudal elite and the new and emergent middle class. One of the characters in the opening scene is a brahmin who is enamoured by the Tamil tradition of musical plays. The name of the theatre group is lampooned as '*Kusala Kolahala Leela Vilasini Natak Sabha*', the cacophony in the name suggesting disharmony and discord as the defining features of the old aesthetic.

The same kind of satire is employed by one of the first novels in Malayalam, *Indulekha* by Oyyarathu Chandu Menon (1847–99). First published in 1889, the novel instantly became a literary classic, and was translated into English within six months, by a colonial administrator in Calicut (now Kozhikode). In the preface to the novel, Menon says that he was in the habit of narrating to his friends storylines of the English novels he had read and that their demand had become so insistent that he decided to translate an English novel into Malayalam. But he soon realised the problems involved in translating a massive English novel and decided to write an original Malayalam novel, 'more or less after the English fashion' (Jain 2011, 74). The novel narrated an imaginary story, but in doing so Menon 'described only the ordinary affairs of the modern life without introducing any element of the supernatural' (76). It was in the use of an everyday version of the language that the novel made a breakthrough, setting new standards for the 'literary':

> The language I have used in this book is the language I would ordinarily speak at home. Although I have some knowledge of Sanskrit, I have as a rule employed Sanskrit words only in the manner and to the extent in which they are employed colloquially by Malayalis. . . . I have made no attempt to abandon, in favour of a style modelled on pure Sanskrit prose, the diction of Malayalis conversing at home. (77)

In fact, the full title of the novel is *Indulekha: A Story Written in the Manner of English Novel.* It became an iconic Indian novel of the nineteenth century for its ability to stage the cultural contest between the Sanskrit cosmopolis and the emergent English-centred colonial modernity. This kind of cultural production cannot be understood without reference to a language of comparatism which is implicit in the very aesthetic that produced and legitimated the new cultural products in Indian languages. One of the characters who is lampooned throughout this novel is a brahmin who embodies the feudal past of Kerala. The relations between brahmins and nairs were further complicated through the marital alliances that existed between the two castes which, in effect, framed nair women as objects of sexual desire for brahmins. The novel challenges this sexual practice through its assertive heroine, Indulekha, whose knowledge of English gives her an aura of invincibility, which reduces the brahmin suitor to a laughing stock. The novel critiques the neo-classical world of Sanskritised Malayalam by using an Anglicised syntax that signifies a new set of values concerning culture, education, individualism and authority. In his Preface, Menon articulated his position in favour of a new aesthetic of realism, which he had found in oil paintings of the 'European style', as opposed to the stylised unreality of two-dimensional Indian painting. His literary authority came from the fact that the novel, as a new genre, derived a mode of address that was aligned with the new public sphere. *Indulekha* marked a moment of privileging the intermediate caste of nairs, whose cultural capital did not depend on their knowledge of Sanskrit but on their access to English education.

The contours of the conflict we outlined above, is nowhere better seen than in the new discipline of literary criticism which was still in its formative stage in the late nineteenth century. Many of the early critics voiced their strong disapproval of literary works rooted in Sanskrit conventions. C. P. Achutha Menon, for instance, is ruthless in his criticism of the verse-play *Manoramavijayam*, which was modelled on old Sanskrit plays with neither coherence nor any dramatic vigour. His review is dismissive of the play for its corrupting influence on the young. Throughout this period, the question of 'taste' is repeatedly invoked, and discrimination and judgement are seen as essential aspects of the critical process of evaluation. In 'Poetry and Verse', C. Antappayi refers to the general view that melodious diction is an essential attribute of poetry. He quotes Hegel to disagree with him and mentions the *Quarterly Review* which had described Walter Scott's works as 'poetic works'. Here it may be added that one of the raging debates in Malayalam literature at that point in time centred on whether it was essential to use second-syllable rhyme in a poetic line. Antappayi's emphasis on the poetic as a dimension that exceeds and transcends the merely verbal and outward embellishments, moves away from the neo-classical model of poetry.

Another piece of criticism during this phase which takes a similar view of poetic composition is C. V. Kunhiraman's defence of Kumaran Asan's *Karuna* (1923), a masterly critique of P. K. Narayana Pillai's contemptuous dismissal of the poem. This long narrative poem is considered a path-breaking work of great poetic rigour. Pillai had held up a traditional poem based on the mythological figure of Krishna, *Kuchelavrittam*, as a great poem, without paying any attention to its conventional treatment of a worn-out theme and lack of social relevance. Asan's *Karuna*, on the other hand, was a modern poem that raised several issues regarding marital relationships and individual responsibility, apart from underlining the human conflict between desire and non-attachment. Pillai's judgement of Asan seems to have been motivated by caste prejudice, as the latter belonged to a lower caste. Pillai had commented that 'it would have been much more unsettling if Asan had turned Vasavadatta into a Muslim'. C. V. Kunhiraman draws our attention to the 'scorpion's sting' concealed in the comment, basing his argument on the need for a cosmopolitan discourse. Here the liberating potential of colonial modernity is deployed in the service of a new aesthetic opposed to feudal and neo-classical values.

What occasions the emergence of a literary critical discourse in Malayalam is the pluralising of the idea of the literary as a result of the breakup of an order rooted in classical Sanskrit paradigms and the ascent of the modern backed by the institutional control of the colonial regime. The dominant aesthetic, which had held sway for centuries, now comes to be contested from a vantage point provided by colonial modernity. There is an epistemological charge that these critical discourses transmit, animating new cosmologies that can only be expressed through the new genres of prose or the lyric poem or the polemical essay.

Here the role of translation in shaping the new idea of the 'literary' has to be highlighted. A series of social novels written in Malayalam on the plight of lower-caste communities (Dalits), such as *Saraswativijayam* (1893) and *Sukumari* (1897), shows how the translations of the Bible, *The Pilgrim's Progress* and other Christian tracts have contributed to a critique of caste system in Kerala. (This is also true of other parts of the country.) Through the medium of print, which was introduced by Christian missionaries, the idea of an ideal society where the lower castes are not discriminated against was disseminated among the literate community.

## 3

The homogenisation of India through new colonial institutions gave rise to a logic of standardisation which imposed a normative subjectivity on people belonging to different sections of the society. Those who did not subscribe to this normative subjectivity imagined their community differently, and the Malayalam novel of the nineteenth century dealing with Dalit experience allows us to configure such alternative world views circulating in the public sphere of the time. In Malayalam, translations of the Bible and Christian tracts and the advent of the printing press brought about a new idiom of writing that was different from the prevalent Sanskritised version. Of the twenty or so novels published in Malayalam in the nineteenth century, five were directly concerned with the Dalit struggle for social justice, which often took the form of conversion into Christianity.

It has to be remembered that slavery was prevalent in Kerala during the nineteenth century. A memorandum submitted by British missionaries to the king of Travancore, on 26 March 1847, stated that 1.64 lakh of people out of a total population of 12.8 lakh were slaves. By the middle of the nineteenth century, there were about 4.25 lakh slaves in Kerala (Mohan 2015, 63). Buying and selling of slaves was prohibited in Kerala by 1911, but this benefitted only those belonging to the *avarna* castes, such as the ezhavas, and not members of the lower castes considered to be 'untouchables', such as the parayars, pulayars, kuravars, pallars and the malayars. In 1843, slavery was banned in British India which included North Kerala (Malabar). These legislations owe a lot to the tireless efforts of missionaries. It is against this background that conversion figures in some of the novels dealing with the Dalit experience as an act of resistance and ethical positioning of a new subjectivity. Colonial modernity empowered Dalits in Kerala by giving them access to rudimentary literacy. This enabled them to recognise their own subhuman condition as man-made. In the prevalent feudal system, the landlords – who belonged to nair, brahmin and Syrian Christian communities – feared that the awakening of the lower castes would deprive them of their cheap labour and, hence, they opposed their conversion to Christianity, and this led to social conflicts.

The nineteenth-century Malayalam novels that addressed questions of slavery and Dalit emancipation and saw conversion as a means of resisting poverty and exploitation include *Ghatakavadham* (The slayer slain, 1877), *Pulleli Kunju* (1882), *Saraswativijayam* (The triumph of knowledge, 1893) and *Sukumari* (1897). *Indulekha* (1889) had captured the imagination of the Malayali elite by embodying an ideal of individualism, of the emergent bourgeoisie class, around its principal characters. But the moral underpinnings of this code of self-advancement came into conflict with the tenets of social contract which demanded an inclusive ethic. The rise of Dalit novels points to a context in which two irreconcilable ideals of freedom and justice – one elitist and selective and the other inclusive and open – became available to Kerala society. The Dalit novels call into question the process of 'othering' that was implicit in the construction of an elitist nation grounded in a middle-class ideology.

For the lower castes, the nationalist discourse was not emancipatory. The aesthetics of *Indulekha* is grounded in the middle-class world of desires, the embodiment of which is an imagined community consisting of English-knowing middle-class groups belonging to the upper castes. It is important to note that these Dalit novels were not received as part of the mainstream till recently, as the issue of caste was not seen as central to the reading of literature in the nineteenth century. Yet, the Dalit novel problematised the mystique of the 'literary novel' represented by *Indulekha.* The critical spirit that questioned the hermetic idea of the 'literary' text opened up a new discourse of the literary which gained ground subsequently in the twentieth century. Hence, comparatism is built into the project of the Dalit novel, since it creates a new reader and sanctions a new mode of writing.

The lower-caste Dalit novel is concerned with the 'soul-making project' of those who were denied humanity. For them, it was important to subvert the symbolic spaces that invested the hegemonic structures of power with inviolability. For instance, *Saraswativijayam* opens with an incident where a Dalit boy is brutally punished for singing loudly when a brahmin's entourage is passing by. The boy's family is evicted from the small piece of land they owned in the village. The Dalit boy is abandoned for dead, and subsequently, a decayed dead body that was recovered from a nearby river is taken to be that of the same boy. The colonial administration registers a case of murder against the brahmin who now flees the village. The nair servant who had committed the crime is arrested and sentenced to fifteen years of imprisonment. Years later, the brahmin is arrested from Banaras, where he was living under an assumed name. He is brought to trial, and here the story takes an unexpected turn. The Dalit boy had escaped from the village and gone to Mangalore, the seat of the Basel Mission, where he converted to Christianity and received modern English education. He becomes a judge in the colonial administration, and it is in his court that the murder trial finally comes up. The novel ends happily as the brahmin comes to know that his daughter, who had left home as the family was excommunicated, has now become the wife of Yesudasan, the judge.

*Saraswativijayam* is written with a view to project conversion as a means of upward mobility for the lower castes. Each chapter begins with a quotation from canonical Hindu literatures. These epigraphs from classical Indian texts – such as the *Mahabharata,* the *Ramayana* and the *Manusmriti* – highlight the nature of 'right' conduct; but the narratives that follow them demonstrate the injustice and brutality of caste system. There is an implicit comparatism here – through intertextual gestures, the novel points to the context of social asymmetry where ethical questions cannot be answered within the prevailing codes of morality. Values such as democratic rights, social justice or equality do not become transformative agents in society, unless they are mediated through texts that can turn them into public emotions. Martha Nussbaum, in her *Political Emotions: Why Love Matters for Justice* (2013), makes a strong case for the role of literature in fostering commitments to shared goals in the service of justice, in order to create a liberal society. Principles such as equality and justice do not enter the experiential frame of everyday world for the masses, unless literary works embodying them in narratives address them directly. This is why these Dalit novels acquire a dialogic character, debating and questioning the moral codes that prevail in a caste system.

In the second half of the nineteenth century, pamphlets and tracts published by Christian missionaries, providing a critique of the caste system, often took the form of dialogues between an elite Hindu and a lower-caste character converted to Christianity. In *Neetimargam* (The way of justice), for instance, we have a dialogue between Dharma and Satyavadi. In another pamphlet, Raman, who hails from an upper-caste community, confronts Satyavadi. This argumentative discourse informs both *Pulleli Kunju* and *Sukumari*. In the former, we come across the following statement: 'When people cannot relate to each other as human beings, they remain separate like grains of sand.' This is an insightful argument for a participatory space in a democratic society. Dalits had no means of making an emotional investment in the nationalist discourse constituted by selective exclusions.

Apart from the dialogic nature of the novelistic discourse, the chronotope of the public space is central to these Dalit novels. *Indulekha*, for instance, is a domestic novel where most of the action takes place in the interiors of upper-caste homes. However, the Dalit novel is marked by confrontations which are staged in the public space, when the lower castes try to claim their right to equality. Public roads, schools, courts and offices figure in these novels as places where the self-fashioning of a new Dalit subject is narrated. These narratives also present the chronotope of the house in an altered context. For instance, in *Sukumari*, the central character, Sukumari, is deeply impressed by the cleanliness and tidiness of a Christian devotee's house. Similarly, in *Ghatakavadham*, there is a long description of how neatly Koshy Kurian had organised his tiny plot and thatched house. The lower castes were considered a source of 'pollution' and were seen as 'unclean'. By stressing the hygienic nature of their surroundings, their modernity is symbolically coded into the narrative. In another interesting instance, the sixth chapter of *Sukumari* describes the syllabus of a course that is offered in an orphanage run by missionaries: home science, economics, scriptures, Malayalam reading, mathematics, handwriting, English reading, geography, history, physical hygiene, stitching and music. Obviously, the new Dalit subject narrated in these novels is constituted by a cosmopolitan world view that transcends boundaries of caste, region and religion. Collectively, these elements clear a space of ethical resistance that calls into question the 'othering' of the lower castes by the project of colonial modernity.

## References

Anthappayi, C. 2013. *Naluperiloruthan adhava natakadyam kavitvam.* Thiruvananthapuram: Chinta Publications. (Orig. pub. 1893.)

Chakrabarty, Dipesh. 2000. *Provincializing Europe: Postcolonial thought and historical difference.* Princeton: Princeton UP.

———. 2008. The public life of history: an argument out of India. *Public Culture* 20: 143–68.

Cohn, Bernard. 1985. The command of language and the language of command. *Subalterns Studies IV.* New Delhi: Oxford UP: 276–329.

Collins, Mrs. 2004. *Ghatakavadham.* Kottayam: D. C. Books. (Orig. pub. 1877.)

Deshpande, Prachi. 2007. *Creative pasts: Historical memory and identity in western India, 1700–1960.* New Delhi: Permanent Black.

Jain, Jasbir, ed. 2011. *The writer as critic: Essays in literature, history and culture.* Jaipur and New Delhi: Rawat Publications.

Koshy, Archdeecan. 2013. *Pulleli Kunju.* Thiruvananthapuram: Chinta Publications. (Orig. pub. 1882.)

Kunjambu, Potheri. 2013. *Saraswativijayam.* Thiruvananthapuram: Chinta Publications. (Orig. pub. 1893.)

Lelyveld, David. 1993. Colonial knowledge and the fate of Hindustani. *Comparative Studies in Soceity and History* 35. 4: 665–82.

Mappilai, Kandathil Varughese. 1972. *Kalahinidamanakam.* Kottayam: National Book Stall. (Orig. pub. 1893.)

Menon, O. Chandu. 1964. *Indulekha.* Calicut: Mathrubhumi Publications. (Orig. pub. 1889.)

———. 1965. *Indulekha.* Trans. W. Dumergue. Calicut: Mathrubhumi Publications. (Orig. Pub. 1890.)

Mohan, Sanal P. 2015. *Modernity of slavery: Struggles against caste inequality in colonial Kerala.* New Delhi: Oxford UP.

Mooliyel, Joseph. 2013. *Sukumari.* Thiruvananthapuram: Chinta Publications. (Orig. pub. 1897.)

Naregal, Veena. 2001. *Language politics, elites and the public sphere.* New Delhi: Permanent Black.

Nussbaum, Martha. 2013. *Political emotions: Why love matters for justice.* Massachusetts: Harvard UP.

Pollock, Sheldon. 2002. *Literary cultures in history: Reconstructions from South Asia.* Berkeley: U of Columbia P.

———. 2006. *The language of Gods in the world of men.* New Delhi: Permanent Black.

CHAPTER THIRTEEN

# Beyond Canons and Classrooms: Towards a Dialogic Model of Literary Historiography

The idea of the canon has been contested by recent developments in literary theory. An essentialist view of the literary is no more tenable. Reception of a text is mediated by the social context as well as the reader's expectations. In the Indian context, the long tradition of orality and the prevalence of multilingual traditions that shape individual texts further complicate this process. The colonial intervention that forced a rupture in the perception of the literary relegated the pre-modern into the realm of 'folk', disregarding the deeper continuities that shape the literary field in Indian languages. In India, literary history has to conceive of texts differently. Regional literatures are plural and multiple as they have been shaped by conflicts within. The radical and the regressive in regional literatures vary from region to region. Literary histories tend to homogenise regions into harmonious wholes, ignoring their separate social and cultural dynamics. Literary histories need to reflect the dissent and resistance built into the dynamics of each literary tradition. This requires an interdisciplinary approach to literary historiography. This is further illustrated with examples from Malayalam literature.

The discourse of literary historiography is informed as much by developments in social sciences as by those in arts and literature. It is important to note the fact that literary history comes into being as part of the institutionalised study of literature. Hence, the nature of inclusion or exclusion – operating within literary historiography – can be understood only with reference to institutional power structures that ordain their legitimacy. The classroom and the canon are central to this discussion of literary historiography – because literary histories are shaped by the institutions which also shape the classroom and the canon.

The idea of the canon has come to be questioned by recent developments in the study of culture and society. Traditionally, teaching literature meant teaching the canon. This was largely an insular exercise that stressed the formal features of the text, the period or contexts, and the genre. The idea of 'literariness' was an unambiguous category, derived from canonical texts that upheld 'literary tradition' in an essentialist manner. However, with the shift in focus, from the text to the reader, this essentialist way of understanding tradition has given way to multiple ways of reading texts. It is a critical commonplace now to say that 'literary' values are not inherent in a work of literature but are produced in collaboration with a community that actively participates in the creation of the idea of the 'literary'. The social dimension of literature is, thus, fulfilled only when the literary experience of the reader enters into the horizons of expectations projected by the text. Hans Robert Jauss has argued that the reception of any work of art is conditioned as much by the social context that mediates between the text and the reader as by the expectations of the reader from the text (Jauss 1982). But Jauss does not help us comprehend the nature of the reception in social contexts where the production and circulation of literary texts are largely oral and multilingual. The example of *Jñānēśvarī* in Marathi may illustrate the point further. This thirteenth-century commentary on the Bhagavat Gita, composed by Jñāneśvar, galvanised the imagination of an entire population through its powerful use of Marathi, which was yet to evolve as a literary language. By using the everyday language of Marathi for his philosophical poem, Jñāneśvar created a community of listeners for whom literature was speech, performance and worship. As Ganesh Devy explains, Jñāneśvar's imagination could reconcile the conventions of oral tradition with the requirements of textual writing (1998, 51).

In Indian contexts, literature and the community in which it circulates cannot be separated. Literary historiography in India has to deal with the complex nature of utterance and the enunciation of the text, whether it is in the poetic texts of the Alvars and the Lingayat poets of the South, the Jaina scholars of Gujarat, the Vaishnava poets of Bengal, the Sufi mystics, or Kabir and Tulsidas, who had their own following in central India. The clue to understanding literary production in the subcontinent has to be sought in the community formation where sects that question hegemonic structures of power have articulated their dissent in everyday languages. We encounter this phenomenon variously in every part of India. Behind the rise of modern Indian languages – such as Kannada, Marathi, Bengali, Oriya and Malayalam – are such collective expressions of social dissent. Often in the everyday cultural practices of these communities, literature and worship are inseparable. The complex negotiations within caste structures and performance traditions also require careful study. Simon Charsley has this to say on the caste status of performing artists in India:

> We see them as rituals specialists, bards, members of acting troupes and event managers. We see how performing has been organized, and still is in many cases, as integral part of a caste system which has differentiated and fixed occupations within in-marrying groups, as hereditary and defining possessions. . . . In this social universe shaped by caste, performance has been linked with Brahmins and their learning, but the performing itself has mainly been the concern of those placed low in the system. (Charsley and Kadekar 2006, 41)

The evaluation of the production and consumption of 'texts' in such societies cannot follow the norms of reception and cultural production that are encountered in Western societies. In his essay on literary historiography in Malayalam, P. P. Raveendran argues that 'the concept of literature in pre-modern Kerala was wide enough to accommodate all written discourses, indeed all discourses, there being little room for the privileging of a specifically aesthetic discourse. An aesthetic discourse gets crystallized only in the ideological environment produced as a result of prolonged colonial intervention' (2009, 71). Genres such as *vachana*, *quissa* or *kilippattu* cannot be understood without reference to the dynamics of their transmission and preservation. Literary historiography in India will have to conceive of texts differently, if they are to be studied against the context of social formation in India.

The division between the pre-modern and modern phases in Indian literatures cannot be absolute as the forms of an earlier period continue to circulate in Indian society and also inform later compositions and cultural productions. In the modernist phase in Indian poetry and drama, the renovation of genres was made possible by the assimilation of pre-modern modes of articulation. In his essay on 'Tensions in Kannada Literary Culture', D. R. Nagaraj observes that 'the absent and the invisible have to be taken as parties in the construction of literary cultures in South Asia' (Pollock 2003, 335). Nagaraj argues that the institutional beginnings of literatures in languages such as Malayalam, Telugu, Kannada and Tamil involved the repression of poetry as a 'natural' activity, as opposed to its formalisation in the service of a courtly culture. When poetry was codified into 'poetics', texts such as *Kavirajamarga* in Kannada or *Leelathilakam* in Malayalam performed acts of standardisation and exclusion that involved transactions between the cosmopolitan pan-Indian *marga* and the regional-local *desi*. Nagaraj says that 'the notion of a universalizing cultural order such as that of Sanskrit has played a crucial role in the making of vernacular literary traditions' (335). A [illegible]ge such as Malayalam resisted the hegemonic elements present in both Tamil and Sanskrit in fashioning its self-identity, and this process involved selective assimilation of the local and the universal. It is through a dialogic model of acceptance and rejection that Malayalam located its cultural space in the prevailing hierarchical structures of power. This process involved translations as rewritings and adaptations, at several levels. Such transactions and transformations are part of a dialogic process that reconstitutes the local and the universal in the context of a specific speech community. Elsewhere I have shown how the mainstream poetic tradition in Malayalam has defined a lexicon of social experience which responds to the conflicting demands of its socio-cultural contexts (Ramakrishnan 2009, 29–41).

This selective assimilation of the local and the universal in the regional cultural tradition further raises issues regarding the very content of regional cultures. It is to be noted that they are not constituted along identical lines across India. This also means that what is radical or regressive in a culture can vary from region to region. The regional has to be seen as multiple and plural, if we are to understand its social and cultural dynamics. The histories of 'Indian Literature' tend to integrate the regions into a homogenous, self-contained whole. However, the region is a site of power struggle between several competing points of view, and these struggles inform their cultural productions. Literary historiography in India has to take into account the dissent and resistance built into the dynamics of each literary tradition. For instance, the addressivity of *vachana* in Kannada or *kilippattu* in Malayalam is a response to the latent conflicts between the dominant and marginal voices in the field of culture. This, in turn, reflects the larger social inequalities based on caste, gender and power. A literary historiography which seeks legitimation from the endorsement of the canonical erases the conflictual elements in the field of culture.

For a clear delineation of the dynamics of cultural politics in India we would need an interdisciplinary approach to the questions of culture and history. We need to recover the subliminal voices that inform the production of literature, and this will involve looking beyond the canon. Literary historiography in India is deeply implicated in the formation of the nation, and this meant the construction of canons that endorsed a selective view of history and culture. The canonical world of classics and the grand narrative of culture mutually reinforced each other. This effectively excluded several traditions that were not considered elitist. Dipesh Chakrabarty has argued that when history became a popular subject in India at the turn of the twentieth century, Indian scholars, who believed that historians in India and Europe belonged to the same republic of letters, joined together in a common bond of trust in the universality of the empire (2008, 143). Little did the Indian historians know that they were being co-opted in an imperial project. The noted Indologist R. G. Bhandarkar, in a public lecture titled 'The Critical, Comparative and Historical Method', delivered on 31 March 1888, said, 'It is no use ignoring the fact that Europe is far ahead of us in all that constitutes civilization. And knowledge is one of the elements of civilization' (qtd. in Chakrabarty 2008, 147). Bhandarkar advised Indian scholars to follow the European 'critical, comparative and historical method'. Jadunath Sarkar was another scholar who advocated a scientific approach to history, along the same lines. By aligning themselves with Western scholars, Indian historians saw the cultural productions of India through Western eyes. To be fair to them, they were also uneasy about their affiliation to the imperial project. They resisted the rationality that the empire represented in matters of culture and politics. This ambivalence is best illustrated by the Indian nationalist discourse, which looked towards the future as well as the past. While endorsing rationality in matters of the public world in general, the nationalist discourse resisted it in the private domain of personal life and the field of culture. This resulted in an inability to accommodate cosmologies that were divergent and deviant. As Chakrabarty observed, 'this vision of the nation was predicated on the assumption that elites were capable of overcoming deep-seated social conflicts to usher in an age of social harmony' (150). The literary historiography of the late nineteenth and early twentieth centuries also shared this blindness inherent in the nationalist discourse. We need to recover texts that are missing from the literary historiography of this period.

To provide an example, *Kerala sahithya charithram* (Literary history of Kerala, 1955) by Ulloor S. Parameswara Iyer (1877–1949), one of the most influential literary histories of Malayalam, has very little to say about the cultural productions of the marginalised. Iyer shows a patronising attitude towards women writers or writers of the lower castes, when they are mentioned in his work. He hardly has anything to say on the social context of colonialism, though he was a civil servant under the king of Travancore. He does not relate the shifts in literary sensibility in the modern context to the arrival of the printing press, the struggle of the lower castes for civil rights or the emergence of a public sphere. In other words, the 'literary' is seen as autonomous and self-contained with its own internal codes. None of the major translations that appeared during the period finds a mention here, though the latter half of the nineteenth century saw a spate of translations in every genre. Another prominent work of the period, R. Narayana Panikkar's seven-volume *Kerala bhasha sahitya charithram* (Literary history of the Malayalam language, 1956), is highly critical of the progressive movement as it eschews moral instruction, which is seen as the primary objective of all literature. Panikkar sees the mid-twentieth-century phase of Malayalam literature as a period of decline. Such value judgements are rooted in the literary historiography of the nineteenth century, where Victorian world views tended to dominate. For instance, Raveendran has observed that Panikkar borrows from W. H. Hudson's views on the relation between language and literature while formulating his own approach to literary historiography (73).

Now that historians have begun to contest the term 'history' from within, we need to interrogate the terms and conditions that are implicit in literary historiography. Social and cultural histories have to be incorporated into histories of literature. They are not 'backgrounds' to the study of literature, but integral to the study of texts. Texts that are canonised into a dominant literary tradition have turned literary history into a biography of a pantheon of authors. In contrast, a dialogic model of literary history will not define 'literariness' in exclusivist terms. We need to reclaim, as cultural products of a community, texts that are relegated to the backyards of 'folk literature'. In Indian literature, the distinction between 'folk' and 'mainstream' literatures was the product of colonial world views infiltrating the domains of culture. There are multiple pasts to be recovered. As in the case of translation, the question of equivalence is of great significance here. Our 'Romanticism' or 'modernism' may not share the contents of the Western typologies. However, the existing literary historiography has synchronised our literary texts with the temporal templates of Euro-centric notions of literariness. This has alienated our cultural products from us, assimilating these texts into narratives that dislocate and distort them. We need to reimagine literary historiography to relocate ourselves in its narratives. This will be the beginning of addressing the strange case of the 'missing' texts. In the field of history, one notices that the nationalist consensus on historiography has given way to 'combative narratives' from previously colonised communities. Badri Narayan's *Women Heroes and Dalit Assertion in North India* (2007) is an example of the new 'combative history' which interrogates received models of writing histories. Such narratives are answers to the demand for alternative models of history, which are based on representations of the 'pasts' that were not considered legitimate by elitist views on history. They may not conform to the rigorous methodologies used in 'academic' history, but they participate in the public sphere by interrogating elitist notions of identity.

Our alienation from certain kinds of cultural pasts may be illustrated through an anecdote. Once in Kerala, a few 'folk' poems were prescribed in a postgraduate course in Malayalam. But when it came to introducing these poems to students, no teacher had any clue as to what these long narratives were about or what they meant. One of these teachers voiced his frustration openly during a discussion in the staff-room. This was overheard by a woman employed in the college as a sweeper and she volunteered to explain those poems to the teachers. She could recite from memory more than three hundred long oral narratives belonging to the rich oral traditions of Kerala. Subsequently, she became a sought-after speaker in colleges and refresher courses organised by academic staff colleges in Kerala. This Dalit Christian woman knew these narratives from within and could explain the subtle nuances of those texts in detail and relate them to ritualistic performances, and contexts of performance and social history. This story illustrates that cultural products of oral traditions are yet to be reclaimed as part of our 'mainstream' literary history. This would also help us remap the complex inter-relations between the canonical and the non-canonical.

We need micro-histories that go into the complex matrix of relations that a text embodies. We also need to relate the non-literary to the literary. For instance, a comprehensive history of the print revolution in India is yet to be written. The nineteenth century saw a massive shift, not only in literary sensibility but in the use of literary genres. Though much has been written on early novels, the shift from what is considered 'pre-modern' forms towards the novel, the short story, the essay, the modern proscenium play and the autobiography, marks an unprecedented move towards a new paradigm of representation. In those few years, our mental landscapes were reconstituted in accordance with Western codes, when these forms came to represent something vital for our speech communities. It amounted to redrawing the social contract with a new 'fine print' attached. The implications of the investment we made in these forms need to be critically evaluated. What D. R. Nagaraj says about the codification of poetry into poetics, and the consequent repression of cultural forms, may be relevant to the study of the nineteenth century too. The colonial context introduced alien codes of representation that recast the relations between our language and reality. This also involved acts of standardisation and exclusion that established a new hierarchy between the alien traditions and the already existing regional-local and pan-Indian traditions. Literary forms are related as much to social formations as to the dialogic potential of a society. They are part of a larger dialogue that takes place in any society. The reorganisation of our literary forms involved setting new paradigms for addressing contemporary society, and this excluded large sections of people from the dialogic process of self-articulation. Hence, a new literary historiography, which will address issues of the kind discussed above, would necessarily be a dialogic one, in the sense that it would investigate the codes that make literary representation possible.

## References

Chakrabarty, Dipesh. 2008. The public life of history: An argument out of India. *Public Culture* 20. 1: 143–68.

Charsley, Simon, and Laxmi Narayan Kadekar. 2006. *Performers and their arts: Folk, popular and classical genres in a changing India.* London: Routledge.

Devy, Ganesh. 1998. *Of many heroes: An Indian essay in Indian literary historiography.* Hyderabad: Orient BlackSwan.

Iyer, Ulloor S. Parameswara. 1955. *Kerala sahitya charithram* [Literary history of Kerala]. Thiruvananthapuram: Department of Publications, Kerala University.

Jauss, Hans Robert. 1982. *Toward an aesthetic of reception.* Trans. Timothy Bahti. Sussex: The Harvester Press.

Nair, S. Guptan, ed. 1994. *Malayala niroopanam innale* [Malayalam literary criticism in the past]. Thiruvananthapuram: Kerala Bhasha Institute.

Narayanan, Badri. 2007. *Women heroes and Dalit assertion in North India: Culture, identity and politics.* New Delhi: Sage India.

Panikkar, R. Narayana. 1956. *Kerala bhasha sahitya charithram* [Literary history of the Malayalam language]. Thiruvananthapuram: Vidyavilasini.

Pollock, Sheldon. 2003. *Literary cultures in history: Reconstructions from South Asia.* Delhi: Oxford UP.

Ramakrishnan, E. V. 2009. Translation as resistance. In *Decentering translation studies: India and beyond,* ed. Judy Wakabayashi et al, 29–42. Philadelphia: John Benjamin's Publishing Company.

Raveendran, P. P. 2009. *Texts, histories, geographies: Reading Indian literature.* Hyderabad: Orient BlackSwan.

**CHAPTER FOURTEEN**

# Habitations of Resistance: Role of Translation in the Creation of a Literary Public Sphere in Kerala[*]

The eventful decades of socio-political turmoil between the 1930s and 50s in India coincided with major shifts in literary discourses that called into question the very notion of the 'literary'. The reasons for the emergence of the 'progressive' literary movement have to be sought in the gathering social ferment at the repressive apparatus of colonialism and the exploitative regime of feudalism. Encounters with European literature, particularly social realist fiction, through various forms of translation, enabled Indian writers to articulate their sense of resistance in contemporary terms. This chapters takes up the case of Malayalam literature during its 'progressive phase', to map the nature of contestations and confrontations that defined its trajectory. In the context of this chapter, 'translation' has to be understood in the larger sense of 'refraction' or 'rewriting' that, according to André Lefevere, includes commentary, critical summaries, historiography, anthologising and theatre production. The chapter argues that the process of rewriting which accompanied the progressive literary movement called into question the prevailing norms of the 'literary' and 'prestige styles' that had legitimated earlier social systems. The debates and dialogues that followed in their wake pluralised the literary public sphere and radicalised Malayalam literature, redefining the relation between the literary and the socio-political.

This chapter examines a critical moment of transformation in the literary sensibility of modern Indian literatures in general, and of Malayalam literature in particular, from the larger perspective of the role of translation in radicalising the literary discourse. During the period between the 1930s and 50s, India witnessed momentous events in the political field as the nationalist freedom struggle gathered momentum and impacted cultural productions, from theatre to painting and

*This article was originally published with the title 'Habitations of Resistance: The Role of Translation in the Creation of a Literary Public Sphere in Kerala' in *Translation and Global Asia: Relocating Networks of Cultural Production*, pp. 169–181.

literature. As Priyamvada Gopal notes, 'The years from about 1936 to 1954 were the heyday of a hugely influential radical cultural movement that spanned several regions and languages across India (as well as the region that became Pakistan)' (2005, 1). The writers responded to the massive socio-political changes that swept across India in the wake of anti-imperialist resistance movements, by radicalising the role of literature in society and interrogating prevalent modes of representation. Translation played a significant role in this process of radicalisation.

The 1930s and 40s were marked by socio-political upheavals across the world, as was evidenced by the economic depression in America, the rise of fascism in Europe, and the intensification of the struggle against imperialism in Asia and Africa. It was against this backdrop that a group of writers from fifteen countries met in Paris in the spring of 1935 under the banner, 'International Writers for Defence of Culture'. Among the writers who participated in the conference were André Gide, André Malraux, André Breton, Tristan Tzara, Aldous Huxley, E. M. Forster, Boris Pasternak, Isaac Babel, Bertolt Brecht, Julien Benda, Heinrich Mann and Gustav Regler. The conference set 'the guarding of our civil liberties, the organization of writers to safeguard their own economic interests and to render help to the writers exiled by fascism' as its larger goals (qtd. from Anand 1979, 13). Mulk Raj Anand and Sajjad Zahir, both young writers from India, participated in the conference and felt the need to disseminate the radical ideas highlighted in the conference in India. Zahir had already edited a volume of Urdu short stories, *Angaaray* (Live coals), in 1932, which had caught the attention of the young readership in the country. The influence of European avant-garde of the 1930s was apparent in these stories. This volume raised a storm in the Urdu-speaking Muslim community as most of the stories were highly critical of 'the middle-class Muslim mores and practices of the period' and later the book was banned by the United Provinces' legislature (Coppola 1986, 21). Zahir was forced to leave India as a result of the controversy surrounding *Angaaray.* He went to London to study, and there, along with Mulk Raj Anand, formed an organisation called the Progressive Writers' Association. The Association drafted a manifesto which appeared in English in the *Left Review* in February 1936, and in Hindi in *Hans,* a journal edited by Premchand, in October 1935.

## I

Anand and Zahir were instrumental in organising the 1936 Lucknow conference of the All India Progressive Literary Association, presided over by Premchand. Zahir mobilised support for the Association by forming local chapters at several places including Allahabad, Lahore, Hyderabad and Aligarh. The conference was planned at Lucknow in early April 1936 for a reason – a national convention of the Indian National Congress was scheduled to take place in Lucknow at around the same time. The organisers hoped to rope in Jawaharlal Nehru to preside over the All India Progressive Literary Association. But, eventually, it was Premchand, the most eminent Hindi writer of his generation, who presided over the conference, which was attended by writers from all over India, including Kerala. The conference galvanised the popular anguish against the oppressive apparatus of colonialism, the exploitative regime of feudalism, and the regimentation of society along the lines of caste, class and gender. The manifesto, which was prepared to commemorate the 1936 conference, explicitly spelt out the social role of writers:

> We believe that the new literature of India must deal with the basic problems of our existence today: the problems of hunger and poverty, *social backwardness and political subjection*. All that drags us down to passivity, *inaction and un-reason* we reject as reactionary. All that arouses in us *the critical spirit*, which examines institutions and customs *in the light of reason* which helps us to act, to organize ourselves, to transform, we accept as progressive. (Anand 1979, 20–21; emphasis added)

The statement identifies the 'social backwardness' of India as the reason for its 'political subjection'. The writer, as an activist, is also a rationalist, interrogating tradition and orthodoxy. His/her critical spirit enables the transformation of literature. Some of these ideas were reiterated in the presidential address by Premchand. He declared that a writer is, by nature, progressive, and 'the greater the intensity of his pain the more powerful his writings and the more realistic his portrayal' (Jain 2010, 123). He added, 'Progress, to me, is that situation which generates in us the resolution and the will to act, which makes us aware of our pain, which helps us identity the various internal and external reasons that have led to this condition of desolation and decline, and which impels us to try and overcome them' (124). He wanted writers to redefine their ideas of 'beauty' in the context of a changing society and inculcate in them openness to new knowledge. He concluded his speech with these words:

> But we do not consider literature as a means of enjoyment and luxury alone. Real literature for us is one which consists of high philosophy, a desire for independence, the essence of beauty, the instinct for creativity, and which is illuminated by the realities of life—one which can generate a momentum in our lives, make us restless and generate in us the will to fight; it should not put us to sleep, for to sleep any more now is a sign of death. (131)

The credo of social realism, thus, became a mode of embodying the social ferment and gathering its potential for intervention in the direction of a radical poetic. Most of the literatures in India came under the spell of this radical poetic during the period from the mid-1930s to the late 50s. Sisir Kumar Das, in his history of Indian literature, has observed that the impact of the progressive movement was felt in all major literatures of India: 'The most positive impact of the [All India Progressive] Association was on the growth of literature which can be loosely described as "socialist" so far as its themes and moods are concerned. There was hardly any growing literature in India now which did not respond to the growing and expanding socialist ideas" (1995, 88). We will take up the case of Malayalam literature here for a detailed study, as it will illustrate the nature of the contestations that defined the trajectory of this transformative poetic.

## 2

Translation had played an enabling role in the development of Malayalam fiction, even before the arrival of the progressive literary movement on the scene. In 1925, the publication of the Malayalam translation of Victor Hugo's *Les misérables* brought about a shift in the prevailing literary sensibility. Hugo may be better known as a Romantic poet in France, but for the Malayalam reader, his *Les misérables* opened up possibilities of imagining alternative models of reality. The Malayalam novel, after the pioneering efforts of social reformist writers such as O. Chandu Menon in the late nineteenth century, had become stereotyped in their approach to reality. While Malayalam poetry had responded to the anti-colonial nationalist movement in the 1920s with a new poetic, the novel in Malayalam merely reproduced formulaic plots. Against such a backdrop, the translation of Hugo's novel, based on its English version, by Nalapat Narayana Menon (1887–1954), proved a creative intervention. Menon employed the 'foreignising' mode of translation which had the effect of defamiliarising the very syntax of Malayalam. Many of his literal translations have become part of the everyday idiom in the language. This translation provided a new set of subtexts that could render into a tangible narrative the unfocussed disquiet of a period that was yet to find expression. *Les misérables* problematised the conflict between law and justice, suffering and survival, dehumanising repression and the redemptive epiphany of human dignity, against the turbulent period of revolutionary France. This translation revamped the apparatus of fictional representation by making available to the reader a new discourse about *being* human. This amounted to making visible the inner contradictions of a stratified society divided along the lines of caste, class and gender.

A meeting of Progressive Literary Association was held at Thrissur in Kerala on 20 April 1937, under the leadership of K. Damodaran, who had attended the 1936 Lucknow meeting, and a few political activists and writers such as P. Kesava Dev, K. A. Damodara Menon, E. M. S. Namboodiripad, C. Narayana Pillai, K. K. Variyar, P. Narayanan Nair and A. Madhavan. It is significant to note that E. M. S. Namboodiripad and K. A. Damodara Menon went on to become well-known political leaders. During the proceedings of the meeting, contemporary Malayalam literature was criticised severely for its elitist bias and lack of social concern. The Association was rechristened 'Jeeval Sahitya Samgham' in Malayalam, to signify its close affinity to life and lived experience (the term '*jeeva*' suggesting 'life'); and 'jeeval sahityam' ('literature of life', literally) was defined as a 'new literature that will promote equality of opportunity, opposing the present exploitative system, in favour of a realistic representation of man's struggles against nature as well as his circumstances' (Sardarkutty 1993, 49). In an article published in the Malayalam daily *Mathrubhumi* on 25 May 1937, the following objectives of the Jeeval Sahitya movement were spelt out: 'to publish literature of the progressive kind, to forge unity among progressive writers, to translate "progressive literature" from other languages and oppose reactionary forces in culture and fight for the freedom of expression' (52). The model provided by Hugo received further legitimation from the endorsement of the social realist mode by progressive writers. As shown by the example of *Angaaray* in Urdu, critical examination of existing social mores was the new role that the progressive movement envisaged for writers. The social realist mode functioned as an oppositional discourse, interrogating the existing attitudes to culture and contemporary social thought.

The trajectory of Jeeval Sahitya Samgham, which held a series of meetings across Kerala in the next decade, is one of bitter controversies and acrimonious dialogues between those who considered freedom of expression as sacrosanct and those who wanted to use literature as a vehicle of social change. In the 1949 meeting held at Thrissur, the eminent critic M. P. Paul, who presided over the gathering, spoke against the main resolution that sought to ensure the writers' allegiance to the political ideology of the communist movement. The progressive movement soon lost its sense of direction and purpose; but by this time, it had succeeded in putting on the social agenda of writers in Malayalam issues related to the writer's commitment to political ideology, the relation between form and content, and the irreconcilable dichotomies of aesthetics and politics in contemporary literature. In effect, the writings that appeared in the wake of the progressive literary movement problematised the very idea of the 'literary' and its relation with the socio-political.

## 3

The radicalisation of the literary discourse, during this phase in Malayalam literature, was largely achieved through the agency of translation. In this section, we will briefly examine the critical role of the writer A. Balakrishna Pillai (1889–1960) who, through his interventions as editor, translator, literary critic and social commentator, shaped a secular, progressive and analytical language to speak of literature and its relation to life. By combining the roles of a political activist, literary critic and social thinker, Pillai redefined the relation between literature and the public sphere in Kerala society. Though Pillai was never part of the progressive literary movement, he supported its radical agenda, articulating its core ideas through commentaries and review articles in his periodicals and prologues to contemporary works. He was arrested thrice by the Travancore government for inciting 'rebellion'. In the 1930s, his periodicals, *Prabodhakan* and *Kesari*, published a wide variety of translations from European avant-garde literature, and were proscribed by the authorities. He encouraged writers like Thakazhi Sivasankara Pillai to translate social realist fiction from European languages. Among the writers Balakrishna Pillai translated and published were Flaubert, Maupassant, Balzac, Stendhal and Ibsen. His editorials dealt with literary subjects, along with social and political topics, and mounted scathing attacks on the king of Travancore and his *diwan* (prime minister). In an editorial written on 21 January 1931, titled 'The Turbulent Malayalam Literature', Pillai argued that free thinking and 'the desecration of idols' (*vigraha dhwamsanam* in Malayalam) were essential for literature to develop. The epic, as a form, he said, was in decline all over the world. Quoting the Italian critic Benedetto Croce, he argued that there was no essential difference between prose and verse. Pillai's essays contained translations from European thinkers and writers – translations clearing a space and breaching the closed world of prevailing literary cultures.

Collectively, these translations of avant-garde authors from Europe and America, belonging to different schools of writing and thought, created a literary public sphere where the discourses of literature were seen as part of socio-political discourses. For instance, Pillai's views on the critical role of literature, particularly the novel, in democratising society can be discerned from these comments, taken from the essay 'The Pitiable State of Malayalam Prose':

> When Malayalam writers produce novels portraying the reality of Kerala society, they will have to be critical of Kerala society. When they do so, the government, the Universities and then text-book committees will withdraw their patronage though they would not send them to jail as Mussolini did in Italy. Real novels can appear only when this state of affairs changes. And the public will have to work very hard to change it. (1991, 11)

Pillai's *Novel prasthanangal* (Movements in the history of the novel) elaborately documents, with examples, the trends in the European novel. The essays in this book carry translations of long passages from European novels to illustrate the narrative styles and techniques of writers such as Marcel Proust, Thomas Mann, André Gide, John Dos Passos,

D. H. Lawrence and William Faulkner. The psychological breakthrough achieved in the treatment of sexuality by Western writers is highlighted in another long section. Pillai's interest in the European avant-garde was prompted by the need to critique the literary field in Malayalam. Central to his project was the creation of a new social imaginary which enabled writers to critique social practices and create a modern secular literary discourse. Pillai also wrote extensively on the trends in European art, illustrating with examples the characteristics of movements such as impressionism, post-impressionism, cubism, futurism, expressionism, surrealism and the abstract art. He wrote essays on Vincent van Gogh, Paul Cézanne, Pablo Picasso and other masters of European art. What this accent on the European avant-garde achieved in the 1930s and 40s in Malayalam was the creation of a new consciousness about the role of art and literature in society. This enabled a new generation of writers to question the existing poetic, and through it, the prevailing 'prestige styles' of literature and its canons. *Thottiyude makan* (The scavenger's son, 1947) and *Randidangazhi* (Two measures of rice, 1948) by Thakazhi Sivasankara Pillai, *Shabdangal* (The voices, 1947) by Vaikom Muhammad Basheer, and stories such as *Pratikaradevata* (The goddess of revenge) and *Kuttasammatham* (Admission of guilt) by Lalithambika Antharjanam partake of this new social imaginary as a metaphorical space that maps the fault lines and fissures of a fractured society and polity. In such works, the nation became a contested space where the false consensus of elitist narratives was critiqued from the margins. Most of the writers of this period – such as Thakazhi Sivasankara Pillai, Kesava Dev and Ponkunnam Varkey – were also translators. In their work, the domain of fiction externalised the oppositional content through marginalised voices which became available for representation through the enabling role played by translation.

## 4

The concept of translation has to be understood in a wider perspective, in the context of this chapter. André Lefevere has argued that literature is a system, 'embedded in the environment of a culture or society' (Venuti 2000, 235) and that 'the degree to which the foreign writer is accepted in the native system will be determined by the need that native system has of him in a certain phase of its evolution' (237). It is the inner dynamics of the native literary system that decides the 'acceptability' of the translated work. Lefevere also argues that we need to expand the very concept of translation to include various forms in which literary cultures receive foreign authors. He uses the word 'refractions' or 'rewriting':

> Refractions are to be found in the obvious form of translation, or in the less obvious form of criticism (the wholesale allegorization of the literature of the Antiquity by the Church Fathers, e.g.), commentary, historiography (of the plot summary of famous works cum evaluation type, in which the evaluation is unabashedly based on the current concept of what 'good' literature should be), teaching, the collection of works in anthologies, the production of plays. (235)

New writing styles and themes come to be validated through the patronage extended to translations, thus facilitating a transformation in the very structure of the sensibility. In the case of Malayalam literature, the patterns of contestations with the prevailing 'prestige styles', initiated by Pillai's critical articles, became an organised form of revolt with the arrival of the progressive literary movement. The debates on the relative merits of the 'old' and the 'new', the role of the artist in society, and the relation between literature and politics, soon defined the direction taken by Malayalam literature in the next two decades.

To illustrate the nature of these debates, we may briefly look at the arguments of those who opposed the progressive literary movement. Kuttikrishna Marar (1900–73), an eminent critic, was outspoken in his contempt for the group. He agreed that literature has a social function, of imparting moral instruction. However, for him, the 'literary' form was primary, and not the content. It is the formal perfection that enabled art to influence society, and not the mere fact of its content. Pillai had argued that a poet or a novelist was only a skilled worker and that he could not claim a greater status than those enjoyed by other skilled workers. Marar countered this by stating that readers had to strive to reach the sublime levels attained by the aesthetic beauty of the artist. He or she has to cultivate 'taste' through education and reflection, since the artist will always remain above and beyond the reader (1990, 354–59). The key words of the debate that continued through the 1930s and 40s were: life, society, reality, commitment, art for art's sake, art for life's sake, proletarian literature versus 'prestige' literature, form and content, and the public role of the artist. In his history of Malayalam literature, N. Krishna Pillai lists more than forty European and American novelists who were translated into Malayalam during the three decades from the mid-1930s (1998, 375).

The social energy generated by these translations and debates democratised literature and widened the literary public sphere. The new fiction could effectively channelise this social energy into narratives of resistance which began appearing in Malayalam from the late 1930s onwards. For instance, Thakazhi's *Thyagathinte pratiphalam* (The reward for the sacrifice, 1939) tells the story of a woman forced into prostitution. P. Kesava Dev's *Otayilninnu* (From the gutters, 1948) narrates the struggles of a rickshaw-puller to lead a life of dignity. Thakazhi's *Thottiyude makan* narrates the story of the lower classes who are condemned to work as scavengers; and *Randidangazhi* focuses on the lives of Dalit farmers in Kuttanad. Vaikom Muhammad Basheer's *Balyakalasakhi* (Childhood friend, 1944) narrates a tragic love story against the background of poverty and suffering set in the Muslim community of Kerala, while *Shabdangal* projected the traumatic memories of an ex-soldier haunted by war and violence. Communities that were hitherto unknown now became visible through fictional narratives. Indian society, which had been immobilised by colonial power structures and the stratified caste system, found its articulation through these oppositional narratives.

## 5

To conclude, it was the agency of translation, in all its various forms of 'refraction'/'rewriting', that mediated the creation of a literary public sphere in Kerala, by legitimating new modes of expression and mapping new contours of experience. Translation negotiates between two literary sensibilities, pluralising centres of authority and opening up possibilities, when a literary system is in a state of ferment. Editorials in periodicals, manifestoes of literary associations, commentaries on new books and authors, descriptions of new artistic and literary movements, debates on the comparative merits of different approaches to art and aesthetics, introductions to anthologies and a new historiography – all these have to be studied in consonance with translations to understand how, during the progressive phase, the literary system in Malayalam and other Indian languages developed a new habitus and a new poetic that reflected as well as engaged the contradictions of a transitional period and formulated a new equation between the literary and the political, by incorporating the marginalised into the literary public sphere.

## References

Anand, Mulk Raj. 1979. On the progressive writers' movement. In *Marxist Cultural Movement in India*, ed. S. Pradhan, 32–48. Calcutta (Kolkata): National Book Agency.

Coppola, Carlo. 1986. Premchand's address to the first meeting of the All India Progressive Literary Association: Some speculations. *Journal of South Asian Literature* 21. 2: 21–39.

Das, Sisir Kumar. 1995. *A history of Indian literature 1911–1956: Struggle for freedom: Triumph and tragedy.* New Delhi: Sahitya Akademi.

Gopal, Priyamvada. 2005. *Literary radicalism in India: Gender, nation and the transition to Independence.* London and New York: Routledge.

Jain, Jasbir. 2010. *The writer as critic: Essays in literature, history and culture.* Jaipur and Delhi: Rawat Publications.

Marar, Kuttikrishna. 1990. *Theranjedutha prabandhangal* [Selected essays]. Thrissur: Kerala Sahitya Akademi.

Pillai, A. Balakrishna. 1991. *Novel prasthanangal* [Movements in the history of the novel]. Kottayam: D. C. Books.

Pillai, N. Krishna. 1998. *Kairaliyude katha* [A history of Malayalam literature]. Kottayam: SPCS.

Sardarkutty, E. 1993. *Purogamana sahitya niroopanam* [A critical history of progressive literature]. Thiruvananthapuram: State Institute of Languages.

Venuti, Lawrence, ed. 2000. *The translation studies reader.* London and New York: Routledge.

## Chapter Fifteen

# Shifting Centres and Emerging Margins: Translation and the Shaping of Modernist Poetic Discourse in Indian Poetry

This chapter examines the role played by translation in shaping a modernist poetic sensibility in some of the major literary traditions of India in the twentieth century, between 1950 and 1970. Translations of major European poets such as Baudelaire, Rilke, Eliot and Yeats contributed towards clearing a space for the modernist discourse in Indian poetry. The chapter will study examples from Bengali, Malayalam and Marathi, to understand how such translations of modern Western poets were used to breach the hegemony of prevailing literary sensibilities and poetic modes. Many of the major Indian poets – such as Buddhadeb Bose, Agyeya, Gopalakrishna Adiga, Dilip Chitre and Ayyappa Paniker – were also translators. Their translations were 'foreignising' translations that disrupted cultural codes that legislated regimes of reading and writing poetry. Also, translations during the early phase of modernism in major Indian languages appeared in little magazines that played a critical role in opening up the poetic discourse. Apart from providing alternative models of thinking and imagining the world, these translations also legitimised experimental writing styles that became a defining feature of modernist Indian poetry. As the contradictions within the 'high' modernist mode deepened in the politically turbulent 1960s, one witnessed a gradual radicalisation of modernist sensibility in these languages. Here, once again, it is translation that enabled poets to turn away from the modernist 'high' style, providing a critique of its elitism and complicity with nationalist discourses. Translations from African and Latin American poetry played a significant role in this phase of modernism. Poets such as Neruda and Parra were widely translated into Indian languages during this phase. In this context, translation enacted a critical act of evaluation, a creative act of intervention, and a performative act of legitimation, in evolving a new poetic during the modernist phase of Indian poetry.

Translation was integral to the project of modernism in Indian languages, in assimilating a new poetic into the horizon of the 'native' reader's expectations as well as in contesting the claims of prevailing aesthetic norms by breaching its autonomy and authority. The Indian modernist form emerged from a socio-political formation that demanded change; and as such, the dynamics of Indian culture was responding to the deeper seismic forces shaped by historical events such as the communal riots and killings that followed the Partition, the perceived failure of the Nehruvian project of modernity and the consequent erosion of idealism which had inspired an earlier generation of writers committed to socialist realism and Romantic nationalism.

This chapter uses the term 'translation' to suggest a range of cultural practices, from critical commentary to creation of intertextual texts. Following André Lefevere's concept of translation as refraction/rewriting, the chapter argues that 'rewritings' or 'refractions' found in the 'less obvious form of criticism . . . , commentary, historiography (of the plot summary of famous works cum evaluation type, in which the evaluation is unabashedly based on the current concept of what "good" literature should be), teaching, the collection of works in anthologies, the production of plays' (2000, 235) are also instances of translation. Hence, an essay on T. S. Eliot in Bengali by Sudhindranath Dutta, or a scathing critique in Malayalam on the poetic practices of Vallathol Narayana Menon by Ayyappa Paniker, can also be described as 'translational' writings as they have elements of translation embedded in them. Both these essays 'carry across' modes and models from an alien Western tradition to interrogate the self-sufficiency of an entrenched poetic. In India, modernism, as a practice, fundamentally differed from that in the West, but it fulfilled a function in the socio-cultural contexts of Indian languages by transforming the relations between the text and the reader, and the modes of writing and reading. Modernist writers were responding to the internal dynamics of their own traditions in selectively assimilating an alien poetic that could be regressive or subversive depending on the context and the content. In this sense, a conservative poet such as Gopalakrishna Adiga in Kannada, or a radical dissident like Gajanan Madhav Muktibodh in Hindi, belonged to the larger modernist tradition which accommodated diverse political ideologies and innovative experimental styles.

## I

An elaboration on the relation between 'modernity' and 'modernism' in the Indian context will need a separate chapter. For the purpose of our discussion, it may be broadly stated that 'modernity' designates an epochal period of wide-ranging transformations brought about by the advent of colonialism, capitalist economy, industrial mode of production, Western models of education, assimilation of rationalist temper, resurgence of nationalist spirit and emergence of social, political, legal, juridical and educational institutions that constituted a normative subjectivity embodied with cosmopolitan and individualist world views. It has also been argued that such a modular modernity, as envisaged in Western terms, brought about a rupture in the social and cultural life of India, separating its 'modern period' from what was 'pre-modern'. Such a view may be disputed but it can be convincingly shown that the dynamics of literary expression and the apparatus of cultural transmission came to be redefined in the 'modern' period.

The project of modernity in India was implicated in colonialism and imperialism. This colonial modernity informed literary and cultural movements, beginning from the reformist movement of the nineteenth century to the modernist movement of the mid-twentieth century. The modernist revolt in India was a response to the disruptions brought about by colonial modernity. As Dilip Chitre observes, 'what took nearly a century and a half to happen in England , happened within a hurried half century' in Indian literatures (1967, 2). The breaching of entrenched traditions resulted in a crisis which had to be tackled creatively by resorting to the resources of alien traditions. While introducing the works of B. S. Mardhekar, a major Marathi modernist, Chitre says, 'The poet B. S. Mardhekar was the most remarkable product of the cross-pollination between the deeper, larger native tradition and contemporary world culture' (2). It has been argued that the idea of a 'self-referential or self-validating' literary text (P. P. Raveendran in Satchidanandan 2001, 60–61), which is central to modernist poetic, is rooted in an ideology of the aesthetic that was complicit with colonialism. But one has to note that modernist sensibility, as it appeared in Indian languages, was essentially oppositional in content. It countered the prevailing ideology of nationalism, which had become the ideology of the nascent nation state. D. R. Nagaraj has pointed out that as nationalism became the ideology of the nation state, writers who had earlier found nationalism to be a form of resistance to colonialism, retreated to individualism. He adds, 'When ideologies like nationalism and spirituality become apparatuses of the state, a section of the intelligentsia has no option other than to seek refuge in bunkers of individualism' (Nagaraj in Ananthamurthy et al 1992, 108). Experimental writings of the modernist period range from the anarchist/avant-garde to the formalist/conventional.

## 2

The term 'modernism' implies a literary/artistic movement that was characterised by experimentation, conscious rejection of the nationalist/Romantic as well as the popular, and the cultivation of an individualist, cosmopolitan and insular world view. In the European context, it signified a set of tendencies in artistic expression and writing styles of the late nineteenth and early twentieth centuries through a new aesthetic that was iconoclastic, insular and elitist. The aesthetics of modernism in the West had a transnational, metropolitan world view that excluded the claims of the local and the national and made no concession to the popular taste. While the modernism that emerged in Indian literatures shared many of these defining features, its political affiliations and ideological orientations were markedly different. Due to its postcolonial location, the Indian modernism did not share the imperial or metropolitan aspirations of its European counterpart. It invested heavily in regional cosmopolitan traditions. It was oppositional in content and questioned the colonial legacies of the nationalist discourse. It was elitist and formalistic and deeply distrustful of the popular domain.

The modernist phase in Indian language traditions has not been recognised as part of the global modernist movement. The discourse of modernism is heavily slanted in favour of Western writers of the late nineteenth and early twentieth centuries. Chronologically, in Indian languages, modernism manifests itself in the second half of the twentieth century. The postcolonial context adds a complex political dimension to the aesthetic of Indian modernism. How are we to evaluate the modernisms that emerged in the postcolonial phase in India? Critics such as Simon Gikandi, Susan Friedman, Laura Doyle and Laura Winkiel, and Aparna Dharwadker have argued that non-

Western modernisms are not mere derivative versions of a European hegemonic practice. The emergence of modernism in societies in Asia, Africa or Latin America cannot be seen in terms of a European centre and non-European peripheries. The Eurocentric nature of the discourse on modernism can be laid bare only by documenting the 'modernisms' that emerged in non-Western societies. This will enable us to reimagine the centre–periphery dialectic in terms of a dialogic between peripheries. This would need a careful consideration of the nature of the circulation of ideas, indigenous contexts of reception, and strategies of contestations and articulation that constituted the modernist style in Indian contexts. The emerging problematic will have to contend with issues of ideological differences between the Western modernism and the Indian one, the different trajectories they traversed as a result of the difference in socio-political terrains and the dynamics of the relations between the past and the present in the subcontinent, which has a documented history of more than five thousand years. The problematic that informs this argument is manifest in the critiques of Eurocentric accounts of modernism by Gikandi, Friedman, Doyle and Winkiel, and Rebecca L. Walkonwitz, in different ways.

## 3

The reception of Western modernist discourses in India was mediated by the dynamics of socio-political upheavals related to the formation of the nation state and the realignment of power structures in society. This is to say that the dynamics of the local has to be factored into any evaluation of Indian modernism. Since each literary tradition has to contend with certain 'givens' that are peculiar to their evolution and internal configuration, it may not be possible to make a general statement on modernism in India without making exceptions. The oppositional content of the modernist sensibility functioned differently in each regional language. In the context of Bengali, as Amiya Dev has observed, 'It was not because they imbibed modernism that the *adhunik* [modernist] Bengali writers turned away from Rabindranath; on the contrary, Modernism was the means by which they turned away from Rabindranath and they had to turn away, for their history demanded it' (in Ananthamurthy et al 1992, 7). Commenting on the role of Kannada modernists, R. Sasidhar writes,

> If European modernism was drawn between the euphoric and the reactive, in Kannada the precipitate modernism was drawn between the Brahminical and the non-Brahminical. Just as the euphoric and the reactive modernisms were part of the internal dynamics of modernism itself, so also the Brahmanical and the non-Brahmanical modernisms in Kannada were part and parcel of a modernism that came as a reaction to the Nehruvian environment. (in Satchidanandan 2001, 34)

Issues of caste, ethnicity, progress, freedom, individualism, region and nation figure variously in different modernist traditions in India. The presence of a father-figure, like that of Tagore in Bengali, is a fact that is not relevant to the development of Kannada or Malayalam modernism.

## 4

Translation enables us to delineate the complex artistic and ideological undercurrents that shaped the course of modernism in Indian literatures. To discuss this, we will look at three representative modernist authors from three separate Indian literary traditions – Sudhindranath Dutta (1901–60) from Bengali, B. S. Mardhekar (1909–56) from Marathi and Ayyappa Paniker (1936–2004) from Malayalam. These authors help us see the chronological trajectory of modernism across Indian literatures. While the modernist shift in Bengali emerged in the 1930s and continued into the 40s and 50s, it manifested itself in Marathi from the 1950s to the 60s. It was in the 1960s that the Malayalam literary sensibility was transformed into the modernist mould, its influence slowly waning by the late 70s, though by that time, it had redefined the relations between content and form in all literary forms.

Translation is central to the modernist poetic as it unfolded in these literary traditions. Each of these three authors was bilingual and wrote essays in English as well as their own languages, outlining their new poetic, thus preparing the reader for new poetic modes. Their essays elaborated the basic features of a new aesthetic against the prevailing Romantic–nationalist or Romantic–mystical traditions. Sudhindranath Dutta translated Stéphane Mallarmé and Paul Valéry into Bengali.

Buddhadeb Bose, another Bengali modernist, rendered 112 poems of Charles Baudelaire's *The Flowers of Evil* into Bengali, apart from translating Rainer Maria Rilke, Friedrich Hölderlin, Ezra Pound, e. e. cummings, Wallace Stevens and Boris Pasternak. Ayyappa Paniker translated European poets into Malayalam, while B. S. Mardhekar's *Arts and the Man* (which was published in England in 1937) was a treatise on formalist aesthetic that legitimated modernist practice. Mardhekar had earlier attempted original poems in English, while he was in England in the 30s. Their profound understanding of Western philosophy and artistic/literary traditions equipped these three writers with the critical capacity to see the significance and limitations of the West. All of them wrote critical studies validating the emergence of a new poetry. It is also important to note that their discursive prose on matters of form in poetry need to be seen as part of an attempt to 'translate modernism' into Indian terms.

## 5

One of the recurring themes in Sudhindranath Dutta's critical essays is the primacy of the word. In 'The Necessity of Poetry', he argues that the persistence of poetry through the ages in all societies, particularly among the unsophisticated and the primitive, attest to its necessity (Chaudhuri 2008, 3). His discussion of Aristotle, Plato, Voltaire, Byron, Mallarmé and Yeats prove his mastery over Western thought. Though he claims himself to be a pragmatist, Dutta believes that 'only the poetic mind, whatever its norm, can intuit associations where reason faces a void' (5). In assigning a higher role for poetry in life, he seems to reject the centrality of the Enlightenment idea of reason in modern society. Thus, the case for the modernist poetic is argued in a persuasive manner in the context of the everyday world and its needs. In another essay, 'The Highbrow', he observes, 'I agree with Virginia Woolf that creative artists must from time to time seek shelter within the much maligned Ivory Tower' (9). This does not mean that Dutta was a formalist committed to a hermetic aesthetic. He constantly invokes the progressive role of the writer in a society, and underlines the role played by the masses in the creation of a literary tradition. He observes in 'Whiggism, Radicalism and Treason in Bengal': 'Not the introspecting intellectuals, but the enduring masses are the guardians of tradition and directors of progress; and whatever be the calibre of the experimenter, unless he passes the pragmatic test of his people, the facts he would establish are febrile dreams, and the truths he would loudly proclaim are a maniac's fancies' (22).

Dutta is critical of the Anglicists, who abdicated the larger responsibility of emancipating the people from the illusions bred by colonialism. He invokes the art of Jamini Roy for having boldly shown the way forward by evolving a universal mode of representation, using elements of traditional Indian art (Chaudhuri 2008, 24). Here, we can see one of the complex contradictions that beset Indian modernists: their pursuit of cosmopolitan and universal values could not be at the cost of a complete disjunction from tradition. In his radio talk on Eliot, delivered on the occasion of the latter winning the Nobel Prize in 1948, Dutta highlights Eliot's commitment to tradition as 'revolutionary in the fullest sense of the term'. He adds, 'But I am convinced that if civilization is to survive the atomic war, Mr. Eliot's ideal must become widely accepted, so that in the oases that may escape destruction it may be cherished through the interregnum' (55). Obviously, Dutta's endorsement of Eliot's world view has to be seen in relation to his critique of contemporary Indian society. Modernism in India was part of a larger decolonising project. It was not a mindless celebration of Western values and the European avant-garde.

In Dutta's well-known poem, 'The Camel-Bird', one may glimpse this critical spirit and desire to reinvent tradition from a cosmopolitan perspective. The poem is about the crisis of perception that can only be remedied by reinventing oneself completely. In the poem, the bird is presented as vulnerable and incapable of defending itself against the hunter. The poem ends with this stanza:

> This ruin is our inheritance:
> A line of spendthrifts went before;
> They picked the pounds, and left no pence:
> Now both of us must pay their score
> And so your self-absorption seems
> Inept: Can blindness cheat a curse?
> The present is no time for dreams:
> By shunning me you make bad worse
> Let each of us then seal a bond
> To serve the other's interest

> You speed me to the world beyond,
> While I propose the human test. (qtd. in Ananthamurthy et al 1992, 28)

The poet locates himself in a threatened landscape of ruins where he and the bird have no access to the glorious traditions of the past. Disinherited and defeated, the poet retreats into his wounded self, which has to devise its own strategies of survival in a hostile environment, bereft of the nourishing streams of the past. The poem speaks of the poet's alienation in the present, his disjunction with the past, his need to recover a bond with the world outside and the angst inherent in the quest for meaning in a world haunted by violence and servility. As a modernist poem, 'The Camel-Bird' moves beyond the personal by embodying the condition of inertia that a colonised community is condemned to. While its voice of anguish is personal and intimate, bearing testimony to a personal crisis, its larger burden is the quest for humanity in a brutalised world, and the recovery of a sense of community in an uprooted world of isolated selves.

## 6

B. S. Mardhekar transformed Marathi poetry and its direction and dynamics in terms of its vision, form and content. Like Dutta, he was deeply aware of the entire 'tradition' of Marathi poetry from its beginnings. He published a treatise on aesthetics, *Arts and the Man*, in London in 1937, and *Two Lectures on the Aesthetic of Literature* in Bombay (Mumbai) in 1944. Together, they make a strong case for a modernist aesthetic in Marathi. P. S. Rege, another major modernist Marathi poet, also had spent time in London in the 1930s and was profoundly influenced by modernist poets like Eliot. Both Rege and Mardhekar went back to the roots of Marathi poetic traditions to reinvent the saint-poets such as Tukaram and Ramdas for a modern audience. One may locate a parallel movement in what Eliot and Pound did with reference to the reinterpretation of the Provencal poets, Guido Cavalcanti, Dante and the Metaphysical poets, in their own time. But the parallel cannot be forced beyond a point.

Mardhekar intervened in Marathi literary tradition as an insider who had mastered the insights given by an alien tradition. Mardhekar's creative reclamation of tradition is a response to the disruption of a moral order in his culture. He had to invent a language to articulate this fragmentation. The existential angst, psychological disorientation and political disillusionment he experienced in the urban turbulence of Bombay may have superficial parallels with what the metropolitan modernists underwent in the West, but Mardhekar's case was more complex. His alienation from tradition and his allegiance to tradition were inseparable. He lived in a society which had an internal discourse of modernity, beginning with Jyotiba Phule in the nineteenth century and extending to Bhimrao Ambedkar in the twentieth. Hence, it would be wrong to say that his modernity did not have any indigenous resources. (This is also true of Dutta and Paniker in different ways.) Mardhekar's own poetic practice, which was much more complex than his critical arguments, problematised the relation between the poet and the reader, contemporary poetry and its past, and poetic form and its ideological function in society. His poetry was deliberately obscure and his devastating irony was a means of negotiating the contradictions that threatened to rip apart his sense of himself as a social being. Mardhekar's poetic line carried echoes of saint-poets like Tukaram, creating a self-reflexive idiom. This enabled him to embody the moral squalour of contemporary society even as he invoked an order of the sacred rooted in tradition.

In Mardhekar, both irony and self-reflexivity are ways of constituting a new reader by freeing him or her from his or her habits of viewing the world. These are strategies to re-inscribe a self-critical attitude towards the material content of art and life. In 'Mice in the Wet Barrel Died', which became the iconic modernist poem of Marathi, Mardhekar goes to the very limits of language to capture an acute state of anguish that is closer to the saint-poet's suffering than the existential crisis of the modern man or woman. The opening lines of the poem capture the wretched nature of their existence:

> mice in the wet barrel died;
> their necks dropped, untwisted;
> their lips closed with lips;
> their necks fell, undesiring. (Chitre 1967, 55)

The metaphor of the mice is meant to evoke the morbid and the malevolent in modern life. In the subsequent lines of the poem,

Mardhekar points to their blind search for survival in a hostile world. The surreal image in the line, 'sadness has poisonous eyes made of glass', sums up the opaqueness of their vision and the toxic nature of their condemned existence unrelieved by any sense of benign order of life. This sense of being trapped with no exit is a characteristically urban/ metropolitan experience one encounters in modern literature. When this poem was originally published in Marathi, in *Abhiruchi*, it was met with several disapproving comments, leading to long discussions and even parodies of the poem in Marathi. The existential horror of urban life had never before found expression in Indian poetry with such force. The poem is replete with references to physical details of decrepitude and degeneration. The rats die hiccupping in the barrel. The daylight that spills on their ash-grey eyes and washes their limbs and phalluses does not revive them. Living and dying become matters of habit, an obsessive compulsion devoid of any rationale. Mardhekar captures the haunting malignancy of modern existence in the line discussed above: 'sadness has poisonous eyes made of glass'. The honeyed corals which gather on the lips are artificial, tinsel. The shock effect of the line is augmented by the dislocation of the word order in the original.

To see how subversive Mardhekar could be in the original, we need to remember that he could address God with such irreverence: 'There is still a choice curse / on my tongue for you.' This is followed by a prayer: 'Grant me, O Lord, just his one boon: Let my tongue never be paralysed.' As Vilas Sarang (1988) points out, in the original Marathi version, Mardhekar uses two separate words, *jibha* and *jivha*, for 'tongue', the former a modern colloquial word and the latter an archaic term suggesting 'devotion'. Mardhekar constantly uses the archaic diction of the saint-poets of the medieval period. He also juxtaposes formal 'poetic' words with everyday English words, creating a collage of images. In the poem 'Although the Lights', Mardhekar uses the words 'punctured', 'pumps', 'rubber' and 'pumps' in unusual collocations. The poem opens with lines that suggest a surge of darkness against lights 'that puncture the night', as a mechanical activity. The night is seen as a synthetic substance that is formless, suggesting a process of dissolution:

The rubber night went suddenly flat
There is no other tyre in space;

> The dogs sit licking the piles
> Of the slough of a coarse mind. (Engblom 1990, 43)

The human and the mechanical/artificial intermingle in the subsequent lines suggesting a loss of the human in the urban landscape. Mardhekar conveys the dehumanised cityscape in images that are stark and quotidian, with searing clarity. The poem develops the central image of bleakness and despair into a vivid landscape of harrowing metaphors. Philip C. Engblom shows how Mardhekar transplants the modernist mode into Marathi: '[The poem] does not make a paraphrasable statement. Its structural principle, rather than based on discursive logic or narrative, is determined by what Ezra Pound called "a governing image"—or really, in this case, two governing images, rubber tyre and dogs—which develop according to their own metaphoric "logic of the imagination". This is characteristic, defining technique of Modernist poetry' (43).

## 7

Like Mardhekar, Ayyappa Paniker also began as a Romantic poet but transformed himself into a modernist with a long poetic sequence titled *Kurukshetram* published in 1960. Paniker was a poet, critic and translator, who, apart from introducing world poetry to Malayalam readers through translations published in his little magazine, *Kerala Kavita,* also created the cultural environment for a shift in the literary sensibility through critical interventions. He published a translation of *The Love Song of Alfred J. Prufrock* in his journal in 1953. Earlier, in 1950, in an article on T. S. Eliot, Paniker had highlighted the idea that it was not form and prosody that created poetry but the invention of rhythm and resonance that befit the emotion. He urged Malayalam poets to reject prosody in favour of rhythmic free verse. In a scathing attack on Vallathol Narayana Menon, a canonical figure of Malayalam Romantic poetry, Paniker brought out Vallathol's lack of intellectual rigour, his dubious political attitudes and adherence to wornout idioms and stale diction. Paniker argued that a writer has to integrate his or her personal and public selves into an emotional apprehension of the totality of relative truths about the world bound by time and space. In a seminal essay on modern Malayalam poetry, he argued that the ideology of the poet is embodied in the syntactic structure of the poem. The modernist poet has to reject the allegorical and the didactic, to articulate his or her complex awareness of the relation between form and content. The Romantic poets had made a shift from Sanskritic traditions to folk metres, which was a movement towards open forms. The experimental poetry of the modernists, on the other hand, opened up poetic forms further, by using imagist, suggestive free verse that affirmed that each poem has its authentic form which cannot be approximated to a metre which functions independent of content. Here, one may also recall the contribution of M. Govindan, a poet-critic who was closely associated with the modernist movement in Malayalam from its very beginning, particularly through his patronage of young writers such as Paniker, through his avant-garde journal, *Sameeksha.* Govindan advocated a return to the Dravidian sources of Malayalam poetry, which he thought could rejuvenate its syntax and rhythm through a robust earthliness that had been curbed by the scholastic Sanskritic tradition.

*Kurkshetram* is a poem of 294 lines in five sections. The opening lines of the Bhagavad Gita are cited as the epigraph of the poem, thus setting a high moral and critical tone in relation to contemporary life and society. As in Eliot's *The Waste Land, Kurukshetram*'s opening lines communicate a pervasive decline of moral values and a disruption of the organic rhythms of society:

> The eyes suck and sip
> The tears that spurt;
> The nerves drink up the coursing blood;
> And it is the bones that
> Eat the marrow here
> While the skin preys on the bones
> The roots turn carnivore
> As they prey on the flowers
> While the earth in bloom
> Clutches and tears at the roots. (Paniker 1985, 14–15)

The title, 'Kurukshetram', signifies the place where the epic battle that forms the central theme of the *Mahabharata* took place. The poem progresses through broken images from contemporary life, but there are also redemptive memories of forgotten harmonies that recur through the metaphor of the dream. The evocative rhythms of the poem provoke a profound disquiet that cannot be particularised. The self is seen as a site of struggle and conflict, but the modern men and women are denied the tragic dignity of epic heroes. The triviality of everyday life drowns all their yearnings to transcend the sense of disintegration. In a revealing metaphor, Paniker speaks of the hordes of devotees tearing their eyes out, to fix them with spectacles of faith. Against the overwhelming pain of dream, desire and despair, and the labyrinth of the daily grind, the entangled wisdom of 'philosophies' looks unreal. The poet describes contemporary society in terms of a market place where people come to bargain, buy and sell.

The second section of the poem retreats into a private space, away from these public images. The inner movement of the poetic structure signifies the undercurrents of a conflict that cannot be paraphrased in moral terms. In this sense, the poem defies the representational structure of the mimetic type. Lines such as, 'Rose of my dream, why do you wear the fevered look? / Singer of my vision, why do you droop and wilt?' (18), invoke subterranean depths of the mind from where memories of an organic community speak to the poet. But this vision of harmony is short-lived, as the self once again relapses into its infernal vision of collapse and disruption. The torments of dream, desire and despair interrupt the poem, and the poet recognises the futility that haunts his existence:

> Athwart the circumambient void
> an expiring meteor hurtles to the earth beneath;
> and this sphere of ours turns on its self-driven axis. (20)

The third section returns to the public world of conflicts. The mythical characters of Sugriva, Vibhishana, Vashistha, Lord Ram, Arjuna and Oedipus are invoked in this section. The wisdom encoded in myths is now inaccessible to modern men and women, who are diminished into fragmented dehumanised figures. Since the self inhabits a violated space, it lacks the power to know itself.

In the fourth section, the poet denounces the promises made by faith as well as politics, to turn towards the inner resources of the self:

> Around us
> The varied visions of a heaven on earth
> Grow dim, and dwindle and die;
> What avails the journeying spirit
> In its onward march?
> What can self sustain?

Let us, then,
Move into a new frenzy
And wage an endless flight
To shape and remould
The world around
Nearer to the heart's desire.
Our own hands must trace the route ahead;
Our own eyes decide where the feet should go. (23)

This is an existential confrontation with the void, where the self recognises its absolute isolation and vulnerability in a hostile world where there are no sages or saviours. It tries to affirm its inner resources to reconstitute the self and reinvent the world. But this resolve is short-lived as the images of mindless violence crowd the poem in the last section, with the figure of Gandhi as a failed prophet standing at its centre. But the poet also addresses the dream which has been haunting him all through. He has wandered after false gods all his life and now, in the hour of acute self-fragmentation, he turns to his dream which shines like a beacon of life. He has to be reborn in the lotus of this dream, which will bloom out of his navel. Here the poem invokes the image of Brahma, the creator of life, who, according to Hindu mythology, sits on the lotus sprouting out of the navel of Lord Vishnu, the God responsible for preserving life and the world. The image of the apocalypse, which animates the poem from the beginning, seems to be held at bay at the end through this desire to redeem oneself through imagination. It is obvious that the poem has no vision to offer, only a desire to reimagine the world after one's own vision.

## 8

It is important to understand the indigenous roots/routes of modernity and modernism in all the three writers discussed above. They partake of the logic of a postcolonial society which had already developed internal critiques of Western modernity. In other words, they had access to the intellectual resources of alternative traditions of modernity that were bred in the native context. This enables them to selectively assimilate resources of a Western modernity on their own terms. They 'translate' modernity/modernism through the optics of postcolonial 'modernities'. There is an internal dialectic and an external dialogic involved here.

Their relations with Western modernism need to be seen in terms of a dialogism that allows them to negotiate its modes of representation without surrendering to its ideological baggage. At the same time, what allows them to enter into this dialogic relationship is a dialectic that operates in their own culture. They can relate to their language and culture only as critical outsiders. They are critical of the provincial nature of their own culture, even as they relate to its cosmopolitan world views. They value the internal critique of Western modernity, which their cultures had developed over a period of time, but they distrust the grand narratives bred by the same powers of resistance. The act of translation answers something deep within their ambivalent existence, as it embodies their complex relation with a fragmented society. Translation allows them to be 'within' their speech community and 'without' it, at the same time. Their bilingual sensibility demanded a mode of expression that could transit between native and alien traditions.

The modernist subject was fragmented and fractured in the Indian context, but not for reasons that constituted fragmented selves in the Western context. Colonial modernity operated within the Indian context as a realm of desire which brought into being a new social imaginary. The formalist poetic of modernist poetry corresponded to an inner world of desire that produced a language bristling with disquiet and angst. Translation enabled the displaced self of modernity to locate itself in a language that was intimately private and, also, outspokenly public. The idiom of their expression afforded the possibility of self-knowledge through epiphanies that brought 'momentary stays against confusion' (Ramanan 1996, 56). Thus, language became, for the modernists, the only reality that they could relate to. Their moment of re-cognition, enabled by the discourses of 'Western' modernism, was postcolonial in its essence. The self-reflexive mo(ve)ment was also made possible by the carrying across of not content or form, but an interior mode of being that questioned the prevailing limits of freedom.

## References

Ananthamurthy, U. R., Ramachandra Sharma, and D. R. Nagaraj. 1992. *Vibhava: Modernism in Indian writing.* Bangalore: Panther Publications.

Brooker, Peter, and Andew Thacker, eds. 2005. *Geographies of modernism: Literatures, cultures, spaces.* New York: Routledge.

Chaudhuri, Sukanta, ed. 2008. *The art of the intellect: Uncollected English writings of Sudhindranath Datta.* New Delhi: Chronicle Books.

Chitre, Dilip. 1967. *An anthology of Marathi poetry 1945–1965.* Bombay: Nirmala Sadanand Publishers.

Doyle, Laura, and Laura Winkiel. 2005. *Geomodernisms: Race, modernism, modernity.* Bloomington: Indiana UP.

Engblom, Philip C. 1990. Modernism in Bombay: Marathi and English versions. *The Bombay Literary Review* 1: 31–48.

Friedman, Susan Stanford. 2006. Periodizing modernism: Postcolonial modernities and the space/time borders of modernist studies. *Modernism/Modernity* 13. 3: 425–43.

Gikandi, Simon. 1992. *Writing in limbo: Modernism and Caribbean literature.* Ithaca, NY: Cornell UP.

Lefevere, André. 2000. Mother Courage's cucumbers: Text, system and refraction in a theory of literature. In *The translation studies reader*, ed. Lawrence Venuti, 233–49. New York/London: Routledge.

Paniker, Ayyappa. 1985. *Selected poems of Ayyappa Paniker.* Trivandrum: Modern Book Centre.

Ramanan, Mohan, ed. 1996. *Four centuries of American poetry.* Madras (Chennai): Macmillan.

Sarang, Vilas. 1988. *The stylistics of literary translation: A study with reference to English and Marathi.* Bombay: University of Bombay.

Satchidanandan, K., ed. 2001. *Indian poetry: Modernism and after.* New Delhi: Sahitya Akademi.

Walkowitz, Rebecca L. 2006. *Cosmopolitan style: Modernism beyond the nation.* New York: Columbia UP.

**CHAPTER SIXTEEN**

# Shifting Paradigms of Literary Historiography: Malayalam Literary History in the New Millennium

Literary historiography is a site where competing cultural and political ideologies intervene in the production of knowledge about the past. The present chapter focuses on the assumptions and attitudes that shaped the mainstream Malayalam literary historiography as it evolved from late nineteenth century, as part of a quest to define the cultural identity of modern Kerala. P. K. Parameswaran Nair's *Malayala sahitya charitram* (Malayalam literary history, 1958) and N. Krishna Pillai's *Kairaliyude katha* (The story of Malayalam, 1958) project an elitist view of Kerala as culturally homogenous and unified, disregarding the literary contributions of its minorities, women and lower castes. Such totalising evolutionary teleologies have been questioned in recent decades by the revisionist trends in literary historiography exemplified by micro-histories contained in *Anjooru varshathe Keralam* (Kerala of the last five hundred years, 1998) and *Nammude sahityam, nammude samooham* (Our literature, our society, 2001). The chapter probes issues of orality, marginality, cultural plurality and modernity from a decolonising perspective, to recover the dynamic relations of the past with the present.

## I

Literary history, as a discipline, was shaped by the nationalist discourse prevalent in Europe in the nineteenth century. As national literatures became important subjects of study in schools and universities, books detailing their histories became a necessity. These 'literary histories' ran parallel to 'national histories', and were based on the principles of 'race, milieu and moment', developed by the French critic and historian Hippolyte Taine, and that of *Zeitgeist,* as outlined by Hegel. The periodisation of literature also reflected an unwavering faith in the idea of *Zeitgeist,* which pointed towards a common spirit that informs all social and literary events of a particular period. These literary histories contributed towards the creation of national identities. But it is notable that these canonical histories excluded the cultural productions of minorities and the oral traditions which were not seen as part of the 'mainstream'. Such literary histories marginalised several authors and texts, the schematic patterns forging false unities at the cost of pluralities. Though there have been several initiatives in the past by critics belonging to the Russian formalist group, and notably by Mikhail Bakhtin, to counter this view of literary history, it was only in the 1960s, with the rise of structuralism and poststructuralism, that a coherent response to the impasse in literary history became available. In 1967, Hans Robert Jauss published an essay titled 'Literary History as a Provocation of Literary Scholarship' which began with a scathing attack on the prevailing modes of literary historiography. He outlined a theory of reception that mediated between the production and reception of literary texts by a living community. The dialogic space of reception where the readers' viewpoints found articulation was now considered an integral part of any investigation into literary history. Further, in the 1990s, the question of literary historiography came to be scrutinised in the context of literary theory by several critics; and the title of David Perkins's 1992 book – *Is Literary History Possible?* – reflected the prevailing mood in the discipline. All 'grand narratives' were now suspect, and histories were seen reflecting teleologies with specific ideological orientations.

This chapter will focus on Malayalam literary histories and the ideological attitudes they project. As mentioned above, most of these narratives were written when it was believed that literature reflected the collective will of the nation and the objective of writing a literary history was to project a unified view of the identity of the Malayalam-speaking people, their cultural boundaries and linguistic territory. The first Malayalam literary history, *Malayala bhasha charithram* (Malayalam literary history), published in 1881 by P. Govinda Pillai, was clearly part of a larger project of nation-building. Pillai claims a history that goes back to the folk traditions of the thirteenth or fourteenth centuries and the *manipravalam* literature of the fifteenth century. The canon, however, excludes a large number of Christian and Muslim writers who were not considered 'literary'. In fact, none of the canonical literary histories bothered to look at compositions in Arabic Malayalam, which had been in circulation in many parts of Kerala for centuries. These oral texts show the influence of Persian and Arabic literary traditions, thus enlarging the scope of Malayalam literary resources. P. J. Thomas wrote *Keralathile christiya sahitya charithram* (The literary history of Kerala's Christianity, 1935) to highlight the literary contributions of the Christian community. Similarly, several histories and essays on Arabic Malayalam literature have come out in recent times.

As multiple assertions of identity from the periphery proliferate, and the forces of globalisation render the cultural boundaries of Malayalam permeable and porous, the assumptions of conventional historiography will be subjected to scrutiny. For instance, the construction of Kerala as a bounded political unit with a homogenous population speaking a single language, Malayalam, will be challenged. P. K. Parameswaran Nair's *Malayala sahitya charithram* (Malayalam literary history, 1958) and N. Krishna Pillai's *Kairaliyude katha* (The story of Malayalam, 1958) share such conventional views and closely follow a linear model of chronology – following Malayalam's emergence as a separate language and Kerala's subsequent development as a separate political category. In these narratives, literature is a means of charting a cultural geography, which is projected onto a territory as a unified language with its own separate history, identity and destiny.

N. Krishna Pillai and P. K. Parameswaran Nair present an essentialist and exclusivist view of history. The historicism that is at the back of their narratives essentialises the notion of the 'literary' as a quality inherent in textual material. It is an insular concept that excludes oral creations and several other forms of writings, such as travelogues, autobiographies, biographies and translations. Historicism considers the socio-political as incidental or external to the literary text. It is unaware of the 'fictionality' of history as a narrative and the 'textuality' of literature as fictions. They are devoid of self-reflexivity, making them totalising narratives claiming complete objectivity. The past is seen here as closed and unalterable, with no echoes in the present. This chapter will examine the nature of stereotypes that inform these narratives.

In contrast to the conventional literary histories discussed above, two volumes of 'micro-narratives' have appeared in the last decade – *Anjooru varshathe Keralam* (Kerala of the last five hundred years, 1998, edited by V. J. Varghese et al) and *Nammude sahityam, nammude samooham* (Our literature, our society, 2001, edited by M. N. Vijayan). They present a revisionist view of literary history, pointing to a change in attitude towards the very idea of literary historiography.

## 2

P. K. Parameswaran Nair's literary history was commissioned by Sahitya Akademi in the mid-1950s and was published in 1958. Nair had the reputation of being a good biographer and was well aware of the challenges posed by the project. He observes in the prologue,

> To write a concise history of Malayalam literature, that is also complete in all respects, raises impossible hurdles. . . . Everything that has a bearing on the literary history of Malayalam, however minor, has to be included. Besides, leading poets and authors who have contributed towards the progress of poetry and prose, along with the literary movements they nurtured, have to be integrated in the right order and evaluated critically by a literary historian. Literature has to be studied against the background of social circumstances. (1958, vii)

In the course of twenty-four chapters, spread over three hundred pages, Nair does a fairly good job of concisely tracing the historical trajectory of the Malayalam canon, as established by earlier literary historians such as Ulloor S. Parameswara Iyer and P. Govinda Pillai. He also shows an awareness of the 'unity-in-diversity' approach advocated by the central Sahitya Akademi, when he emphasises certain parallels between Malayalam literature and other literary traditions in India, particularly when he mentions the Bhakti period and nationalist/progressive phases of modern Malayalam literature.

While examining the origins of the Malayalam language, Nair agrees with the well-established view that Dravidian languages originated from a common proto-Dravidian language spoken south of the Vindhyas. He endorses the view that there was an earlier form of Tamil out of which modern Tamil and modern Malayalam developed. Malayalam has retained much of the vocabulary from this earliest 'Tamil phase' of its development, along with some grammatical features described in *Tolkāppiyam*. *Chilappatikaram* (The tale of an anklet, by Ilango Adigal), the fifth-century classic, refers to Kerala in its concluding cantos. The Sangam period includes the present Kerala within its cultural boundary. Nair is judicious in his appraisal of the relationship between Malayalam and Sanskrit. Regarding the brahmin migration to Kerala, he comments,

'The spread of Aryan culture in Kerala was not a subversive cultural conquest; on the other hand, it was a creative and complementary synthesis' (10). What was a purely Dravidian language was progressively Sanskritised. This view demonstrates how Nair treads a middle path, eschewing extreme positions. However, he does not refer to any histories of Kerala to support his views.

N. Krishna Pillai's *Kairaliyude katha* was composed mainly for postgraduate students of Malayalam. As the author states in the prologue,

> This is not meant to satisfy erudite readers. The present work does not put forward any new findings regarding Kerala literary history. I had in mind the common reader who wants to get a broad view of the development of his language and literature over the centuries till today. I have only included major texts and significant writers in this brief account. (1998, 5)

Pillai's account of the origins of Malayalam is a little more elaborate and goes into certain aspects of social history, while discussing the brahmin migration. He traces the emergence of the hegemonic status of brahmins in Kerala around 800–1000 AD. He shows how temples played a central role in establishing the dominant status of the brahmin. Like Parameswaran Nair, Pillai also discusses at length the origin and rise of *manipravalam* as a poetic mode that was in contrast to the popular realm of *pattu* traditions. What they, however, do not discuss is the social divide that point to differences in status, affiliations and beliefs, between these two traditions. Equally glaring in both these canonical histories is the absence of even a passing reference to *Payyanurpattu*, which was described by Hermann Gundert as the first independent Malayalam literary text. Gundert's dictionary and Malayalam grammar carried several references to the text and raised issues of language and society as reflected in the text. Many of the questions regarding *Payyanurpattu* were finally settled when a copy of the text was discovered in the Tubington Library collection of Gundert's papers by Scaria Zakharia. Zakharia brought out a detailed study of the text. M. G. S. Narayanan, the eminent historian, has argued that *Payyanurpattu* is different from other ballads, or *manipravalam* texts, in its delineation of characters and enactment of psychological drama that has shades of tragic conflict. The concluding sections of the text were not found in the Tubington papers. However, the available portions give valuable information regarding the social structure of North Kerala, details of shipping trades, mosques and the Muslim presence in the area. While there are no references to nambudiries (Kerala brahmins), nairs and ezhavas, Muslims and Buddhists are repeatedly mentioned. References to gold, iron and copper ornaments as well as details of the merchandise sold by the Portuguese make this poem a historical document of great significance. Much of Kerala's literary history will have to be reimagined in the light of such texts.

Both Parameswaran Nair and Krishna Pillai see the past as a closed narrative with fixed meanings. They also use a concept of the literary as a timeless essence transcending shifts in sensibility or changes in social and literary movements. This is one reason why they do not try to correlate available historical material about the various periods under consideration to the evaluation of literary texts. For instance, the period when Thunchaththu Ezhuthachan wrote his master works coincided with one of the most turbulent historical phases in Kerala – the Portuguese and the Dutch forcing a civil war between the kings of Calicut (Kozhikode) and Kochi. These turbulences weakened the brahminic power structure, paving the way for the rise of an *avarna* poet to the centre stage. In the canonical literary histories, one looks in vain for any reference to social or political history. While assessing literary texts which question ideological constructs about Kerala's homogenous identity, these literary historians seem to rely on literary 'merit' as the sole criterion for deciding the relevance of a text. For instance, the question why many of the Kathakali texts put the figure of Ravana at the centre of their performative creations does not bother these historians. In the light of the Dravidian movement in the neighbouring state of Tamil Nadu, such questions have become urgent in present-day Kerala. In recent literary criticism, several critics have talked about an alternative aesthetics deriving its sources from a Dravidian ideology in their treatment of Aryan myths. While commenting on *Ravana vijayam* (The triumph of Ravana), Krishna Pillai would only say that the author of the text was an accomplished artist who articulated his ideas with consummate literary skill. Parameswaran Nair's history, being much more concise, has no space to go into the social aspects of any of the texts in detail.

These two literary histories consider socio-political contexts as 'background', in the tradition of W. H. Hudson. For instance, the complex history of print in Malayalam is discussed without any reference to the contribution made by missionaries, whose role was crucial in defining modernity in the Kerala context. Both the histories refer to the impact of English on Malayalam, but without examining its implications for print or for the standardisation of language and dissemination of its literature. Slavery was prevalent in Kerala for most of the nineteenth century, though it was officially banned in 1835. The revolt of the 'lower' castes against this oppression took many forms in culture and politics – the social reform movement initiated by Narayana Guru being one of the prominent examples. While discussing the rise of the novel in Malayalam, both these histories highlight *Indulekha* by O. Chandu Menon, while they fail to mention the six or seven novels dealing with the oppressive nature of casteism, such as *Saraswativijayam* and *Sukumari*. Further, the advent of prose in Malayalam is seen merely as a literary phenomenon, without any reference to the emergence of the press, periodicals and the public sphere. It is in negotiating such nodal points of transition that these histories fail to do justice to the complex nature of the relations between society and culture.

Another major limitation of the traditional literary history is in recognising translation as an important sub-system of literature. What begins as a trickle in the early nineteenth century becomes a flood by the end of the century, with translations from Sanskrit and English multiplying manifold. Both Parameswaran Nair and Krishna Pillai have much to say on translations from Sanskrit, particularly on translations of Kalidasa's works. Nair devotes an entire chapter to translations, and comments on the literal quality of the translation of Victor Hugo's *Les miserables* by Nalapat Narayana Menon. Menon's translation came at a point when the novel tradition in Malayalam had stagnated; and his translation opened up new possibilities with the life of the anti-hero becoming a model for new kinds of narratives. Nair makes a feeble attempt to compare Ezhuthachan's *Adhyatma Ramayanam* with some of the translations of the *Ramayana* in Hindi and Tamil. But he fails to note how translation forms an integral part of the creative tradition of literature in Malayalam. In a section titled *Ennam perukiya novel paribhashakal* (Countless novel translations), Krishna Pillai lists all the major translations of fictional works into Malayalam that came out in the opening decades of the twentieth century. The list runs into a page and a half, but Pillai makes no attempt to study the contexts that prompted such a deluge of translations, the nature of their impact on the readers and writers, and their literary quality.

These canonical histories show serious lapses in evaluating individual authors, largely due to the historians' outmoded ideas regarding the function of literature. One such instance is their failure to grasp the full significance of Kesari Balakrishna Pillai, whose contribution towards modernising Malayalam sensibility was phenomenal. While praising the critical initiatives of Balakrishna Pillai, particularly his attempts to introduce European literary and artistic movements to readers in Kerala, Krishna Pillai goes on to find fault with his critical method:

> In none of Kesari's works, there has been an attempt to evaluate the literary values of a work based on the emotional impact the work has on the mind of the reader. His critical writings are, of course, objective and analytical. We never feel that his heart beats can match the rhythms of a work of art. He is like a scientist who observes the world dispassionately. . . . His style is colourless, matter of fact and uninvolved. (1998, 310)

Obviously, Krishna Pillai has a long way to go before he can comprehend the critical method practised by Balakrishna Pillai. Balakrishna Pillai's dispassionate critical voice opened up a critical discourse that challenged the textbook view of literature. He was one of the few modern Malayalam critics to value avant-garde writing and advocate radical revisions in the very idea of the literary. He introduced new models and modes of fiction by translating European texts and by illustrating the innovative styles used by writers such as Marcel Proust and D. H. Lawrence. He was very clear that writers need to challenge received notions of truth and question prevailing attitudes towards issues of gender and sexuality. The conventional nature of the canonical literary history fails to recognise the radical departures made possible by a pioneering critic like Balakrishna Pillai.

Both Parameswaran Nair and Krishna Pillai view literary history as static, unitary and closed. They evidence a totalising, evolutionary teleology that is characterised by a univocal world view. The nineteenth-century positivist view of literature informs their ideological moorings. For them, literary texts are autonomous and inhabit what is vaguely understood as a moral sphere. Literary texts enact 'Kerala' as a reality, concretising its lived reality through imaginative productions. In the process, they forget that the past changes as much as the present, as we move forward. In fact, the past signifies a relationship between the past and the present, and not a span of time sealed off from the present. As new configurations of relations between power and culture emerge in the present, the significance of the events in the past changes for a new generation. For instance, Dalit writing recovered several texts which were marginalised for their lack of 'literary merit', and also helped us conceive a literary history from the standpoint of subaltern experience in general and Dalit experience in particular. A full-length history of Malayalam literature from the perspective of the margins is still to be attempted, though there have been critical commentaries on individual authors and movements. The following section will look at a couple of literary histories which deviate from the evolutionary teleology mentioned above.

## 3

The shifting, contingent and contradictory nature of history is captured in the two edited volumes of micro-histories that appeared around 2000 – *Anjooru varshathe Keralam: Chila arivadayalangal* (1998) and *Nammude sahityam, nammude samooham* (2001). The former was published on the 500th anniversary of the arrival of the Portuguese in Kerala. In the preface, Scaria Zacharia, the scholar who helped conceive the volume in its present shape, says, 'The forty-two essays collected here discuss the major transformations in Kerala's life during the last five hundred years in relation to the ideologies of colonisation and decolonisation' (Varghese et al 1999, ix). Thus, the volume has been planned meticulously from the perspective of an ideological view of contemporary history. Since decolonisation provides a definitive cosmology to frame literary texts, the texts are not evaluated from an arbitrary idea of the 'literary' or a false sense of the autonomy of literary texts. The volume is divided into four sections. The first section, 'Histories – Background, Theories, Models', has essays such as 'Colonisation, Industrial Revolution, Nationalism, Knowledge Explosion' by M. G. S. Narayanan, 'The Tradition of Book Writing in Malayalam' and 'Fashion and Its Cultural Onslaught'. The second section, titled 'The Semiotics of Art', has essays such as 'The Cultural Dimensions of Colonialism' and 'The Ocular Ideology of Ravivarma: Colonialism and Modernity'. The third section, 'Feminist Thoughts', has essays such as 'Feminist Translation: An Introduction' and 'The Identity Formation of Women in Kerala Culture'. The fourth section has essays such as 'Urbanisation and the Malayalam Novel', 'The Missing Pages of Literary Histories' and 'Colonisation and Decolonisation in the Reading of the *Mahabharata*'.

Obviously, the book focuses not on literature, but on culture as a way of life. This is why tribal culture, Vedic tradition and 'fashion' come to be discussed. Essays focus on the politics of culture by locating the subliminal layers of texts or cultural phenomena. They bring out how ideological blinkers of various kinds, rooted in caste and gender discriminations, inform spoken Malayalam, the performance tradition of Sanskrit theatre (Kootiyattam), ballads of northern and southern Kerala, and the literary histories composed in the twentieth century. The essay by Geetha, 'Ulloor's Literary History and Women Writers', points out that only fourteen women writers are mentioned in his five-volume literary history, which narrates the history of Malayalam literature between the years 1760 and 1947. The women writers mentioned by Ulloor are from royal families or are closely related to members of such aristocratic families of repute. The author points out that the works of these women hardly find any mention in this history, it is their family reputation that Ulloor comments on. The women are praised for their good conduct, devotion to their husbands, piety and such 'extra-literary' factors. Obviously, Ulloor uses a different set of criteria to evaluate women writers, and this precipitates a distorted view of their social role. As Geetha observes,

> Literary history is shaped by prevailing notions of hegemony. It is clear that Ulloor's literary history has done nothing to resist the biases rooted in caste, race, gender and class. Only the women of prestigious families from the upper castes, reputed for their good conduct, who abided by the rules of patriarchy, have found a place in this history, even when they have written next to nothing. (Varghese et al 1999, 284)

The concluding essay is on a Dalit ballad, *Chengannoorathi,* which is sung by an oppressed community. Its musical and lyrical features make it an outstanding oral epic which has been in circulation among the lower castes for centuries. In the canonical literary histories of Malayalam, from those of Govinda Pillai to Ulloor and that of Krishna Pillai, there is no detailed account of this oral narrative that is remarkable for communicating the revolutionary sentiments of an oppressed community. The poem has many versions in circulation and not all have been collected. The eleven cantos of the ballad consist of more than 6200 lines that give an account of the adventurous life and tragic end of Chengannoorathi, a heroic warrior who was trained in martial arts. He had to break the pledge he had given to his guru that he would never reveal his (guru's) name, while leading an assault against the nineteenth chieftain. The ballad narrated his romantic exploits and heroic courage in a befitting manner. That mainstream literary histories never had space for such oral epics illustrates how they view literature as being solely made up of written texts.

The volume contains essays that critically evaluate the elements of decolonisation in the study of the *Mahabharata* and critical approaches of eminent historians of Kerala culture, such as Elamkulam Kunjan Pillai. V. J. Varghese shows how Kunjan Pillai's historiography reflects resistance towards imperial and colonial epistemology, even as it partakes of the ideology of colonial modernity. As Varghese comments, 'Elamkulam's practice clearly indicates that writing history is not a mechanical ritual but a conscious act with political dimensions. These are reflected in the tones of resistance his work embodies' (1999, 142). Though not all the essays break new ground, new modes and models for understanding the past in relation to the present emerge in the course of the essays collected here.

*Nammude sahityam, nammude samooham,* in two volumes, focuses on the cultural, political and literary history of Kerala during the twentieth century. The first volume gives a timeline of the twentieth century, comprising all major events concerning the world, India and Kerala. The twenty-one essays of the second volume analyse the social and cultural formation of Kerala during this period, in all its manifold manifestations in politics, art and culture. These essays go beyond the literary, as can be seen in the titles of some of the essays – 'Migration and Diaspora in Malayalam Literature', 'Print and Modernity in Malayalam', 'Popular Literature' and 'Environment and Literature'. In a scholarly introduction, titled 'Lessons of the Renaissance', M. N. Vijayan, the editor, brings out the salient features of the literary Renaissance in Kerala, with special reference to a new literary sensibility that manifested itself in Malayalam. He observes that the new interest in the classics of Indian literature, following William Jones's translation of *Shakuntalam*, gave rise to a re-evaluation of such classics in Malayalam. This neo-classical phase has an element of 'exhibition', as the past was valued not for its own sake, but to showcase one's achievements in the past. This marks a rupture with the past. While the literature of the Romantic period celebrated the individual and his/her assertion of freedom, Indian literature of nineteenth-century Renaissance dealt with social issues. Kumaran Asan, a representative poet of Malayalam Renaissance, wrote extensively on love as an emancipatory experience that transcends the norms of a society. Vijayan observes that Asan's Romantic love is not about the individual's quest for freedom but the society's liberation. The fragmentary and the transient now become the subject of the lyric, as opposed to the monarchic values of the feudal regime that found expression in the epic. This confluence of multiple streams of ideas enabled the society in Kerala to reinvent itself. Asan's poems as well as the novels of the time speak of a new social order. The society had begun to transform itself, in response to the aspirations of a large majority of people who had a stake in social reforms. As Vijayan, in his concluding remarks, observes, 'The secular ideal that all human beings are equal and constitute one collectivity is the essence of the Renaissance. Renaissance is not a subject to debate and define. It is a blueprint for action' (2001, 27).

These two volumes mark a transformation of the idea of literary historiography in Malayalam. Questions of oral literature, women's writing, folk literature, tribal literature, subaltern peasant movements, and the history of fine arts and performative traditions are now seen as integral to the understanding of literary sensibility. Literary history is now seen as plural and multiple, as numerous histories converging on the site of literary production. Exclusivist attitudes towards literariness – as constituted by moral values, craftsmanship and allegiance to dominant traditions – have been subjected to critical scrutiny. The construction of 'creative excellence' as a mark of '*pratibha*' or 'genius' is no longer tenable; language and culture are to be seen as repositories of collective experience.

A radical revision of the conventions of literary historiography became inevitable with the emergence of women's writing and Dalit writing, not to mention the influx of literary and critical theory as a mode of critiquing existing categories. A certain Archimedean point outside the discourse of the conventional discipline of literary history now became available to tilt the centre of gravity in literary historiography. For instance, the introduction to the *Oxford India Anthology of Malayalam Dalit Writing*, stated, 'Unlike Dalits in other parts of India, Kerala Dalits were conditioned in a dream that was trans-national, anti-imperialist and anti-bourgeoisie. They were also forced to believe in a Hegelian teleological vision of history, for which the grand narrative known as Marxism supplied the vital political fuel' (Dasan et al 2012, xxiii). What appeared as a radical critique of the mainstream in the 1930s and 40s is now identified with another set of essentialist and exclusivist assumptions. The invisibility of Dalits in mainstream Malayalam is now traced to a set of aesthetic principles that defined the literary to include only certain kinds of expressions. Dalits, who often articulated their experiences in forms which were marginalised, now demand a reconsideration and redefinition of literary history from the margins. Oral traditions which constitute a significant component of literature, beginning with the earliest phase of Malayalam, have to keep in mind the history of Dalit orality, which has been collective and subversive in nature. As the editors of the Oxford anthology observe, 'The central and south Kerala Dalits have had their own oral traditions with immense historiographical potential. *Chengannuradi, Idanadan Pattukal, Krishigeetha* and other folk-songs are instances. It addresses the formation of an agrarian society in which Dalit community produced the subsistence and surplus and still remained subservient to the dominant political authorities' (xxvi). The understanding of the Dalit cosmogony necessitates a rewriting of existing literary histories. Moreover, it demands a reflexive discourse that self-critically views the very act of writing historical narratives.

## References

Dasan, M., V. Pratibha, Pradeepan Pampirikunnu, and C. S. Chandrika. 2012. *The Oxford India anthology of Malayalam Dalit writing.* New Delhi: Oxford UP.

Nair, P. K. Parameswaran. 1958. *A history of Malayalam literature.* New Delhi: Sahitya Akademi.

Pillai, N. Krishna. 1998. *Kairaliyude katha* [The story of Malayalam]. Kottayam: National Book Stall.

Varghese, V. J., N. Vijayamohanan Pillai, Scaria Zakharia, ed. 1999. *Anjooru varshathe Keralam: Chila arivadayalangal* [Kerala of the last five hundred years: Some knowledge indicators]. Changanacherry: Tharathamya Pathana Samgham.

Vijayan, M. N., ed. 2001. *Nammude sahityam, nammude samooham, 1901–2000* [Our literature, our society]. Thrissur: Kerala Sahitya Akademi.

# Index

# Critique and Postcritique

*Edited by Elizabeth S. Anker and Rita Felski*

This book attempts to evaluate the structural, methodological, and political potential and limitations of critique. The contributors assess the merits of the postcritical turn while exploring a range of alternate methods and critical orientations. This volume outlines the state of contemporary literary criticism and shows how this can be updated to include the intellectual and political challenges of the present.

**Elizabeth S. Anker** is Associate Professor of English at Cornell University.

**Rita Felski** is William R. Kenan Jr. Professor of English at the University of Virginia.

336 pages Hardback ISBN: 978 93 86689 62 7

---

# Crossing Borders

Essays on Literature, Culture, and Society in Honor of Amritjit Singh

*Edited by Tapan Basu and Tasneem Shahnaaz*

*Crossing Borders* is a volume of interdisciplinary essays on the paradigm of borders in African American literature, multi-ethnic U.S. studies, and South Asian studies. Written by established and mid-career scholars from across the world, the essays employ a variety of approaches to the idea of "border crossings" and represent important contributions to the discourses on modernity, diasporic mobility, populism, migration, exile, sub-nation, trans-nation, as well as the formation of nationalities, communities, and identities. The volume also honors and celebrates the life and work of Amritjit Singh as a teacher, mentor, author, scholar, and editor.

**Tapan Basu** is Associate Professor in the Department of English at the University of Delhi.

**Tasneem Shahnaaz** is Associate Professor in the Department of English, Sri Aurobindo College, University of Delhi.

376 pages Hardback ISBN: 978 93 86689 36 8

*For more information, visit www.orientblackswan.com*